WESTERN RESOURCES

This publication funded in part by Western Resources,
a company committed to protecting the environment for all living things.

DO SOMETHING WILD!

This publication funded in part by the Chickadee Checkoff of the Nongame
Wildlife Improvement Program of the Kansas Department of Wildlife and Parks.

All persons filing a Kansas income tax form have an opportunity to make
a special contribution, through the convenience of the tax form,
that is earmarked for conservation of nongame wildlife.

Do something wild!

Make your mark on the tax form for nongame wildlife.

Front cover: An adult male Longear Sunfish (*Lepomis megalotis*) from the
Verdigris River, Chase County, Kansas. Photograph by Garold Sneegas,
Lawrence, Kansas.

University of Kansas
Natural History Museum

Public Education Series No. 14
Joseph T. Collins, Editor

FISHES IN KANSAS

With the advice and assistance of

Ken Brunson and Larry Zuckerman
Kansas Department of Wildlife and Parks

Donald A. Distler
Wichita State University

Mark E. Eberle and Thomas L. Wenke
Fort Hays State University

David R. Edds
Emporia State University

Harold E. Klaassen
Kansas State University

Kate Shaw and Edward O. Wiley
University of Kansas

James R. Triplett
Pittsburg State University

Color artwork by Joseph R. Tomelleri

Color photography by Garold Sneegas and Suzanne L. Collins

FISHES
IN KANSAS

SECOND EDITION, REVISED

Frank B. Cross

Natural History Museum
University of Kansas

Joseph T. Collins

Natural History Museum
University of Kansas

Foreword by John E. Hayes, Jr.

Western Resources

UNIVERSITY OF KANSAS NATURAL HISTORY MUSEUM

The Public Education Series is intended to provide semitechnical publications on
natural history for the people of Kansas.
This volume is the result of studies sponsored by
the University of Kansas Natural History Museum,
the Kansas Department of Wildlife and Parks, and the Kansas Biological Survey.

Distributed by the University Press of Kansas,
Lawrence, Kansas 66049

Library of Congress Cataloguing-in-Publication Data

Cross, Frank B. (Frank Bernard), 1925–
        Fishes in Kansas / Frank B. Cross, Joseph T. Collins ; foreword by
John E. Hayes, Jr. — 2nd ed., rev.
                p.   cm. — (Public education series ; no. 14)
        Includes bibliographical references and index.
        ISBN 0-89338-048-2 (cloth)
        ISBN 0-89338-049-0 (paper)
        1. Fishes—Kansas.   I. Collins, Joseph T.   II. Title.   III. Series.
QL628.K3C69   1995
597.092'9781—dc20   95-4094

To F. W. Cragin for
his contributions to our knowledge of
Kansas fishes

FOREWORD

The Natural History Museum at the University of Kansas has a long and distinguished history in the study of Kansas wildlife. The Museum's first vertebrate handbook about Kansas, *Handbook of Amphibians and Reptiles of Kansas* by Hobart M. Smith (1950), was the forerunner to a series that has constantly evolved and today sets an example that other states emulate.

Currently, the Museum offers handbooks covering all vertebrate animals in Kansas—fishes, amphibians and reptiles, birds (two volumes), and mammals. All are illustrated with photographs and county dot distribution maps that enable the reader to determine quickly where any kind of animal is found in Kansas. The latter innovation, based on the maps in H. A. Stephens's *Trees, Shrubs, and Woody Vines in Kansas* (1969), was initiated in 1974 with the first edition of *Amphibians and Reptiles in Kansas* by Joseph T. Collins. Since that time, many other handbooks have adopted this style in states and regions across North America.

In this second edition, revised, of *Fishes in Kansas,* Western Resources is proud to provide the support necessary to include color photographs of many of the different kinds of fishes known to occur in our state. This is the second Natural History Museum handbook about Kansas vertebrates to include color photography; this feature will greatly aid those who spend spring, summer, and fall in outdoor pursuits where they are likely to encounter these animals.

As pressures build on an ever-dwindling natural environment, the handbooks produced by the Natural History Museum are a valuable source of knowledge and represent a strong, ongoing commitment to informing the people of our state about their natural heritage. Fishes are especially important in this regard because they reside in water, a basic necessity for everyone living in the state. Like people, fishes must have clean, free-flowing water; if Kansas water is not clean, our fishes will die and eventually disappear. We ignore their health at our peril.

Western Resources is committed to improving life for all living things, including fishes, and protecting the water on which they depend. We think this book is a compelling expression of the diversity of Kansas fishes, a variety that enriches us, a diversity that stimulates the interest and curiosity of our children. We urge all Kansans interested in wildlife to take this book with them as they fish or visit the streams, rivers, and lakes of our state. Don't leave it behind on the bookshelf—have it at hand when you meet these fascinating creatures for the first time.

John E. Hayes, Jr.
Chairman of the Board, President,
and Chief Executive Officer
Western Resources

PREFACE

A little over a quarter of a century has passed since the *Handbook of Fishes of Kansas* by the senior author appeared in print, recording 131 fish species in the state. In 1975 we wrote the first edition of this book, describing 123 kinds of fishes known to occur in Kansas. In the years since those two books appeared, much has changed. New kinds of native fishes have been discovered in Kansas, and additional nonnative species have been released or have escaped, and have established reproducing populations in our state. Other kinds of fishes have disappeared, maybe forever. They dwindled away in the 1970s and 1980s, and we did not notice until it was too late. Growing public concern about the environment and the creatures found therein has led to an increased awareness of the plight of fishes that inhabit Kansas—a state with too little water being used by too many people at the expense of aquatic wildlife, particularly the fishes that live in the Arkansas River drainage.

The taxonomy of North American fishes has undergone extensive change, as can readily be seen by comparing this second edition to the first. This edition features 135 kinds of fishes that have been verified from Kansas, including those that are now extirpated. Most nonnative fishes that have been introduced and have established breeding populations are included, as are those few species, such as the Rainbow Trout and Brown Trout, that are annually released for sport fishing but that cannot survive in Kansas due to adverse habitat conditions or weather. We have not, however, included the various species of Tilapia and its relatives that are known to have been released or escaped into Kansas waters. Too little is known about their current status in our state.

This book is an update of the first edition of our *Fishes in Kansas*, and draws heavily on the senior author's original handbook from 1967. In addition, we are fortunate to have in this book color illustrations by Joe Tomelleri, nationally acclaimed fish artist. His drawings, along with the photography of Garold Sneegas and Suzanne L. Collins, plus an updated version of the identification key that appeared in the *Handbook of Fishes of Kansas*, are features that will increase the usefulness of this book to the reader. The identification key is enhanced by the illustrations done by Gene Pacheco, Thomas Swearingen, Anne Musser, and Linda Greatorex. Black-and-white halftone drawings that begin each species account are the artwork of F. A. Carmichael, Victor Hogg, Gene Pacheco, Thomas Swearingen, and Joseph R. Tomelleri. Artwork and photography are appropriately credited in the captions. Although less technical in nature than the 1967 handbook, this volume provides a readily available source of information about Kansas fishes. A more technical work, with precise drainage distribution maps for all Kansas fishes, a more extensive key, and detailed historical information about these creatures in Kansas, is being compiled by E. O. Wiley and his colleagues in the Division of Ichthyology, Natural History Museum, the University of Kansas, Lawrence. When published, this work will be of great value to professional ichthyologists and stream biologists working in Kansas and neighboring states.

As in the first edition, general information about the kinds of fishes discussed in this book has been taken, in most instances, from the 1967 handbook and the sources cited therein. To the numerous colleagues and researchers whose works are the basis of this book, we are most indebted and sincerely appreciative.

Many individuals assisted us in the field and in preparing this book. We thank Douglas W. Albaugh, Jim Beam, Ken Brunson, William Busby, Lawrence Cavin, Donald A. Distler, Ray W. Drenner, David R. Edds, Guy W. Ernsting, Tim Evans, Ruth Fauhl, Owen Gorman, Wendy Gorman, Cal Groen, Joe Hartman, Robert Hartmann, Steve Haslouer, Bill D. Hlavachick, Wayne Hoffman, Donald G. Huggins, Kelly J. Irwin, Richard Kazmaier, Harold A. Kerns, Harold E. Klaassen, Amy Lathrop, William Layher, Stuart C. Leon, Glenn Lessenden, Joe Lilly, Leroy E. Lyon, Chris Mammoliti, Vic McLeran, Larry L. Miller, Paul Mills, Randall E. Moss, Carolyn Mouron, James Power, John Rickett, Stanley D. Roth, Richard M. Sanders, Jr., William G. Saul, Eric Schenk, Roy Schoonover, Kate Shaw, Gerald R. Smith, Garold Sneegas, Thomas Swearingen, Vernon Tabor, James R. Triplett, Amy C. Waddle, Jan Wagner, Elaine Webster, Thomas L. Wenke, Edward O. Wiley, E. David Wiseman, Roger Wolfe, Robert Wood, the late Bruce Zamrzla, and Larry Zuckerman.

A special debt of gratitude is owed to Western Resources, Inc., and in particular to John E. Hayes, Jr., President and Chief Executive Officer, and Thomas J. Sloan, Executive Director for Government Relations and Corporate Communications. Their financial support permitted the inclusion of color photographs in this book, and their commitment allows us to continue to offer this field guide as a means of enriching the wildlife experience of all Kansans.

The cooperative sponsorship of this book was brought about by Philip S. Humphrey, Director of the University of Kansas Natural History Museum, Craig Freeman, Acting Director of the Kansas Biological Survey, and Theodore D. Ensley, Secretary of the Kansas

Department of Wildlife and Parks. To these three colleagues we are deeply grateful.

Various portions of our text profited from the scrutiny of the colleagues listed opposite the title page, and the entire manuscript was reviewed by William Pflieger, of the Missouri Department of Conservation; all errors of omission and commission that may have crept into this second edition are our responsibility alone.

Frank B. Cross
Joseph T. Collins
Lawrence, Kansas
November 1994

CONTENTS

Color plates and photographs of Kansas fishes follow page 140

INTRODUCTION

Although Kansas is not famous for its fishes, the state has a fairly rich fauna of 135 species, of which 116 are native and 19 are introduced. This is a larger number of native kinds than occur naturally in any state farther west or directly north of Kansas. Some of these native species are typical of prairie streams, but more of them occur widely in forested regions to the east and reach the western limits of their ranges in Kansas. No species of fish lives only in Kansas, but a few are more abundant here than in any other state. Some species have disappeared from the state since agricultural and industrial development began more than a century ago. About as many species as were lost have been added to our fauna through introductions for sport, food, or bait. More than 40 of the kinds now present can be caught on hook and line; these include a majority of the species recognized as game fish in North America.

Probably a third of all Kansans go fishing, spending more than 30 million dollars each year on their angling activities. Pond facilities of the Kansas Department of Wildlife and Parks in Pratt are among the largest in the United States. This agency developed the methods used in producing Channel Catfish, which now lead all other species in commercial culture in the United States. Several species other than catfish are raised in private commercial fish farms in Kansas.

Most kinds of fishes are not used directly for food or recreation by people, however, and are of interest for reasons other than immediate economic value. The 135 kinds of fishes described in this book vary greatly in size, appearance, and the sorts of places in which they live. Some are large—as long as 150 cm (5 feet) and as heavy as 45 kg (100 pounds); others are small—never more than 5 cm (2 inches) long, and a hundred or more adults would not weigh a pound. Many are colorful—variously transparent (colorless), white, black, red, blue, yellow, green, orange, purple, and brown. One kind of darter in Kansas has fins as red, white, and blue as the American flag. Some fishes are very limited in their movements, perhaps roaming only a few yards from the place where they hatch. Others migrate hundreds or even thousands of miles to complete their life cycles. Most kinds have specific requirements that restrict the areas of their occurrence in Kansas—in some cases to only one or two streams. Several have been drastically reduced in abundance by our intensive use of land and water, while others have benefited from the changes made, becoming much more common than they were when settlement began. A few are astonishingly tolerant of

conditions lethal to other fishes, withstanding water as warm as
35°C (96°F), as salty as the oceans, or so muddy that they live in
darkness. Under some conditions, a few can live out of water for
hours.

The purpose of this book is to present basic information about
the natural history of each kind of fish known to occur in Kansas.
We assume that the reader is seeking one of three things in reading
our book:

1. Information about a particular kind of fish whose name is already known. In this case, find the name in the Contents or the
Index and turn to the page indicated.

2. The name of a fish that has been caught but that cannot be
identified, along with other information about it. In this case, start
with the Key to Families (major groups of related fishes) on page
248. Compare each picture and statement there with the captured
fish until you find the family that matches it most closely. Then go
to the appropriate Key to Species that follows, and use it to identify
your fish by name. Once the fish has been identified, find its Species
Account (using the Contents or the Index) to learn more about
your fish, and make additional comparisons with the black-and-
white drawing. As a final check, turn to the section of color plates
and see if your fish is illustrated. If so, this should assist you in con-
firming your identification. This process will be easy in groups that
have only a few species in the state. In other groups, such as the
minnows, suckers, and darters, the decision may be difficult because
so many species are listed. The size of your fish and the place where
it was caught may be useful in identification. These parts of the account and the map, as well as the picture(s) and description, should
be noted carefully. If you are still uncertain about the name of the
fish at hand, it can be preserved in 10 percent formalin, which is
available full-strength (38 percent) from your local pharmacy (add
nine parts water to one part formalin), and packaged and sent for
identification to the following address:

Division of Fishes
Natural History Museum
University of Kansas
Lawrence, Kansas 66045–2454

3. General information about fishes and their ways of life in
Kansas. In the general accounts of families of fishes and in the various "long" accounts of selected species, you may learn about the interesting adaptations of fishes, factors that control the distribution

and abundance of various kinds, and ways in which our fish fauna has changed within the period covered by historical records.

PARTS OF A FISH AND THEIR FUNCTION

Head and body: Most fishes are football-shaped or spindle-shaped, because this form moves most easily through water, a living space much more dense than air. For this reason, most fishes tend to look alike in having compact bodies without long, stiff appendages. Variations in body form exist, however, depending on the habitats used by different kinds of fishes. Fishes that live near the surface, such as gars, Northern Pike, and topminnows, have a slender, cigarlike form. Species that range through all depths in calm pools or lakes have compressed bodies, flattened from side to side (Bluegill and Gizzard Shad are examples). Fishes that occupy currents, like the Sauger, Rainbow Trout, and Emerald Shiner, are narrowly spindle-shaped to allow the water to slip by them with least resistance; or they are flattened from top to bottom (depressed), so that the force of water flowing over their backs holds them against the stream bottom (as in catfish and sturgeons). A few kinds have long, flexible bodies that allow them to avoid currents by wriggling into crevices between rocks or into holes in the bottom (American Eel, Slender Madtom, Burbot).

Fins: With a few exceptions, fishes have five kinds of fins, as shown in Figure 3: a dorsal fin on the centerline of the back, a tail fin, an anal fin on the underside opposite the dorsal fin, a pair of pelvic fins on the belly, and a pair of pectoral fins behind the head. These fins are supported by rodlike struts of two types: flexible cartilaginous rays, which are commonly branched near their tips; and stiff bony spines, which have sharp tips and are never branched (except in the case of the Banded Sculpin, whose spines are soft and flexible). All fishes have soft rays in their fins, but only the more advanced groups of fishes have fin spines. The spines, when present, are situated in the front part of the fin. The dorsal fin usually has the most spines, and it is divided into two parts—one with spines and one with rays—in many fishes.

The shape and position of the fins, along with their color and the number of spines and rays present, can be used to identify most kinds of fishes. The fishes themselves use fins for recognition, although their primary purpose is to control movement in the water. The tail fin often aids in swimming, but the dorsal and pectoral fins are equally important in propelling some fishes. The

sides of the body provide the main forward thrust in rapid swimming by most species. All of the fins serve to some degree as stabiliz-
ers. The dorsal and anal fins act as keels, as would be expected from
their shape and position. They also help to brake a fish's forward
motion when it changes direction, reducing sideways slippage as it
turns. These three fins (dorsal, anal, and tail) are brightly colored
in males of some species during their breeding season. The anal fin
of the Mosquitofish *(Gambusia)* is used for inseminating the female
for internal fertilization of the eggs; the mosquitofish is the only fish
in Kansas that gives birth to its young rather than laying eggs.

The pelvic and pectoral fins of fishes correspond to the legs and
arms of mammals. In some fishes (sturgeons, suckers, catfish) they
extend outward like stubby wings or elevators. They are also useful in
propping a fish on the bottom or holding it there as currents are de-
flected off the top surfaces of the fins. In other groups of fishes (sunfish, topminnows) the pectoral fins extend outward from the sides
like oars, with their flat surfaces at right angles to the direction the
fish is heading. Fishes having pectoral fins in this position use them
in small maneuvers and in offsetting the propulsive effects of jets of
water from the gills. The position of the pectoral and pelvic fins provides an important means of identifying major groups of fishes.

Scales and skin: The scales are thin bones, overlapping like shin-
gles in most fishes. A few kinds (Chestnut Lamprey, Paddlefish, catfish) lack scales on the body, and others (American Eel, Burbot)
have scales so deep in the skin that the fish appears naked. Some
fish have scales on the head (topminnows, sunfish, and most
perches and darters), whereas others do not (minnows, suckers, and
shads). In most primitive fishes (sturgeons and gars), the scales are
thick and hard. Most groups of fishes, except shads and topminnows, have a single row of lateral-line scales along the middle of
each side. These scales are perforated by small tubes that join a sensory canal in the body of the fishes; its purpose is discussed under
sense organs, below.

The scales are covered by a layer of skin that contains color cells
and secretes the protective film of mucus that causes fishes to feel
slimy. The slime helps fishes maintain their salt content at a higher
level than exists in the surrounding water, and it wards off bacteria
and other disease organisms.

Jaws and teeth: Many primitive fishes (gars, Bowfin, Goldeye, Rainbow Trout, Northern Pike) have jaws closely anchored to other
bones of the skull. Fishes in these groups may have large, needlelike
teeth for grasping their prey. Teeth may be present on the roof of
the mouth and the tongue, as well as on the jaws. More advanced

groups of carnivorous fish (sunfish, for example) have jaws loosely hinged to the skull. Folds of skin allow the jaws to be thrust outward so that the prey is "inhaled" rather than clamped between the jaws. Such fishes may have pads of tiny teeth on the jaws, useful for holding but not penetrating the prey. Some fishes that inhale their food (minnows, suckers) lack teeth in the jaws, but have "throat" teeth behind the gills that tear or crush the food as it is swallowed. If the food is captured near the surface or in midwater, or if it is plucked selectively from rocks and plant stems, the fishes' lips are thin, as in minnows. If the food is sucked off the bottom, the lips are usually thick and fleshy.

A few kinds of large fishes feed almost entirely on microscopic plants and animals that float freely in the water. These fishes generally have weak jaws and teeth, but their gills are equipped with hair-like structures that strain food from water pumped through the mouth for respiration. The Paddlefish, Gizzard Shad, and Bigmouth Buffalo are filter-feeders of this kind.

Visceral organs: Carnivorous fishes generally have a recognizable stomach, a rather short intestine, and white or silvery skin lining the body cavity. Few if any fishes are strictly herbivorous, but those that do feed on plants lack an enlarged stomach, have a long, coiled intestine, and have a black lining in the body cavity. Other internal organs that may be recognizable are the large brownish liver, a small bright-red spleen, and gonads. The male gonads are a pair of slender, straplike, milky organs in most fish, whereas the female gonads are plump, yellow, and coarsely granular, or gray and thick-walled. The heart in a fish is located forward of the other visceral organs, in a chamber below the gills. The heart pumps blood upward through the gills where it gathers oxygen; the blood then flows through the rest of the body before returning to the heart. Most fishes have a low blood pressure with sluggish flow, and no means of maintaining a body temperature different from that of the water around them. The kidneys of fish are thin, dark-colored organs lying against the backbone (in Rainbow Trout) or more compact organs in the rear part of the body cavity (in sunfish). They are the structures most anglers scrape away with a fingernail as a final step in cleaning a fish, to avoid an objectionable flavor after the fish is cooked.

The air bladder, when present, is an obvious organ in the upper part of the body cavity. It is basically equivalent to the lungs in other vertebrate animals, and it functions like a lung in some fishes (gars, Bowfin). In most fishes, the air bladder is a thin-walled, hollow sack that allows a fish to adjust its internal pressure to match that of the surrounding water. Thus, a fish becomes "weightless" and can float freely at any depth without having to expend energy to maintain its position. The air bladder also amplifies vibrations (sounds) received from the water and increases the range of hearing in some fishes—especially suckers, minnows, and catfish. In the Freshwater Drum, the air bladder is used to produce sounds.

Sense organs: Like other animals, fishes have five major senses: sight, smell, taste, hearing, and touch. Sight is important to fishes, but the reduced amount of light underwater and the difficulty in focusing light rays there limit vision to short distances. Sight is nearly useless in muddy water, so fishes that depend on sight to find their food are greatly handicapped in turbid lakes and streams. Fishes detect odors in the water by means of cells beneath their nares (nostrils)—pits on top of the head between the eyes and the front of the snout. The nostrils open into chambers containing densely folded skin, like a stack of plates. The nares of fishes are strictly sensory, having no respiratory function, and the sense of smell is highly developed in most fishes. Some kinds of fishes recognize their home area mainly by its odor.

Taste is an important sense in fishes. Taste buds line the mouth, as in other vertebrates, but are not limited to that area. Because the skin is always bathed in water and is not subject to drying (as in land animals), fishes can have taste organs scattered over other parts of the body. The whiskers or barbels of catfish are covered with taste buds, as are the long snouts of Paddlefish and sturgeons. Taste and sight tend to be alternate means of selecting food in fishes. All fishes have both senses, but those that seek food in well-lit water usually have large eyes and few taste buds. Fishes that feed in darkness have small, weak eyes and taste buds generously distributed over the entire head.

Fishes have good hearing, despite the absence of visible ears. Water conducts vibrations better than air does, and fishes perceive sounds both by the inner ear, which is embedded against the skull, and by the lateral-line system. The lateral-line system is a series of canals on the head and along each side of a fish. We have no sensory structures exactly like the lateral-line system, so its function is more difficult to understand than that of other senses. It has been described as a sense similar to touch, as a "pressure receptor" or "current detector," and as a hearing organ. Any motion in the water causes vibrations of very low frequency (sounds far below our range of hearing) and causes variable pressures on different parts of the surface of a fish. The lateral-line nerves are affected by stimuli of this sort.

ENVIRONMENTAL FACTORS THAT AFFECT FISH DISTRIBUTIONS

In keeping with their structural differences, the many kinds of fishes in Kansas occupy different habitats within the state. Some factors that affect their distribution are drainage basin, size of the stream or lake, permanence of flow, kind of material on the stream bottom, and water-quality factors such as temperature, clarity, and salinity or hardness.

Drainage basin: Kansas has two major river systems: the Missouri and the Arkansas. The Kansas, Marais des Cygnes, Little Osage, and Marmaton rivers, together with their tributaries, flow to the Missouri River; all other streams flow to the Arkansas River. Knowing in which drainage basin a fish was found or caught greatly increases the chances of identifying it.

Size of stream: Few fishes are adapted for life in both large rivers and small creeks at the same latitude. About forty species are essentially "large-river" fishes in Kansas. About fifty species live mainly in tributaries and avoid large rivers unless forced there during drought (when the large rivers become small). Less than one-fourth of all Kansas fishes are found regularly in both types of streams.

Permanence of flow: Sustained flow is not a limiting factor in and of itself, but a temporary absence of flow does limit many kinds of fishes. Thus nearly all kinds of small-stream fishes occupy permanent streams, but a smaller number inhabit intermittently flowing creeks. The fishes that predominate in temporary creeks are mostly

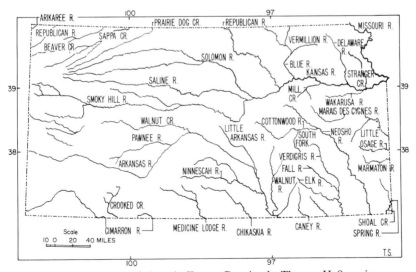

The principal streams and rivers in Kansas. Drawing by Thomas H. Swearingen.

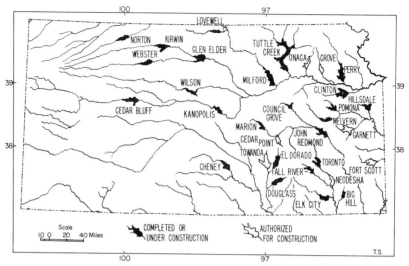

The principal reservoirs in Kansas. Drawing by Thomas H. Swearingen.

widespread, tolerant species. In streams with permanent flow, as
many as forty kinds of fishes occur at any one locality, whereas those
with temporary flow seldom have more than ten to fifteen species.

Bottom type: Most large rivers in Kansas have sandy bottoms. Sand is
a less productive substrate for fish food-organisms than other types
of bottom, and sand has the further disadvantage of leveling itself
when the flow is constant. Therefore, most sandy streams lack variety
in the habitats they provide for fishes. The number of species in
them is lower than in rocky streams, but the kinds that are present
may be abundant. Streams with channels that cross rock outcrops
generally provide several habitats for fish—shallow riffles and pools,
and bottoms varying from large stones through gravel to silt. Small
rocky streams in southeastern Kansas commonly have as many as
thirty kinds of fish, whereas sandy streams of similar size in the western part of the state may have no more than six to ten species, even if
the flow is permanent. Shallow, rocky riffles are important to fish in
many ways—as sites where the water gains oxygen, as spawning sites
for many species, and as food-producing areas in the stream.

Physical and chemical quality of the water: Temperature and turbidity
(muddiness) significantly affect the ranges of fishes in Kansas. All
Kansas fishes tolerate low temperatures, but many species are eliminated if the water warms to 29°C (85°F), 32°C (90°F), or 35°C (95°F)
in summer. Such warming is most likely in shallow streams that lack
tree cover along their banks, and in streams with intermittent flow.
Turbid streams are less productive than clear streams because the

lack of light inhibits plant growth, and because the fish fauna is limited to species that feed effectively by means other than sight. Many turbid streams are in areas having tight, clay soils that shed much water following rains and lack springs to sustain flow at other times. Such streams also fluctuate drastically and become intermittent; they are our least productive waters. Fishes differ in their tolerance of salts dissolved in the water. A few species, like the Gizzard Shad, Plains Killifish, Red Shiner, Fathead Minnow, and Plains Minnow tolerate high salinities. They thrive in naturally salty streams or in those polluted by oil-field brines, but most of our native fishes are eliminated by these conditions.

MAJOR TYPES OF STREAMS AND THEIR FISH COMMUNITIES

Certain kinds of fishes are commonly found together and are rarely if ever found with other kinds, depending on the ecological adaptations of the species involved. One expects to find a particular group of species along a sandbar in the Arkansas River, a different group of species on a rocky riffle in a Flint Hills stream, and so forth. These groups are sometimes called communities; their membership is controlled by the river system (access to the area) and by the general nature of the habitats available (see Plate 1). The major habitat types and fish communities in Kansas are described next.

Sandy Streams

Missouri River: The Missouri River is the largest stream in Kansas, and it has the most distinctive fish fauna. In its natural condition, the Missouri had a wide, shallow bed over which the stream flowed in braided channels divided by sand islands. The channels varied in depth and speed of current, from swift chutes to calm sloughs, backwaters, and oxbows. (Oxbows are channels that are cut off from the river except at flood stage, by minor changes in the course of the stream.) The Missouri River never ceased to flow, but its volume varied enormously and its water was muddy except at low stages. Fishes characteristic of the Missouri River are sturgeon; Paddlefish; Goldeye; Gizzard Shad; buffalofish; Blue Sucker; Channel, Blue, and Flathead Catfish; Burbot; Sauger; and Freshwater Drum. The abundant minnow fauna consists of species adapted to muddy water—Flathead Chub, Sicklefin Chub, Sturgeon Chub, Speckled Chub, Plains Minnow, Western Silvery Minnow, Silverband Shiner, River Shiner, and Sand Shiner. Only a few of these species are common elsewhere in Kansas.

Other large, sandy rivers: The Kansas River, the Arkansas River, and their larger western tributaries are small editions of the Missouri River, but with fewer deep chutes, sloughs, and oxbows. These streams retain as common species the Gizzard Shad, buffalofish, Channel and Flathead Catfish, and Freshwater Drum. Other characteristic fishes are gars, carpsuckers, Silver Chub, Speckled Chub, Emerald Shiner, Red Shiner, Sand Shiner, and Plains Minnow. Various kinds of sunfish are present but rare, as are madtoms (Stonecat). The Plains Killifish is a dominant species in the western part of both river systems.

Spring-fed, sandy brooks: In south-central and western Kansas, as well as in the glaciated area of northeastern Kansas, are scattered small streams with sandy beds that flow permanently because of shallow water tables. Groundwater seeps into the streams along their banks, sustaining clear, cool flows year-round. The generally flat, sandy streambeds afford little variety of habitat, and these streams have no really distinctive communities of fishes. Nevertheless, a few species occur mainly in these sandy brooks: the Bigmouth Shiner in the northeast; the Brassy Minnow in the northeast and northwest; and the Arkansas Darter in the south-central region. Plains Killifish are abundant in most of these streams. The bulk of their fauna consists of widespread species such as Sand Shiner, Red Shiner, Fathead Minnow, Suckermouth Minnow, Central Stoneroller, Green Sunfish, and Orangespotted Sunfish. Isolated populations of Topeka Shiner, Common Shiner, and Creek Chub occupy the limited pool habitat in the northwestern streams of this class.

Streams on Limestone Soils

"Ozark-border" streams of southeastern Kansas: The most diverse habitats for fishes in Kansas (and the largest number of species), occur in streams tributary to the Arkansas and Osage rivers in the southeastern part of the state, westward to the Flint Hills. Rainfall is greatest there, and the land is hilly, with beds of limestone outcropping at the surface. Many streams, both large and small, flow continuously through pools and across rocky riffles. Most darters and many minnows are confined to streams in this area. About twenty species occur only in the Spring River drainage of Cherokee and Crawford counties; others occur only there and, as isolated colonies, in spring-fed creeks of the Flint Hills, especially in Chase County. Still other species occur generally northwestward to Morris, Marion, Butler, and Cowley counties, but not beyond the western limits of the

Flint Hills. Characteristic fishes are Redhorse Suckers, catfish (including several species of madtoms), most kinds of sunfish, and most species of darters. Among minnows, the Gravel Chub, Rosyface Shiner, Redfin Shiner, Cardinal Shiner, Bigeye Shiner, Bluntface Shiner, Mimic Shiner, Slim Minnow, Bluntnose Minnow, and Central Stoneroller are characteristic of this area. Gars and buffalofish are common in large rivers here, as elsewhere.

Upland tributaries of the Kansas River system: From the Flint Hills eastward, the Kansas River receives several small, permanent, rocky tributaries that have distinctive fish communities. These groups of species are more like fish communities in the southeastern ("Ozark border") streams than those in the main sandy rivers, but different species are dominant in the Kansas and Arkansas basins. Characteristic species in the Kansas River tributaries are the Creek Chub, Hornyhead Chub, Southern Redbelly Dace, Common Shiner, Topeka Shiner, White Sucker, and Blackside Darter. Other species common in these streams, as well as in southeastern streams, are the Shorthead Redhorse, Redfin Shiner, Red Shiner, Bluntnose Minnow, Central Stoneroller, Suckermouth Minnow, Green Sunfish, Orangespotted Sunfish, Logperch, and Orangethroat Darter.

Temporary Streams

Many small drainageways in Kansas flow intermittently. These streams vary in the length of time they are dry each year, in the number and size of pools that remain, in the type of stream-bottom materials, and in the diversity of their fish fauna. Some intermittent streams maintain slight flow during winter and during the spring breeding periods of most fishes; these streams support several species. Other intermittent streams dry quickly after rains, and the water in the pools that remain becomes turbid and warm. Fish trapped in the pools are subject to disease, heavy predation by land animals that move along the dry channels, freezing in winter, and death due to decay of organic matter that accumulates in their pools. The Red Shiner, Fathead Minnow, Black Bullhead, and Green Sunfish usually dominate these habitats in Kansas. All are very widespread species, tolerant of many conditions unfavorable to other fishes.

THE EFFECT OF PEOPLE ON FISHES IN KANSAS

Prior to 1850, so few people lived in Kansas that they probably had no impact on the fish fauna of this area. During the latter half of the nineteenth century, the human population and use of land and water in the state increased rapidly to a level almost equal to that of the present. On the basis of early records, it appears that some kinds of fishes may have disappeared during that period—the Lake Sturgeon, Mooneye, Blacknose Shiner, Trout-perch, Western Sand Darter, and Iowa Darter. The ranges of other species—notably the Hornyhead Chub, Topeka Shiner, Common Shiner, Smallmouth Bass, and Sauger—were greatly reduced. Two species seemingly were lost in the major drought of the 1930s—the Bigeye Chub and the Pugnose Minnow. Further reductions in the ranges of other fishes occurred, and the loss of diversity of fishes in the state reached an alarming level. More recently, the Pallid Sturgeon, Sicklefin Chub, Sturgeon Chub, Flathead Chub, Plains Minnow, Western Silvery Minnow, Silverband Shiner, and Arkansas River Shiner have nearly disappeared from the rivers of Kansas, victims of manipulation of their habitat.

The activities of humans that have had the greatest effect on fishes are agriculture, consumption of water, impoundment of water in lakes, and introduced fishes from outside Kansas. Pollution from industrial and urban development have had great local effect but less apparent general effects in Kansas than the factors just cited. In addition, the state's largest river (the Missouri) has been altered greatly by channelization.

Agriculture (including livestock production) and consumption of water probably have been the factors most harmful to the fish fauna. These two factors are related to each other. Much of Kansas has limited water supplies. Water is the essential resource that is sometimes least available, the limiting resource for people and all other forms of life in Kansas. Many small streams in the state retained a permanent flow of clear water only so long as the prairie sod was undisturbed. When the land was plowed, rapid runoff from rains carried loose soil from cultivated land into the streams, filling pools and muddying their waters. Use of water from springs, streams, and wells, for household purposes, livestock, and irrigation of crops, further depleted the streams. Water tables declined, springs failed, and streams became intermittent. Pollution from agricultural and industrial chemicals has added to the problems in our streams, killing thousands of fish in some cases.

The fish fauna of nearly every stream has been changed in this process. Most endangered or threatened species in the state have been put in danger by changes in their habitats attributable to altered stream flows and agricultural development. Agriculture is, of course, the largest and most important industry in Kansas; some people accept these losses as inevitable. Recent improvements in agricultural practices to conserve water and reduce erosion provide hope that further losses of native fishes can be avoided.

Human efforts to conserve water and to seek relief from the effects of flood and drought (which were aggravated by the pattern of early agricultural development) have also had an important effect on the fish fauna of the state. Since the 1930s, nearly 100,000 lakes and ponds have been built in Kansas for storage of water and regulation of flows downstream. Impoundments reduce peak flows and increase flow at other times, because water trapped by a dam enters the stream more slowly, prolonging its period of discharge. Impoundments may also reduce the turbidity of streams, because much of the soil carried into a lake settles there. That reduction in siltload may be offset a few miles downstream, however, by increased erosion of stream banks. Streams that are fully protected from floods discharge all of their annual flow through the channel, with increased erosive effect. If the bed of the stream and its banks are in soils that are easily eroded, the stabilized flow levels the stream bottom, reducing the number of pools and creating a monotonous habitat for fishes. The diversity of the fish fauna is thereby reduced.

The new lakes provide habitats for fishes, of course. Lake habitats were rare in Kansas, where the only natural lakes were small oxbows along streams, a few "sinkholes," and temporary "playa" lakes and marshes. The state now has about 200,000 acres of lake habitat, much of it in central and western Kansas where surface-water formerly was least plentiful. Native fishes that occupy quiet water—including most kinds of sunfish, catfish, suckers, and Freshwater Drum—have spread westward by natural means and through introduction as these lakes were built.

Most introductions of fish into Kansas lakes have involved species native to some part of the state—Largemouth Bass, Bluegill, White Crappie, and other sunfish, together with Channel Catfish and the bullheads. Other introductions have involved species common in nearby parts of the Mississippi valley, where they occur with species native to Kansas; in this group are the Walleye, Yellow Perch, White Bass, Northern Pike, and Mosquitofish *(Gambusia)*. Some of these species inhabited Kansas before settlement. A few introductions— Common Carp, for example—have been truly exotic species with which the native fishes had no previous contact. Most of the native and "near native" (Mississippi valley) fishes that were introduced have established populations in their new lake habitats, and in rivers above and below the impoundments. Of the exotic species introduced, the

Common Carp has prospered beyond all expectations, to the great detriment of native species (especially buffalofish). The Common Carp now occupies a large and prominent position in the Kansas fish fauna.

Impoundments and nonnative fish introductions have been beneficial to native fishes in many ways, but harmful in others. Together they have increased the total diversity of fish populations, especially in central and western Kansas. They have added greatly to sport fishing opportunities. They have changed the local fish communities, not only in the small areas permanently flooded by the lakes, but also in the streams above and below the impoundments. White Bass, Walleye, crappies, and other species in the lakes have become common in creeks and rivers where they were not found many years ago. Predation by these species has reduced the abundance of some stream fishes. Dams restrict movements of many stream fishes, inhibiting the normal dispersal that maintains their populations where suitable habitats remain. Truly migratory species, such as the American Eel, have disappeared from drainages above large impoundments. Other species have benefited from the sustained flow in streams that would be intermittent without gradual releases of water from reservoirs.

Some dangers to nearly all fish are inherent in our ability to regulate the flow of streams, controlling floods. This ability invites intensive use of all land along the streams, by restricting their channels to straight and narrow ditches (channelization). But such an extreme level of development would be disastrous to most kinds of fishes, many other forms of wildlife, and important aesthetic values of life in Kansas. An alternative is possible: management of our water supplies to benefit wildlife and to improve recreational values, as well as to serve economic necessity. Conservative development that leaves untouched a strip of land for the stream course and its protective vegetation will be worth most to us in the long run.

ENDANGERED AND THREATENED SPECIES

In 1974, Dwight R. Platt, along with members of the Conservation Committee of the Kansas Academy of Science and other biologists, prepared a list of rare or endangered Kansas fishes for the purpose of attempting to identify those species in danger of extirpation. In 1975, the Kansas Legislature passed the Kansas Nongame, Threatened and Endangered Species Act. This act invested the Kansas Department of Wildlife and Parks with the authority to establish an official list of endangered or threatened species in the state. As a result, an official list of endangered species, threatened species, and species in need of conservation (SINC) for Kansas was created in 1978. As of May 1994, the list contained 37 species of fishes, 14 of which are protected by state and/or federal law. The 37 endangered, threatened, or SINC species (32 percent of the native Kansas fish fauna) are as follows.

Endangered (federal and Kansas):
    Pallid Sturgeon *(Scaphirhynchus albus)*
Threatened (federal and Kansas):
    Neosho Madtom *(Noturus placidus)*
Endangered (Kansas only):
    Speckled Chub *(Extrarius aestivalis tetranemus)*—Arkansas River
      only
    Sicklefin Chub *(Macrhybopsis meeki)*
    Arkansas River Shiner *(Notropis girardi)*
Threatened (Kansas only):
    Chestnut Lamprey *(Ichthyomyzon castaneus)*
    Western Silvery Minnow *(Hybognathus argyritis)*
    Sturgeon Chub *(Macrhybopsis gelida)*
    Redspot Chub *(Nocomis asper)*
    Hornyhead Chub *(Nocomis biguttatus)*
    Silverband Shiner *(Notropis shumardi)*
    Flathead Chub *(Platygobio gracilis)*
    Arkansas Darter *(Etheostoma cragini)*
    Blackside Darter *(Percina maculata)*
Species in need of conservation (Kansas only):
    Spotfin Shiner *(Cyprinella spiloptera)*
    Gravel Chub *(Erimystax x-punctatus)*
    Brassy Minnow *(Hybognathus hankinsoni)*
    Plains Minnow *(Hybognathus placitus)*
    River Shiner *(Notropis blennius)*
    Ozark Minnow *(Notropis nubilus)*
    Topeka Shiner *(Notropis topeka)*
    Blacknose Dace *(Rhinichthys atratulus)*
    Highfin Carpsucker *(Carpiodes velifer)*
    Blue Sucker *(Cycleptus elongatus)*
    Northern Hogsucker *(Hypentelium nigricans)*
    Spotted Sucker *(Minytrema melanops)*
    River Redhorse *(Moxostoma carinatum)*
    Black Redhorse *(Moxostoma duquesnii)*
    Tadpole Madtom *(Noturus gyrinus)*

Banded Sculpin *(Cottus carolinae)*
Greenside Darter *(Etheostoma blennioides)*
Bluntnose Darter *(Etheostoma chlorosomum)*
Slough Darter *(Etheostoma gracile)*
Stippled Darter *(Etheostoma punctulatum)*
Speckled Darter *(Etheostoma stigmaeum)*
Banded Darter *(Etheostoma zonale)*
River Darter *(Percina shumardi)*

The designation "endangered" indicates a higher priority than the designation "threatened." The fourteen species listed above as endangered or threatened are protected by state regulations, and a permit issued by the U.S. Fish and Wildlife Service and/or the Kansas Department of Wildlife and Parks is required to collect them for scientific purposes. These designations and protection represent a major step by the people of Kansas toward conserving these creatures. They are a vital aspect of the wildlife heritage of our state.

EXPLANATION OF SPECIES ACCOUNTS

Each account contains information about a species of fish. Although brief, an account provides the basic information needed to identify a fish (when used with the accompanying map and illustrations), shows its range in Kansas, and summarizes its natural history. For continuity and ease of reading, we have avoided citing most sources in the text. The accounts are arranged by order and family in the same sequence used by Robins et al. (1991); within families, the species accounts are alphabetical by genus and species.

Common and scientific names: Each of 23 families of fishes known from Kansas is presented as a unit. For families represented in Kansas by one or two species, information about the family is contained in the species accounts. For families represented in Kansas by several species, a general family account precedes the species accounts.

Each species account begins with the standardized common name according to Robins et al. (1991). We urge use of that name only, when referring to a particular fish. This prevents much confusion and allows for easy recognition of a fish in conversation and reading.

The scientific name is the formal Latin name of each species and subspecies. Two or three words make up a scientific name. The first word always begin with a capital letter and is the genus (plural: *genera*). The second word never begins with a capital and designates the species (plural: *species*). A genus may contain many species, but a species belongs to only one genus. Sometimes a scientific name has a third word. This identifies the subspecies. A species may have many subspecies, but a subspecies belongs to only one species. An example of the structure of the scientific name is as follows:

> Genus—*Etheostoma* (a group of darters)
> Species—*Etheostoma spectabile* (Orangethroat Darter)
> Subspecies—*Etheostoma spectabile pulchellum*

Thus, the genus *Etheostoma* refers to a group of fishes called darters; the species *E. spectabile* refers to a particular darter within the genus, called the Orangethroat Darter; and the subspecies *E. s. pulchellum* refers to a particular race found in Kansas. It should be noted that North American fish subspecies do not have standardized common names; we do not use common names for subspecies in this book.

After each scientific name comes the name of the person or persons who originally described the species. These names may or may not be in parentheses, depending on whether the species was originally described in the same genus in which it is currently placed (no parentheses needed) or in a different genus (parentheses present).

Illustrations: All color drawings in this book are by Joseph R. Tomelleri. Black-and-white drawings of fishes are taken from Cross (1967) and Cross and Collins (1975). Color photographs of streams and rivers are by Suzanne L. Collins; those of fishes are by Garold Sneegas.

Maps: Each species account includes a small Kansas map showing the outline of each county. A circle (solid or open) centered in a county indicates that the species has been collected (voucher specimen or photograph available), verified (identification made by a professional ichthyologist; no voucher), or stocked in that county by the Kansas Department of Wildlife and Parks (mostly game species). No attempt has been made to show the exact locality where a species has been collected. To determine the correct drainage system for a species within a county, consult the habitat section in the account. For information on the range of each species outside Kansas, refer to Page and Burr (1991). On our maps, the distributional records backed by preserved vouchers are based on specimens deposited in the Natural History Museum at the University of Kansas, the University of Michigan Museum of Zoology, and the National Museum of Natural History. Solid circles indicate collections or vouchers made since 1900. For a few species, open circles are used to represent collections or vouchers prior to 1900, in parts of the state where the fish has not been found in this century. Because the records mapped cover a period of time in which many changes in stream habitats have occurred, they may not accurately reflect the current range of a species in Kansas—especially those listed earlier as endangered or threatened—but instead show the species' historical range.

Description: Characters used to distinguish each species and a brief color description are presented in this section. For some species, this section contains sufficient information to make an accurate identification. For all minnows, suckers, catfish, topminnows, sunfish, and darters, however, we urge the use of the Technical Keys to the Fishes of Kansas (see page 247).

Size: Length is expressed as total length (tip of snout to tip of tail fin) in centimeters (cm) and inches. Weight is given in kilograms (kg), and pounds and ounces. Record lengths of Kansas specimens are based, in most instances, on measurements given by Cross (1967); but for some species, fishes were measured and maximum length was determined by us. State records for game species were made available to us by the Kansas Department of Wildlife and Parks. The maximum size of a species throughout its entire range was taken from Page and Burr (1991).

Habitat: The habitat of each species is defined in this section in terms of the specific streams or the kinds of streams in which the species is found most often. Special requirements (clear water, permanent flow, riffles, or pools) and habits (schooling, migration, and so on) are indicated as they apply. Comments on historical changes in abundance are included in this section as well.

Reproduction: Information on the usual time and place of spawning is presented in this section, based on observations in Kansas and elsewhere, by us or by others.

Food: The general food preference of each fish, based on information published by many authors, is recorded in this section.

Subspecies in Kansas: This section is included if recognized subspecies are known to occur in Kansas; recognized subspecies are those that appear in Page and Burr (1991).

Remarks: This section designates introduced species and includes observations of unusual or interesting behavior. Species regarded as endangered or threatened, at either the state or the federal level, plus those considered by the Kansas Department of Wildlife and Parks to be species in need of conservation (SINC species) are indicated here.

ORDER PETROMYZONTIFORMES

LAMPREYS (Family Petromyzontidae)

An adult Chestnut Lamprey *(Ichthyomyzon castaneus)*. Drawing by Victor Hogg.

Chestnut Lamprey
Ichthyomyzon castaneus Girard (Plate 3)

Description: Round, sucking-disk mouth. Fins absent except for a keellike, rayless fin along back and around tip of tail. Row of seven pits (gill pouches) in "neck" region on each side. Color gray, greenish gray, or yellowish tan with pale belly.

Size: Maximum length for an adult of this species is 38 cm (15 inches).

Habitat: For the past forty years the Chestnut Lamprey has been found only in the Missouri River and the Kansas River near its mouth. Reports from the late 1800s indicate that the species occupied the eastern third of 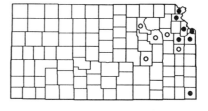 Kansas at the time of settlement. Adults attach themselves to large fishes, and may be carried nearly anywhere by their hosts, but most have been found in large rivers.

Reproduction: Like other lampreys, adult Chestnut Lampreys move upstream in late winter and spring to suitable spawning sites, where they prepare nests in shallow riffles. They remove small stones with their mouths or dislodge them by vigorous swimming movements, to form a depression in the stream bottom. The lampreys then attach by their mouths to stones on the upstream edge of the nest. The eggs are expelled and fertilized. The eggs lodge in crevices in the gravel, and may be covered further as the spawning adults continue to excavate and fill the nest area; but the eggs and young receive no further parental attention. When the young hatch and emerge from the nest, they drift downstream into gentle eddies or backwaters. The larval lampreys, called *ammocoetes,* then burrow into mud and organic sediment near the bank of the stream. The larvae may move to new sites as they grow, but most of a lamprey's life is spent as an ammocoete in burrows, where it feeds and grows in the summer that follows. Ultimately, the ammocoete transforms into an adult lamprey during fall and winter, gaining functional eyes and a cup-like, toothed mouth. After it matures, the lamprey migrates, spawns, and dies soon thereafter.

Food: While in burrows, the ammocoetes feed on micro-organisms and bits of organic debris that are carried to them by currents. Adult Chestnut Lampreys attach themselves to large fishes (carps, buffalofish, redhorses, Paddlefish, catfish, Freshwater Drum), use their toothed tongue to rasp a shallow wound, and withdraw body fluid from the host.

Remarks: THREATENED SPECIES IN KANSAS. The decline of the Chestnut Lamprey probably is due to deterioration of small streams in which the eggs and young are produced. The larvae perish if the streams stop flowing or if floods scour out the organic sediments in which they burrow.

ORDER ACIPENSERIFORMES

STURGEONS (Family Acipenseridae)

An adult Lake Sturgeon *(Acipenser fulvescens)*. Drawing by Thomas H. Swearingen.

Lake Sturgeon
Acipenser fulvescens Rafinesque (Plate 3)

Description: Snout short and bluntly V-shaped, not upturned at tip (except in some small specimens), with fleshy mouth underneath. Smooth barbels beneath snout. Five rows of large, bony scutes (hooked scales) on body. Caudal peduncle, in front of tail fin, short, rounded, and not fully scaled. Anal fin rays 25–30.

Size: The largest (and only) Lake Sturgeon caught recently in Kansas was 101.7 cm (40 inches) long and weighed 5.7 kg (12.5 pounds). It was caught on rod and reel in the Missouri River, Atchison County, by Larry Goodman of Lansing on 23 May 1988, and was subsequently released. Elsewhere in its range, this species grows to a maximum length of 274 cm (9 feet), may weigh over 90 kg (200 pounds), and lives eighty years or more.

Habitat: The Lake Sturgeon prefers to live on the mud, sand, and gravel bottoms of large lakes and rivers, in waters 5–9 meters (16–30 feet) deep. In Kansas, it is now found only in the Missouri River along the northeastern border of our state.

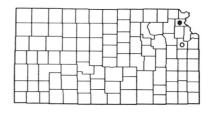

Reproduction: Spawning occurs in late spring on the gravel bottoms of streams or in the shallows of large lakes. Female Lake Sturgeons do not mature until twenty or more years of age.

Food: The Lake Sturgeon eats aquatic insects, mollusks, crayfishes, and small fishes.

Remarks: Lake Sturgeons underwent a widespread decline in abundance around 1900, due partly to pollution and siltation of rivers, which adversely affected spawning sites and one of its food sources (mollusks). In addition, construction of dams restricted access to spawning areas, and the species was severely overexploited by fishing.

An adult Pallid Sturgeon *(Scaphirhynchus albus)*. Drawing by F. A. Carmichael.

Pallid Sturgeon
Scaphirhynchus albus (Forbes and Richardson) (Plate 3)

Description: Like Shovelnose Sturgeon, except: row of scutes on middle of side narrower than space between that row and lower row of scutes. Belly usually scaleless. Four fringed barbels not in a straight line across snout; the two center barbels farther forward and only about half as long as the outer barbels. Dorsal fin rays 37–43; anal fin rays 24–28.

Size: The largest Pallid Sturgeon we have seen from Kansas was approximately 76 cm (30 inches) long. However, outside the state this species attains a length of 168 cm (66 inches) and a weight of nearly 32 kg (70 pounds).

Habitat: The Pallid Sturgeon inhabits the mainstream of the Missouri River and the lower Mississippi River. It enters the lower part of the Kansas River during floods. Thus it is confined to large, muddy rivers with

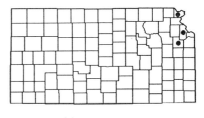

swift currents. Its body form enables it to move along the bottom with ease, maintaining its position against the current. The abrasive effects of water-borne mud and sand are reduced by the tough hide and small eyes of this species.

Reproduction: Nothing is known about the breeding habits of the Pallid Sturgeon in Kansas.

Food: A few Pallid Sturgeons from the Kansas River contained insect larvae and small fishes in their stomachs.

Remarks: FEDERALLY ENDANGERED SPECIES IN KANSAS. The only rivers in which the Pallid Sturgeon occurs have been greatly modified for control of floods and improvement of navigation. The species has long been rare, but its numbers have declined greatly in the past 30–40 years. It recently was designated for protection by the U.S. Fish and Wildlife Service.

Sturgeons are among the most bizarre and most ancient of all the world's fishes. They probably have existed for eighty million years or more, a span of time long enough to cover the disappearance of the dinosaurs and the development of modern mammals and flowering plants. Except for the two species (in the genus *Scaphirhynchus*) included here, the only living "shovelnose" sturgeons occupy tributaries of the Aral Sea in Kazakhstan and Uzbekistan.

An adult Shovelnose Sturgeon *(Scaphirhynchus platorynchus)*. Drawing by F. A. Carmichael.

Shovelnose Sturgeon
Scaphirhynchus platorynchus (Rafinesque) (Plate 3)

Description: Five rows of large, bony scutes (hooked scales) on body. Caudal peduncle, before tail fin, slender, flattened, and fully covered by bony scales. Flat, rounded snout, with fleshy mouth underneath (the scientific name means "flat-snouted spade-snout"). Row of scutes on middle of side taller than space between that row and lower row of scutes. Belly with small bony scales. Four fringed barbels beneath snout in a straight line and nearly equal in length. Dorsal fin rays 30–36; anal fin rays 18–23.

Size: Adult Shovelnose Sturgeons are usually 51–63 cm (20–25 inches) long. The largest one reported from Kansas was 81.4 cm (32 inches) long and weighed 2.0 kg (4.5 pounds). It was caught on rod and reel in the Kansas River by Danny Freeman of DeSoto on 16 May 1989. Elsewhere in its range, this fish attains a maximum length of 86 cm (34 inches).

Habitat: This species has been taken in the Missouri, Kansas, and Republican rivers, and in the lower parts of the Blue and Smoky Hill rivers. In addition, there is a single, recent record from the Arkansas River in Sedg-

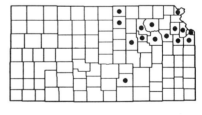

wick County. It occurs only in rivers having broad, sandy channels. Shovelnose Sturgeons are found most often on clean sand bottoms in strong currents; they move into deep, calm pools in winter.

Reproduction: Shovelnose Sturgeons migrate upstream in the Kansas River, preliminary to spawning, in March and April. Actual spawning has not been observed here, but reports elsewhere indicate that reproduction takes place in swift water over rocky bottoms, between April and June.

Food: The stomachs of a few Shovelnose Sturgeons from the Kansas River contained larval insects of many kinds, some of which live on silted bottoms and others on firm, rocky riverbeds.

Remarks: Shovelnose Sturgeons have some importance as a commercial food fish, and they are caught frequently by anglers using worms as bait.

PADDLEFISHES (Family Polyodontidae)

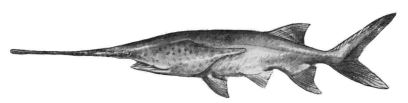

An adult Paddlefish *(Polyodon spathula)*. Drawing by F. A. Carmichael.

Paddlefish
Polyodon spathula (Walbaum) (Plate 4)

Description: Snout long and spatulalike. Jaws toothless. Body scaleless. No other fish in North America resembles it.

Size: The largest Paddlefish caught in Kansas weighed 36.7 kg (81 pounds) and measured 174.2 cm (68½ inches) in total length. It was snagged with a rod and reel by George Elliott of Oswego in the Neosho River below the dam at Chetopa, Labette County, on 1 May 1983. Elsewhere, this fish is known to reach a length of 221 cm (87 inches).

Habitat: Paddlefish live in large rivers and lakes, including the Missouri, Kansas, Marais des Cygnes, Neosho, and Arkansas rivers in Kansas. Many of those caught by anglers are present only temporarily, below dams, 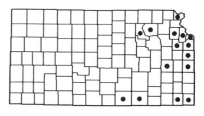 during their spring spawning runs. Paddlefish prefer large, deep pools where the water is calm or flows slowly. They occupy oxbow lakes (old river channels that have been cut off from the mainstream) as well as rivers. Reservoirs provide habitat suitable for Paddlefish, but the species must leave these impoundments to reproduce.

Reproduction: During high water in spring, when the temperature is about 15°C (60°F), Paddlefish migrate up rivers to spawn over submerged gravel bars in swift currents. The eggs stick to stones on the river bottom, where they develop rapidly. After hatching, the young swim upward into the strong current, which sweeps them downstream into pools before the gravel bars are exposed by receding water levels.

Food: Although the Paddlefish is one of the largest freshwater fishes, it feeds mainly on microscopic organisms (plankton) that it strains out of the water as it swims. Clusters of taste buds on the snout and sides of the head aid the Paddlefish in locating concentrations of these food organisms.

Remarks: The Paddlefish has commercial importance as a food fish and increasing recreational importance. It is normally caught only by "snagging." Because it has no scales or internal bones, it is easily prepared for eating: it can simply be gutted, laid flat, and chopped into steaks with a large cleaver. Because its eggs now have commercial value as caviar, illegal fishing for the Paddlefish has become a serious recent problem. Changes in river habitats, including reduction of suitable spawning sites, may also threaten this species.

ORDER LEPISOSTEIFORMES

GARS (Family Lepisosteidae)

Their appearance and behavior are repulsive to some people, but gars are fascinating fishes. They differ from other living fishes about as much as a platypus differs from a dog, or a pelican from a robin. Obvious features of gars are their thick, bony, interlocking scales, and their menacing jaws armed with needlelike teeth. Also, gars have gas bladders that function as lungs, in addition to having gills, and they have vertebrae unlike those of any other fish. The slender, tubelike form of the body, together with the rearward position of the dorsal and anal fins, adapt gars to operate effectively at the very surface of the water. The toothed beak is a primitive but successful mechanism for capturing other fishes, which are almost the only food gars ever eat.

In general, gars inhabit slowly flowing streams or their backwaters and floodpools. Gars sometimes enter swift currents, but they linger most often in the margins of eddies, relatively calm water along river banks, the mouths of tributary streams, or pools below dams. Gars can survive in shallow, weedy, warm waters that hold little oxygen in summer, by swallowing air to fill their lunglike gas bladders. Gars can also survive longer than most other fishes out of water. They can be carried for hours in a moist burlap bag in the trunk of a car, and survive. Gars are tough fishes, durable enough that they have survived all of the happenings on earth for a hundred million years: the drifting apart of continents, the spread of inland seas and massive glaciers, the creation and erosion of mountain ranges, and the competition of all the other fishes that have evolved around them in that span of time. Gars may be slow and ugly, but they are also patient and careful, and they have endured.

In large part, gars feed by lying in wait for unwary prey to approach them too closely. At most, the gar aids its own cause by maneuvering so slowly that the prey is not frightened into flight. Then, with a lateral slash of the jaws, the gar pinions the prey on its teeth, usually crosswise between the jaws. After the victim has quit its struggles, it is worked slowly backward along the jaws, turned, and swallowed. The capture and consumption of a single fish may take gar several minutes, in contrast to the split second required by a bass to ingest a fish. The feeding mechanisms of the gar and the bass are quite different, and that of the bass seems much more efficient. The two methods are roughly comparable to picking up marbles with tweezers or with a strong vacuum cleaner. The gar's tweezers are not the better and faster way, but they work well enough.

Gars reproduce by scattering their eggs over clean, rocky bottoms or in vegetation, in late spring, often after migration upstream. No care is given the eggs after they are deposited. The young hatch before they are able to swim actively, but they have an adhesive organ on the snout with which they attach themselves to rocks until their larval development is completed. By the time they are about two inches long, their food consists mostly of the fry of other fishes, and they grow rapidly. For the first several weeks of life, gars have another peculiar feature: a featherlike extra fin above the main tail fin. This small fin is an extension of the spinal axis; it is undeveloped or disappears at an embryonic stage in other fishes. In young gars, the finlet is kept in constant vibratory motion while it persists, but it diminishes gradually in size and disappears by the time the gar is 20 to 25 cm (8 to 10 inches) long.

Gars can be caught on hook and line. While we have never caught them in that way, we have heard of several methods devised for their capture by ingenious anglers. Gobs of worms laced on treble hooks are one way, but the bony mouth of a gar is not easily penetrated by a hook. Loops of thin steel wire, with a short hook attached and baited with a minnow, are sometimes used. That method depends on the angler's ability to "lasso" the upper jaw of the gar when it takes the bait. We have heard that gars can be caught on baits of raveled nylon cord in which their teeth become entangled. Gars are rather easily "snagged" despite their bony hide, because a well-sharpened hook will penetrate between adjacent rows of scales, which tend to hold the hook in place.

Gars have limited use as food fishes in some parts of their range. Although their flesh is edible, their eggs are poisonous. These are the only Kansas fishes having toxic parts that might be eaten. The scales of gars have been used decoratively, in shell jewelry. Their shape is somewhat leaflike, and the scales are usually arranged with mollusk shells into flowerlike sweater-pins, earrings, and similar items.

An adult Spotted Gar *(Lepisosteus oculatus).* Drawing by Thomas H. Swearingen.

Spotted Gar
Lepisosteus oculatus (Winchell) (Plate 4)

Description: Snout short and broad. Jaws less than twice as long as the rest of the head, from front of eye to back edge of gill cover. Upper jaw wider, near its tip, than diameter of eye. Differs from Shortnose Gar in having round, dark spots on the top and sides of the head.

Size: The largest Spotted Gar from Kansas weighed 3.5 kg (7.75 pounds) and was 85.2 cm (33½ inches) in length. It was taken with bow and arrow by Charles Harbert of Arma in the Neosho River below the dam at Chetopa, Labette County, on 13 May 1983. Elsewhere in its range, this fish attains a maximum length of 112 cm (44 inches).

Habitat: The Spotted Gar lives in backwater pools, oxbow lakes, and reservoirs. In Kansas, it may be confined to the lower part of the Neosho and Verdigris basins. Spotted Gars appeared in the shallow pools of the Neosho Waterfowl Refuge, Neosho County, and in Elk City Reservoir, Montgomery County, soon after their impoundment. It has a decided preference for warm, calm waters.

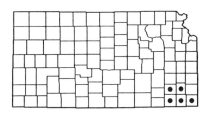

Reproduction: The Spotted Gar probably spawns in weedy shallows, or over vegetative debris.

Food: The Spotted Gar eats other fishes. See the family account for gars.

Remarks: Because of its localized occurrence in Kansas, the Spotted Gar was listed as a peripheral species by Platt et al. (1974), along with threatened species in the state. Preservation of some oxbows and overflow ponds in the floodplain of the Neosho River would ensure the survival of this species, and benefit other kinds of wildlife as well. Such habitat is becoming rare in Kansas.

An adult Longnose Gar *(Lepisosteus osseus)*. Drawing by Gene Pacheco.

Longnose Gar
Lepisosteus osseus (Linnaeus) (Plate 4)

Description: Jaws slender, their length more than twice the distance from the front edge of the eye to the back of the head. Width of upper jaw at its narrowest point (near its tip) less than eye diameter. Color greenish, sides often with dark streaks or spots.

Size: The largest Longnose Gar taken in Kansas weighed 14.7 kg (31.5 pounds), length unknown, and was caught by Ray Schroeder of Topeka at the outlet of Perry Reservoir, Jefferson County, on 21 May 1974, using a rod and reel. Maximum length for an adult of this species is 183 cm (72 inches).

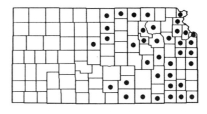

Habitat: The Longnose Gar inhabits most rivers and creeks in the eastern half of the state. It is the most abundant of the three species of gars in Kansas, and the only one likely to be found in small streams. Longnose Gars occur with Shortnose Gars in large rivers, and in oxbow lakes and reservoirs. In winter they leave the shorelines and shallow backwaters to congregate in the bottom of deep pools.

Reproduction: In spring, Longnose Gars migrate upstream into rocky tributary streams and rivers for spawning, or into the shallow, weedy margins of lakes. The eggs adhere to the substrate and are abandoned. See also family account.

Food: Longnose Gars feed almost entirely on other fishes. Young gar chiefly prey on minnows but change to Gizzard Shad or small suckers as adults. The species is one of the largest and most widespread predatory fishes in Kansas. It performs an important and beneficial function by helping to keep the abundance of the prey species within desirable limits. See also family account.

An adult Shortnose Gar *(Lepisosteus platostomus)*. Drawing by Gene Pacheco.

Shortnose Gar
Lepisosteus platostomus Rafinesque (Plate 4)

Description: Jaws less than twice as long as the rest of the head, from front of eye to back edge of gill cover. Upper jaw wider than eye diameter, throughout its length. Differs from Spotted Gar in never having dark rounded spots on the head.

Size: The largest Shortnose Gar from Kansas weighed 2.7 kg (5.94 pounds) and was 87.1 cm (34¼ inches) in length, apparently the longest example on record. It was taken with bow and arrow in Milford Reservoir on 4 May 1985 by Jack M. Frost of Manhattan.

Habitat: The Shortnose Gar inhabits the largest rivers in Kansas: the Missouri, Kansas, Blue, Republican, Marais des Cygnes, Neosho, and Arkansas rivers. It is most common in the Kansas River. Shortnose gars usually

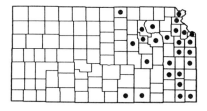

avoid the quiet backwaters, oxbows, and impoundments that are often inhabited by Longnose Gars and that are the main habitat of the Spotted Gar. Records of Shortnose Gar in Milford Reservoir and Republic County State Lake are exceptional.

Reproduction: The Shortnose Gar spawns in spring, probably over bottoms of bedrock or gravel, but possibly over vegetation or woody debris where this is available. See the family account.

Food: The Shortnose Gar eats other fishes and larval aquatic insects. See the family account for gars.

Remarks: This and other gars make novel aquarium pets, easily kept if supplies of small fishes are available as food. Their food requirements are not great, so daily feeding is not essential. Because of their predatory habits, we recommend against placing them in community tanks.

ORDER AMIIFORMES

Bowfins (Family Amiidae)

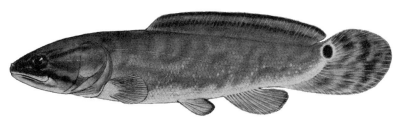

An adult Bowfin *(Amia calva)*. Drawing by Victor Hogg.

Bowfin
Amia calva Linnaeus (Plate 5)

Description: Dorsal fin long and low, with at least forty rays, separate from tail fin. Tail fin rounded. No stiff, bony spines in any fins. Snout blunt, mouth large, with toothed jaws extending backward below eye.

Size: Maximum length for an adult of this species is about 109 cm (43 inches); weight 3.7 kg (8 pounds), but rarely more than 1.8 kg (4 pounds).

Habitat: The Bowfin inhabits clear, calm water in low areas, especially in backwaters of rivers and oxbows and in lakes that have much aquatic vegetation. Bowfins were said to be in the Missouri, Marais des Cygnes, and

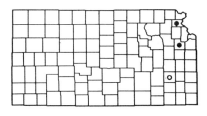

Neosho rivers in the late 1800s, but we have found no specimens to prove those reports. We are sure of only two records: a Bowfin caught near the mouth of Independence Creek in the floodplain of the Missouri River in Atchison County in 1965, and another in Hughes Lake, a private "fee-fishing" pond in Douglas County in 1971. Hughes Lake was restocked regularly with fishes hauled from Minnesota or northwestern Iowa, where Bowfin are common, so that record represents an accidental introduction.

Reproduction: Spawning occurs in spring when the males prepare and defend nests, usually in vegetation. The eggs adhere to sticks or stones on the floor of the nest. On hatching, young Bowfins, like gars, have an adhesive pad on the snout, which they use to anchor themselves to objects in the nest until the yolk sac is absorbed. Thereafter the young gradually range farther in search of food until they depart permanently from the nest and the influence of the attending male parent.

Food: The Bowfin eats other fishes.

Remarks: Bowfins can be caught on some artificial lures, but are more often taken on natural baits, especially at night. They are strong fighters, but not good food fish. They are also hardy fishes, with a lunglike air bladder that enables them to withstand oxygen shortage in shallow, weedy waters. They have been reported to bury themselves in the mud of drying pools, where they survive until rains restore the habitat.

ORDER OSTEOGLOSSIFORMES

Mooneyes (Family Hiodontidae)

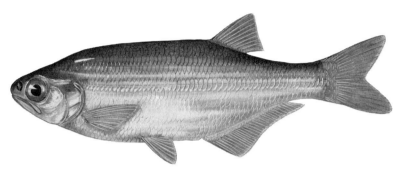

An adult Goldeye *(Hiodon alosoides)*. Drawing by Gene Pacheco.

Goldeye
Hiodon alosoides (Rafinesque) (Plate 5)

Description: Slender, plain white body. Belly not knife-edged. Strong teeth on jaws and tongue. Dorsal fin over anal fin. Anal fin long, with thirty or more rays. Eye very large, iris yellow, pupil shiny.

Size: The largest Goldeye from Kansas weighed 1.0 kg (2.25 pounds) and was 45.3 cm (17¾ inches) in length. It was taken with rod and reel in Milford Reservoir on 19 June 1980 by Mike Augustine of Junction City. Elsewhere in its range, this fish attains a maximum length of 51 cm (20 inches).

Habitat: The Goldeye occurs in large rivers. Our records are from the Missouri, Kansas, Blue, and Republican rivers plus the lowermost parts of the Solomon, Smoky Hill, Marais des Cygnes, Marmaton, and Arkansas rivers. Goldeyes are common in the lower Kansas River but seem scarce elsewhere in the state. Their numbers vary seasonally at Lawrence, being greatest in the cool part of the year and when the river is high. They have been found in small tributary streams only during their reproductive migrations, usually in March or April.

Reproduction: Goldeyes move up rivers, sometimes for many miles, to spawn in flowing water over rocky or gravel bottoms. They also use shoal waters of lakes as spawning sites.

Food: The Goldeye eats insects, both aquatic larval stages and winged forms that fall onto the water surface. Large adult Goldeyes also consume other fishes.

Remarks: The "eye shine" of the Goldeye results from reflective tissue beside the visual cells. It and the large size of the eye enable this fish to make effective use of the dim light available in muddy rivers. Most other fishes that live in turbid water have reduced their dependence on sight by improving other senses such as taste and hearing; the Goldeye, Walleye, and Sauger have improved the sensitivity of their eyes. Goldeyes can sometimes be caught with minnows, small spinning lures, and worms.

ORDER ANGUILLIFORMES

FRESHWATER EELS (Family Anguillidae)

An adult American Eel *(Anguilla rostrata)*. Drawing by Victor Hogg.

American Eel
Anguilla rostrata (LeSueur) (Plate 5)

Description: American Eels are slender, slightly compressed fishes with one continuous fin along the back, around the tip of the tail and forward to the vent. They also have small pectoral fins just behind the head. Water passing across the gills is discharged through a short slot in front of the pectoral fins. These eels have jaws like other fishes, differing from Chestnut Lampreys in that respect. American Eels also have scales, but these are so small and so deeply embedded in the skin that the body appears naked. These fishes are gray or brownish, fading to yellow ventrally.

Size: The largest American Eel from Kansas weighed 2.0 kg (4.44 pounds) and was 89.7 cm (35¼ inches) in length. It was taken with rod and reel in the Kansas River on 23 June 1987 by Ralph B. Westerman of Manhattan. Elsewhere in its range, this fish reaches a maximum length of 152 cm (60 inches).

Habitat: No American Eels ever began life in Kansas, although they formerly occupied streams throughout the state. Their initial habitat is more than 3,000 miles away, in black, cold water more than half a mile deep in

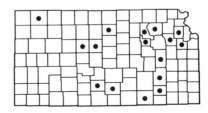

the Atlantic Ocean, where their parents go to spawn and die. Thus young American Eels begin life as orphans, with a long way to go to find a home. They float to the surface and begin feeding on microscopic animals as they drift in ocean currents. The larval American Eels are then flat, transparent creatures, invisible except for their two dark eyes. Within a year they arrive at the coastline, become wormlike in shape, and enter rivers. Only females go very far inland.

All American Eels that we have heard about from Kansas were large—at least 32.5 cm (13 inches) long—indicating that they may have worked their way upstream slowly over a period of years. Historical records indicate that these fishes were more common 100 years ago than they are now. In 1875, F. H. Snow wrote that American Eels were "occasionally taken by the hook, sometimes of 6 lbs. weight" in the Kansas River at Lawrence. In 1885, F. W. Cragin cited reports of fishermen that these fishes were "not uncommon" at Topeka; and I. D. Graham, writing in the same year, believed American Eels to be "common throughout the State."

Seemingly, more American Eels entered Kansas by way of the Arkansas River than the Missouri River, because most of our early, verified records are from the Arkansas basin in southern Kansas: the Neosho, Verdigris, Walnut, and Ninnescah rivers. Eels cannot ascend those streams any longer. High dams across the Arkansas River and its tributaries in Oklahoma and Arkansas now block their migrations. Because they are long-lived, a few American Eels were caught in Kansas for several years after the first of those reservoirs were impounded. They normally spend at least six years in freshwater before returning to the sea to spawn, and captive examples have lived more than twenty years in freshwater. But none persist in southern Kansas today.

In the Kansas River basin, American Eels have been reported as far west as Beaver Creek, Rawlins County. Dams now block their access to that area also, but this fish is still able to reach streams in northeastern Kansas. Several of the records mapped in the Kansas River basin are relatively recent.

Reproduction: Female American Eels mature at an age of six or more years. They begin their spawning migration in autumn, moving down rivers to the Gulf of Mexico, where they are joined by males that have spent their lives in brackish coastal waters. By spring they arrive at their breeding site in the Sargasso Sea, southeast of Bermuda and nearly a thousand miles from the North American coast. So far as known, this is the only place where reproduction occurs, by either American or European Eels. The adults die after releasing and fertilizing the eggs, which developed during the course of the journey.

Food: During their life in Kansas streams and rivers, American Eels eat crayfishes and other fishes. The young eat aquatic insects.

Remarks: American Eels will disappear from the state unless the Missouri and Mississippi rivers remain free of high dams between Kansas and the Gulf. Eels are a luxury food fish, regarded by many people as a supreme delicacy. American Eels can be caught on hook and line, but that happens so rarely in Kansas that few anglers are prepared for the experience. Not surprisingly, the fish writhes like a snake in an effort to escape. It is remarkably strong, and slick, and impossible to hold bare-handed. It may bite. If a burlap sack is handy, the eel can be lowered into that and grasped through the sack, and the hook can then be retrieved from its mouth. Lacking a sack, one can pin the eel against the ground with a hand full of sand or grass, and string it on a cord like any other fish. Or one can clip the line and let it go, hoping it will shed the hook and find a way back to the sea, to complete its extraordinary life cycle.

ORDER CLUPEIFORMES

HERRINGS (Family Clupeidae)

An adult Skipjack Herring *(Alosa chrysochloris)*. Drawing by F. A. Carmichael.

Skipjack Herring
Alosa chrysochloris (Rafinesque) (Plate 6)

Description: Slender, bright silvery body with knife-edged belly. Mouth terminal, with thin jaws and weak teeth. Dorsal fin above pelvic fins. Last dorsal fin ray not elongate. Anal fin short, with about eighteen rays.

Size: Maximum weight for a Skipjack Herring is 1.6 kg (3.5 pounds); maximum length for an adult of this species is 53 cm (21 inches), but this fish is usually less than 40 cm (16 inches) long.

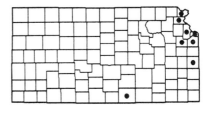

Habitat: The Skipjack Herring is migratory in large rivers. It invaded the Missouri and Kansas rivers only after construction of several large reservoirs caused the flow of those rivers to be clearer and less variable than in the past. Skipjacks also occur in the lowermost part of the Marais des Cygnes drainage. A record from Wellington, in 1942, accounts for the dot in Sumner County, but no Skipjack Herring have since been reported from the Arkansas River basin in Kansas.

Reproduction: Skipjack Herring spawn in river channels following migrations upstream in spring; beyond that, the reproductive habits of this fish are unknown.

Food: Minnows and other small fishes are the favored food of the Skipjack Herring.

Remarks: The Skipjack Herring can be caught on hook and line, with small flies, spinners, or minnows. Platt et al. (1974), in compiling their list of endangered and threatened species, included this fish as a peripheral species in Kansas.

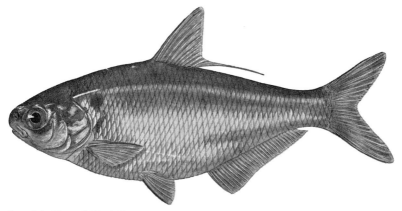

An adult Gizzard Shad *(Dorosoma cepedianum)*. Drawing by Gene Pacheco.

Gizzard Shad
Dorosoma cepedianum (LeSueur) (Plate 6)

Description: Flattened, silvery body with knife-edged belly. Snout blunt, mouth small and subterminal, jaws fragile and toothless. Dark shoulder spot near upper edge of gill cover present in young and subadults. Limp, threadlike extension of last dorsal fin ray; anal fin rays 25–36.

Size: Maximum length for an adult of this species is 52 cm (20½ inches), weight 1.4 kg (3 pounds); rarely more than 0.4 kg (1 pound).

Habitat: The Gizzard Shad occupies most large streams and lakes throughout the state. Introductions into reservoirs have greatly increased the range and abundance of Gizzard Shads since 1950. Vast schools of young shad may be seen near the surface of reservoirs on calm days in summer. The adults seldom cruise near the surface. Shad of all ages commonly move into rivers from the reservoirs, and are sometimes found in creeks.

Reproduction: The Gizzard Shad spawns pelagically, meaning that the eggs are released in open water. Large groups of shad spawn together, usually in May or June. There are no nest-sites and no care of the eggs and young.

Food: Gizzard Shad begin life as tiny predators, capturing single "water fleas" or other animal plankton. At this stage the young are slender, their mouths are large and toothed, and their gut canal is short. After growing to a length of about an inch, the young become slab-sided like the adults. They develop a long gut and a comblike filtering structure on their gills; thereafter they consume micro-organisms (both plant and animal) that are strained from the water as it passes over the gills or settles to the bottom ooze.

Remarks: The Gizzard Shad is now one of the most abundant Kansas fishes. Shallow bays in reservoirs may have as much as 1,000 pounds of Gizzard Shad per acre, more than the total weight of all other species. They are important as forage for game fish.

Threadfin Shad
Dorosoma petenense (Günther) (Plate 6)

Description: Like the Gizzard Shad, but snout more pointed and mouth terminal. Jaws toothless and shorter than in Skipjack Herring. Limp, threadlike extension of last dorsal fin ray; anal fin rays 17–27.

Size: Maximum length for an adult of this species is 23 cm (9 inches).

Habitat: The Threadfin Shad occurs in roving schools in the open water of lakes and rivers.

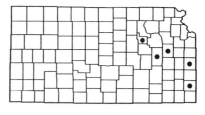

Reproduction: The Threadfin Shad spawns in spring when water temperatures have risen to at least 21°C (70°F). Egg-laying takes place from dawn until shortly after sunrise; the eggs adhere to submerged objects and hatch in about three days.

Food: Like the Gizzard Shad, the Threadfin Shad is primarily a filter feeder, indiscriminately dining on microscopic plants and animals.

Remarks: INTRODUCED SPECIES. The Threadfin Shad has been stocked at various times in Kansas lakes and ponds because of its high value as a forage fish for basses, crappies, and other game fish. It was first introduced into a federal fish hatchery at Farlington, Crawford County, in the 1950s. Although it reproduced abundantly during the summer of introduction, the entire population died in the following winter. This is a southern species that cannot tolerate temperatures below 4°C (40°F). Threadfin Shad were stocked in the 1970s in LaCygne Lake, Linn County, where limited brood stock was expected to survive overwinter in the heated water that is discharged constantly by the power plant for which the reservoir was built. This population perished, however, when the power plant's electric generators were shut down for brief intervals in cold weather. In the 1980s, small numbers of adult Threadfin Shad were stocked experimentally in Osage and Lyon county state fishing lakes, counting on their high reproductive potential to provide forage for game fish through the summer and fall. Although successful in that regard, such management was discontinued, partly because reliable sources of brood fishes for annual spring stocking are so distant from Kansas.

ORDER CYPRINIFORMES

Minnows (Family Cyprinidae)

"Minnows," like other systematic groups of animals, resemble each other in structures that suggest an evolutionary relationship. Small size is one characteristic of most minnows, but size is not really an important systematic character. Other kinds of fishes remain as small as "minnows" throughout their lives, and minnows remain minnows no matter how large they grow. The Common Carp is a minnow that grows more than 91 cm (3 feet) long. The characters that make a fish a minnow are bony structures that are not apparent unless the fish is skeletonized: specialized bones along the spinal column and specialized "throat" teeth behind the gills. Fortunately, most minnows in Kansas can be recognized as members of this family by four characteristics: (1) short, triangular or squared dorsal and anal fins that lack bony spines (except in the introduced carps and the Goldfish); (2) lack of scales anywhere on the head; (3) lack of teeth on the jaws, which usually have thin, U-shaped lips without grooves or other irregularities; and (4) presence of a "lateral-line," a row of scales with small tubes or pores that runs along each side of the fish from head to tail.

More than a third of all the different kinds of fish in Kansas are minnows. Because some species of minnows are extremely abundant, much more than half of all the individual fish in the state probably are minnows. If we judge importance or success in terms of numbers alone, minnows must be the most important and most successful group of fish in Kansas and in most other freshwaters of the world.

All of our streams and some of our lakes contain several kinds of minnows. About thirty kinds occur in the Kansas River or its tributaries, and just as many kinds live in the Neosho River system. Six to ten kinds may be caught by seining along a single sandbar or gravel bar in these streams. Unless one already knows these species on sight, proper identification of them may be difficult. It requires counts of scales, fin rays, or careful measurement of other parts—measurements not easily made without magnifying equipment and use of the key for identification included in this book. While a few of the common kinds of minnows can be recognized by comparing the fishes with the drawings and descriptions in the following species accounts, most require use of the key. If this fails to put a name to the fish, take it (frozen, or preserved in 10 percent formalin) to a local office of the Kansas Department of Wildlife and Parks or to the University of Kansas Natural History Museum in Lawrence for identification.

Despite their similar appearance, various kinds of minnows differ greatly in the habitats they occupy, the foods they eat, and the ways in which they raise their young. Some, like the Red Shiner and the Fathead Minnow, are rugged pioneers found nearly everywhere and capable of making their way where few other kinds of fish survive. Other species have very definite habitat requirements that are satisfied in only one or two streams in the state. Some species live entirely in the swift currents of large rivers, others only on shallow, rocky riffles of small streams, still others only in clear pools or muddy backwaters. Some feed only on microscopic animals (zooplankton) that drift with the current. Others feed mainly on algal films that they scrape off rocks in the channel, or glean from soft sediment in pools. Some kinds feed largely on flying insects that fall onto the water surface. A few kinds of minnows grow large enough to eat other fishes. Most minnows find their food at least partly by sight, but many depend also on the senses of smell and taste to locate food. A few kinds (Common Carp, Creek Chub, Hornyhead Chub, Common Shiner, Golden Shiner) can be caught on hook-and-line.

Minnows have more varied reproductive habits than any other group of fishes in Kansas. The Common Carp, Golden Shiner, and others merely scatter eggs over the stems of aquatic plants and depart. Several kinds go to the other extreme, spending much time and effort in preparing nests for the eggs and young, which they defend vigorously and care for in other ways. Some minnows, like cowbirds, use the nests of other species as a place to put their eggs. The reproductive habits of many kinds of minnows are not known.

Minnows are the main food of most predatory fishes in Kansas streams, including many game fish. Thus they are major converters of microscopic organisms to fish flesh of a kind that we can use or enjoy catching. Minnows are commercially important as bait. Golden Shiners, Fathead Minnows, Red Shiners, and a few other species are produced in ponds and sold for that purpose, but many other minnows are caught in the wild for use as bait. Several kinds of native minnows (Red Shiners, Rosyface Shiners, Southern Redbelly Dace, Redfin Shiners, Fathead Minnows) are active, attractive aquarium fishes that readily accept prepared fish food available from pet shops.

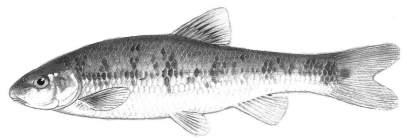

An adult Central Stoneroller *(Campostoma anomalum)*. Drawing by Victor Hogg.

Central Stoneroller
Campostoma anomalum (Rafinesque) (Plates 2, 7)

Description: Head blunt, snout overhanging mouth. No barbels. Lower lip fleshy, not quite covering the hard, chisel-edged lower jaw. Color greenish gray with scattered dark flecks. Fins short and rounded. Gut very long, coiled around air bladder, lining of body cavity black.

Size: The Central Stoneroller grows to a maximum length of 22 cm (8½ inches).

Habitat: This species originally inhabited small streams through-out Kansas and occurred occasionally in rivers. It was most abundant in permanent, clear creeks in the Flint Hills, and in other streams where exposed rock strata cause high gradients, clean stream bottoms, and frequent small riffles. Central Stonerollers tolerate moderate siltation and pollution with organic wastes, so long as the water remains reasonably cool, clear, and well oxygenated.

Reproduction: The Central Stoneroller spawns from March until May when water temperatures are 15°C (60°F) or higher. Nest sites are on bottoms of small gravel with moderately clear water and a deeper pool nearby. Males prepare a nest by digging in the gravel with their snouts, pushing aside stones, and lifting pebbles with their mouths. Nests are often large and clearly visible as light-colored patches on the bottoms of shallow riffles. Several males may prepare the nest and receive females singly to spawn.

Food: This fish feeds on the film of micro-organisms that grow on the surface of stones or debris in the stream.

Subspecies in Kansas: A western race, *Campostoma anomalum pullum.*

Remarks: In central and western Kansas, the distribution and abundance of Central Stonerollers has changed during the past 25 years, due to construction of impoundments, land-use practices (including expanded irrigation), and widespread reduction in stream flows. Headwater streams in the state have dried, and some river channels have acquired characteristics of their tributaries: greatly reduced but more stable flows, clearer water, and stable streambeds. Under these conditions, light penetrates to the firm substrate, allowing development of the algal films needed by Central Stonerollers. Therefore, this species has increased in channel segments of the Arkansas, Cimarron, Smoky Hill, and Solomon rivers, where moderate flow persists in Kansas. In those channel segments, Central Stonerollers have replaced the Plains Minnow, an ecological analogue that predominated when flows of the larger plains rivers fluctuated widely, were usually turbid, and had riverbeds consisting mainly of loose, shifting sand.

An adult Goldfish *(Carassius auratus)*. Drawing by Gene Pacheco.

Goldfish
Carassius auratus (Linnaeus) (Plate 7)

Description: Dorsal and anal fins each with a saw-edged spine at leading edge. Mouth opening forward rather than downward; lips thin; no barbels. Color gray to brassy to orange. Most closely resembles Bigmouth Buffalo and Common Carp.

Size: The Goldfish grows to a length of 41 cm (16 inches) and attains a maximum weight of 1.4 kg (3 pounds), but it is rarely more than 25.5 cm (10 inches) long.

Habitat: The Goldfish is found occasionally in streams and impoundments. It might be caught almost anywhere in the state, but it is not a common fish at any localities known to us.

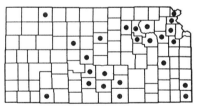

Reproduction: This species scatters eggs on vegetation in shallow water in spring. It doesn't build a nest or provide parental care for eggs or young.

Food: Goldfish feed mainly on zooplankton and larval insects.

Remarks: INTRODUCED SPECIES. The Goldfish has been introduced in Kansas many times since the turn of the century, often as bait. It has not been as successful as the Common Carp in establishing itself in the state. Nevertheless, use of this fish as bait should be discouraged. Its appropriate place is in aquariums and garden pools, as exotic varieties that are least likely to survive if released into lakes and streams.

Grass Carp
Ctenopharyngodon idella (Valenciennes) (Plate 7)

Description: Broad, blunt head with terminal, transverse mouth; dorsal fin spineless, short, pointed, and with eight fin rays; anal fin lacks spine at leading edge; caudal peduncle short and deep; size large.

Size: The largest Grass Carp from Kansas weighed 23.1 kg (51 pounds) and was 117 cm (46 inches) in length. It was taken by bow and arrow in Clark County State Lake on 19 June 1992 by Gregg Lawrence of Minneola. In other states, this fish attains a maximum length of 125 cm (49 inches).

Habitat: The Grass Carp lives in rivers and impoundments. In Kansas, it has been found in the Missouri and Arkansas rivers, as well as in many ponds and lakes where stocked.

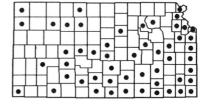

Reproduction: This species spawns in the channels of large rivers, where many thousands of eggs are released to be carried on strong currents.

Food: Young Grass Carp feed on small crustaceans and other invertebrates. The adults of this fish prefer aquatic vegetation (particularly vascular plants properly termed *macrophytes,* but commonly known as "moss" or "weeds").

Remarks: INTRODUCED SPECIES. As early as 1963, the Grass Carp was brought into the United States and released (in Arkansas) as a proposed biological control for aquatic vegetation in ponds and lakes. But elimination of aquatic plants destroys habitat for native animals and alters food chains for fishes in ponds and lakes. The effect of this large fish on the habitat of native river fishes is not yet known. The Grass Carp is strong and active, and will leap over a seine if trapped or cornered.

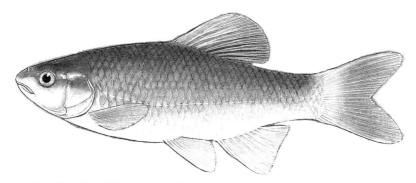

An adult Bluntface Shiner *(Cyprinella camura).* Drawing by Victor Hogg.

Bluntface Shiner
Cyprinella camura (Jordan and Meek) (Plate 8)

Description: Pale area at base of tail fin. Dorsal fin rounded, with black streaks between last few rays. Anal fin with nine rays. Mouth not quite terminal (tip of snout extending slightly forward beyond jaw). Sides compressed (flattened). Color bluish silvery; when spawning it has reddish fins and shoulder patch. Most resembles Red Shiner and Spotfin Shiner.

Size: The Bluntface Shiner has a maximum length in Kansas of about 13 cm (5 inches).

Habitat: This fish is common in the small and medium-size streams in the Flint Hills (Neosho and Verdigris basins), in the Spring River drainage in Cherokee County, and in the Chikaskia River in Kingman and 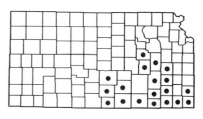 Sumner counties. It prefers moderately fast, clear water and avoids streams with low gradients and mud or sand bottoms.

Reproduction: The Bluntface Shiner spawns in late spring and summer at water temperatures of about 26°C (80°F) or slightly cooler.

Food: Food preferences of the Bluntface Shiner are not known.

An adult Red Shiner *(Cyprinella lutrensis)*. Drawing by Victor Hogg.

Red Shiner
Cyprinella lutrensis (Baird and Girard) (Plate 8)

Description: Body compressed (flattened side-to-side), sides plain silvery or bluish. Mouth terminal. Dorsal fin over or slightly behind pelvic fins, rather low, without distinctive dark streaks between the last rays. Tail fin often red. Breeding males with blue sides and rosy crescent behind head; lower fins and top of head red. Anal fin with 8–10 (usually 9) rays.

Size: Maximum length for an adult of this species is about 9 cm (3½ inches).

Habitat: The Red Shiner is a remarkably hardy, adaptable fish. Whereas most species "specialize" in their habitats and activities, the Red Shiner seems to accept any available living space, so long as it stays wet. This species is ubiquitous in Kansas. It thrives in large rivers (the Missouri, Kansas, and Arkansas); in shaded, rocky Flint Hills streams; in the sunlit runs of shady western creeks; and in the muddy pools of gullies that flow only after rains. We have yet to find it in drinking fountains or swimming pools, but we believe that Red Shiners occur at some time in every natural body of water in Kansas. Within weeks after pollution from feedlots killed nearly all fishes in several miles of the Cottonwood River some years ago, Red Shiners were common in that stream. A few days after a large oil spill passed down the Marais des Cygnes River in 1974, the Red Shiner was the only living thing we found there.

Red Shiners are not equally abundant in all habitats. They are most numerous where few other kinds of fishes occur—where conditions are unfavorable for the more specialized, habitat-limited species. Red Shiners are abundant where conditions are unstable due to irregular flow, frequent muddy water (high turbidity), or pollution. None of the changes people have caused in our streams have discouraged Red Shiners; where other species have been depleted, Red Shiners have increased.

Reproduction: Red Shiners spawn from May to September, at water temperatures between 15° and 29°C (60° and 85°F). Many sites are used by Red Shiners for depositing their eggs: vegetation or woody debris in midwater or at the surface; coarse sand or gravel on the stream bottom; and the nests of other fishes.

Food: The Red Shiner eats small aquatic animals—mainly microcrustaceans and insects—that it gleans from midwater, the surface, or the bottom. It is mainly carnivorous but also consumes some algae.

Remarks: Several adaptations of the Red Shiner work together to account for its success in plains streams. First, it is small, so only limited space and resources are needed to sustain it. Second, it occurs in schools, which aid the individuals in finding one another and the resources each one needs. Third, it is an active, vagile (free-ranging) fish that moves rapidly into all accessible water, such as renewed flow in streams after rains. Fourth, it is short-lived, matures rapidly, and produces large numbers of young. Its populations consist mainly of one-year-old individuals, but these are reproductively mature, and they spawn repeatedly over a long period. These adaptations allow for rapid increase of its population. Finally, the Red Shiner has a remarkable tolerance of conditions that cause many other fishes stress, such as warm temperatures and low levels of dissolved oxygen.

Because of its exceptional resistance to the hazards of aquatic life, the Red Shiner may always be with us, no matter how badly we mistreat our water. We do not mean that Red Shiners cannot be killed by pollution, siltation, floods, and drought; they often die in great numbers. But they are not likely to be "wiped out" at any place and time, as other species are. As other species disappear, the nucleus of surviving Red Shiners occupies the habitats of all of them, and they become more abundant than ever.

The Red Shiner is an excellent aquarium fish, because of its active disposition, "toughness," and the handsome coloration of adult males. It should not be placed in tanks with "tropical" species such as tetras.

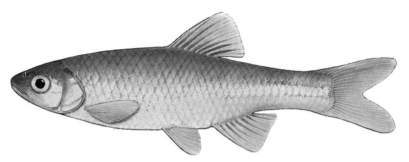

An adult Spotfin Shiner *(Cyprinella spiloptera)*. Drawing by Victor Hogg.

Spotfin Shiner
Cyprinella spiloptera (Cope)

Description: Dark streaks between last few rays of dorsal fin. Body slender but sides flattened. Snout sharp, mouth terminal. Anal fin with eight rays. Sides plain silvery. Breeding males steely blue with dusky streak on sides before tail fin, lower fins yellow. Most resembles Red Shiner and Bluntface Shiner.

Size: This species grows to a maximum length of 12 cm (4¾ inches).

Habitat: The Spotfin Shiner is restricted in Kansas to the Spring River drainage in Cherokee County. It prefers moderate currents adjacent to gently sloping, clean gravel bars at depths of 30–122 cm (1–4 feet).

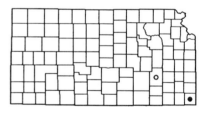

Reproduction: The Spotfin Shiner probably spawns from late May to July in Kansas. Reports elsewhere state that the eggs are laid on submerged logs near riffles, in a slight current. The logs must have loose bark or crevices for egg deposition.

Food: The food of the Spotfin Shiner consists of small insects and crustaceans, mostly captured as "drift" at the surface or in midwater.

Remarks: SINC SPECIES. The Spotfin Shiner was listed along with threatened species by Platt et al. (1974) because it has only limited, peripheral populations in Kansas. It may formerly have occurred in the upper parts of the Neosho and Verdigris drainages.

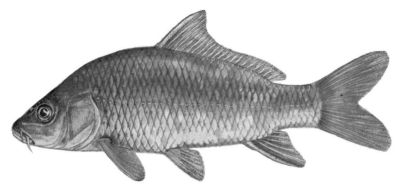

An adult Common Carp *(Cyprinus carpio).* Drawing by F. A. Carmichael.

Common Carp
Cyprinus carpio Linnaeus (Plate 8)

Description: Long, sickle-shaped dorsal fin with one saw-edged spine at leading edge; similar spine at front of anal fin. Two barbels on each side of mouth. Color brassy, fins may be reddish-orange.

Size: The Common Carp normally grows to an average length of 30–65 cm (12–24 inches). The largest example of this fish from Kansas measured 104 cm (41 inches) in total length and weighed 21.1 kg (46½ pounds). It was caught by Michael L. Pembleton of Olathe on rod and reel in the Olathe Waterworks Lake, Johnson County, on 30 May 1989. Elsewhere in its range, this fish attains a maximum length of 122 cm (48 inches).

Habitat: The Common Carp inhabits nearly every body of water in Kansas, other than the small farm ponds for which it was originally introduced. It is most abundant in large lakes and rivers. During floods this species spreads rapidly with the rising water.

Reproduction: The Common Carp breeds any time from March to July, a lengthy spawning season when compared with that of other species. The eggs are scattered over vegetation or debris in shallow water, usually following rises in water level. No nests are prepared, and parent fish afford the eggs no protection. The high reproductive potential of the Common Carp is demonstrated by a 7.7-kg (17-pound) female that contained more than two million eggs.

Food: The Common Carp eats microscopic organisms and plant and animal material, especially insects and refuse. It seldom preys on other fishes, but it does compete with them for food and alters habitats in ways detrimental to native fishes.

Remarks: INTRODUCED SPECIES. The Common Carp was first released in Kansas in 1880 and spread rapidly throughout the state. It is a food and game fish, being stronger and more tenacious than most other gamefish of equal weight. Specimens known as "mirror carp" (with a few enlarged scales) and "leather carp" (without scales) are sometimes caught. These are simply variants of the Common Carp.

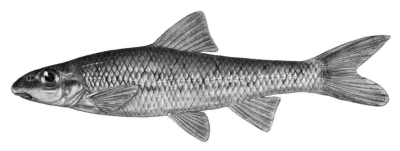

An adult Gravel Chub *(Erimystax x-punctatus)*. Drawing by Gene Pacheco.

Gravel Chub
Erimystax x-punctatus (Hubbs and Crowe) (Plate 9)

Description: Body slender, with dark flecks, some resembling x's. Eye large. Mouth small, beneath snout, one small barbel on each side. Color greenish, not silvery.

Size: The Gravel Chub grows to a maximum length of 11 cm (4¼ inches).

Habitat: This fish resides in deep riffles over gravel bottoms in the Neosho and Spring rivers.

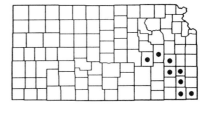

Reproduction: Gravel Chubs spawn in April at water temperatures around 15°C (60°F), generally at a depth of 60–90 cm (2–3 feet). Spawning sites are on gravel bars in swift current.

Food: Food preferences of the Gravel Chub are not known.

Subspecies in Kansas: The nominate race, *Erimystax x. x-punctatus.*

Remarks: SINC SPECIES. To protect this species, Platt et al. (1974) recommended control of pollution, especially influx of nutrients. Permanent flow needs to be maintained over long stretches of clean gravel bottom, and the water must be clear.

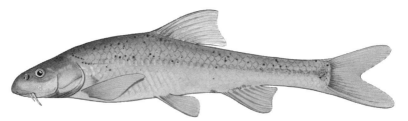

An adult Speckled Chub *(Extrarius aestivalis).* Drawing by Victor Hogg.

Speckled Chub
Extrarius aestivalis (Girard) (Plate 9)

Description: Slender, nearly transparent body with scattered dark dots, like flyspecks on back. Snout long, eye small, mouth small and ventral, with one or two prominent barbels on each side.

Size: Maximum length for an adult of this species is 7.6 cm (3 inches).

Habitat: The Speckled Chub inhabits the shallow channels of large, permanently flowing, sandy streams. It prefers currents over a substrate of clean, fine sand, and avoids areas of calm water and silted stream bottoms.

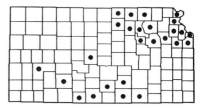

Reproduction: The Speckled Chub seems to spawn only when rivers and streams rise abruptly, between May and August, when water temperatures exceed 21°C (70°F). The eggs drift downstream with strong currents.

Food: The diet of this fish is not known, but it probably consists of larval insects.

Subspecies in Kansas: Two populations of the Speckled Chub, currently recognized as subspecies, occur in Kansas. They are *Extrarius aestivalis hyostoma,* found in the Missouri River and eastern part of the Kansas River basin, and *Extrarius aestivalis tetranemus,* found in the Arkansas River and its western tributaries. Two barbels are present in *E. a. hyostoma,* four in *E. a. tetranemus.*

Remarks: ENDANGERED SPECIES IN KANSAS (Arkansas River populations only). Since the 1960s, the Arkansas River population of this fish, *Extrarius aestivalis tetranemus,* has been decimated, due to precipitous declines in stream flow.

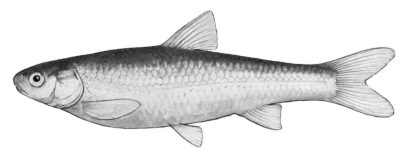

An adult Western Silvery Minnow *(Hybognathus argyritis)*. Drawing by Victor Hogg.

Western Silvery Minnow
Hybognathus argyritis Girard

Description: Resembles the Plains Minnow except that the eye is larger, the scales are larger, and the body is somewhat heavier and more streamlined (less flattened ventrally). The two species are most easily distinguished by examining a bony process above and behind the gills, the bone to which muscles operating the throat teeth are attached. This process is rodlike in the Plains Minnow and expanded in the Western Silvery Minnow.

Size: Maximum length for an adult of this species in Kansas is 15 cm (6 inches).

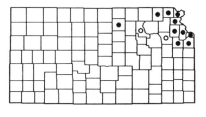

Habitat: The Western Silvery Minnow occurs commonly only in the Missouri River and in the creeks and backwaters of its flood-plain. The species formerly oc-curred in the lower part of the Kansas River, especially during high water, but it was never so abundant there as its close relative, the Plains Minnow. It prefers relatively deep water where flow is sluggish and bottoms are silted, but it can be taken also in strong currents of the mainstream.

Reproduction: Breeding habits of the Western Silvery Minnow are not known.

Food: See the account of the Plains Minnow.

Remarks: THREATENED SPECIES IN KANSAS. No Western Silvery Minnows have been taken in the Kansas River for many years.

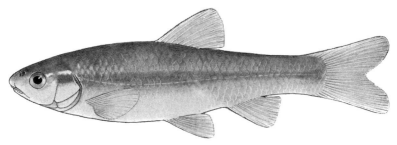

An adult Brassy Minnow *(Hybognathus hankinsoni)*. Drawing by Victor Hogg.

Brassy Minnow
Hybognathus hankinsoni Hubbs

Description: Stout, rounded body (sides not compressed). Head short, snout blunt. Mouth small, its cleft (with jaws closed) forming a shallow crescent rather than a deep U-shape. Sides usually with a dusky streak. Dorsal fin low, rounded, directly above pelvic fins. Anal fin with eight rays. Gut long and coiled, lining of body cavity black.

Size: Maximum length for an adult of this species is 9.7 cm (3¾ inches).

Habitat: The Brassy Minnow is known only from the upper part of the Smoky Hill and Republican rivers in northwestern Kansas, and from the Missouri River and one of its tributaries in Atchison County, northeastern

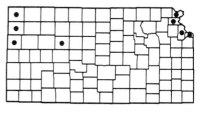

Kansas. It prefers small, clear streams having sluggish current and sandy bottom overlain by organic sediment, or weedy pools.

Reproduction: The Brassy Minnow spawns in May. Little else is known of its reproductive habits.

Food: Food of this fish probably consists of micro-organisms skimmed off the bottom ooze, or attached to detritus.

Remarks: SINC SPECIES. The unusual distribution of this species suggests that it occurred more widely in Kansas at some time in the past. Prior to 1970, Brassy Minnows still occurred in a few small streams in northeastern Kansas, but in that region we have since found them only in backwaters along the Missouri River. In 1986, this fish still inhabited the South Fork of the Republican River and its tributary, Cherry Creek, in Cheyenne County, extreme northwestern Kansas. The Sternberg Museum at Fort Hays State University has one specimen that was caught in the Smoky Hill River in Trego County in 1994. Fossil remains of the Brassy Minnow have been found in the Cimarron River basin in southwestern Kansas.

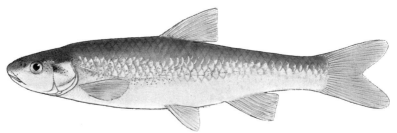

An adult Plains Minnow *(Hybognathus placitus)*. Drawing by Victor Hogg.

Plains Minnow
Hybognathus placitus Girard (Plate 9)

Description: Slender body, flattened ventrally. Mouth thin-lipped, ventral, without barbels. Cleft of mouth (with jaws closed) forming a shallow crescent rather than a deep U-shape. Gut long and coiled, lining of body cavity black. Dorsal fin high and pointed, directly over pelvic fins. Anal fin with eight rays. Straw-colored with sides yellowish-white or dull silvery, not transparent.

Size: Maximum length for an adult of this species is 13 cm (5 inches).

Habitat: This species was formerly abundant in all large Kansas streams that had broad beds of sand and shallow, braided flow. Within such streams, the Plains Minnow is most numerous where sediments accumulate in shallow backwaters, gentle eddies, and along the deeper edges of sand "waves" that are formed on the shifting substrate by the action of the current.

Reproduction: The Plains Minnow spawns between April and August. Its reproductive habits are not fully understood, but its eggs have been collected in strong currents, drifting downstream during their development. Abrupt rises (flood flows) may stimulate spawning in this species. In one instance, we observed Plains Minnows gathered in large schools, ready to scatter their eggs in shallow backwaters.

Food: This fish is partly herbivorous, feeding along the bottom on the thin layer of microscopic plants (diatoms or other algae) and animals that occur in calm, shallow backwaters.

Remarks: SINC SPECIES. The Plains Minnow formerly was a common bait fish in Kansas, due to its wide occurrence, abundance, and large size, but it has declined precipitously over most of its range in the state. It has not been found at all in the lower Kansas River in recent years, although it was abundant there until the 1970s.

An adult Bigmouth Shiner *(Hybopsis dorsalis).* Drawing by Gene Pacheco.

Bigmouth Shiner
Hybopsis dorsalis (Agassiz)

Description: Body stout, not compressed. Back arched and with small, crowded scales along nape behind head. Mouth large, horizontal, extending backward below eye. Sand-colored, sides silvery, no bright spawning coloration. Resembles Sand Shiner, but mouth larger and more nearly horizontal, snout longer, and dorsal fin higher. Anal fin with eight rays.

Size: Maximum length for an adult of this species is 8 cm (3¼ inches).

Habitat: Bigmouth Shiners in-habit small, sandy tributaries of the Missouri River and the head-waters of Stranger Creek and the Nemaha River in the loess-man-tled rolling hills of the Glaciated Region in northeastern Kansas.

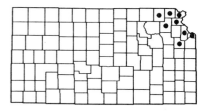

"Strays" are found rarely in the lower Kansas River, and recently (1989 to 1993) this fish was taken in the Delaware River drainage.

Reproduction: The Bigmouth Shiner spawns in June and July.

Food: This species eats larval insects, microcrustaceans, and some algae.

Subspecies in Kansas: The nominate race, *Hybopsis d. dorsalis.*

Remarks: Although not considered to be endangered or threatened in Kansas, the Bigmouth Shiner was listed as peripheral by Platt et al. (1974) because of its highly localized occurrence. The Kansas records are at the southern limit of the range of this species.

   This taxon only recently was placed in the genus *Hybopsis.* Many ich-thyologists have retained it in the genus *Notropis,* pending further study.

Bighead Carp
Hypophthalmichthys nobilis (Richardson) (Plate 9)

Description: Large, laterally compressed, deep-bodied fish with eyes that are very low and well forward on a proportionately big head (head length about one-third of body length). Body scales very small, nearly 100 in the lateral line. Mouth terminal, lower jaw projecting forward beyond the upper. Dorsal fin short, without anterior spine. Pectoral fins long, extending backward beyond base of pelvic fins. Anal fin with 13–14 rays. Upper body dark gray; lower sides and belly white. Resembles Grass Carp, but scales are much smaller and caudal peduncle narrower.

Size: Maximum length for an adult of this species is about 92 cm (36 inches); maximum known weight is about 27.2 kg (60 pounds). An example weighing 14.5 kg (32 pounds) is the largest reported to us from Kansas.

Habitat: The Bighead Carp inhabits the open water of large rivers and lakes in its native range, southern China. Although it can live in lakes and ponds, it does not reproduce in these habitats.

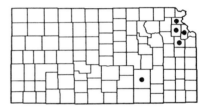

Reproduction: Bighead Carp spawning usually occurs at times of rising water levels, from April to June, in large rivers where the current velocity exceeds 78 cm (2.6 feet) per second. The eggs drift downstream and hatch.

Food: The Bighead Carp is a filter feeder with long gill rakers, consuming large quantities of plankton, mainly microcrustaceans but also some algal plankton.

Remarks: INTRODUCED SPECIES. Bighead Carp were brought to the United States in 1972. Their primary use is in aquaculture (in combination with Channel Catfish), partly for control of pond water quality. Bighead Carp are also sold as food or as live stock for other ponds. They escaped into the Missouri River and, since 1990, have increased and spread into the lower Kansas River. Several were caught in the spring of 1994 in the Kansas, Delaware, and Wakarusa rivers.

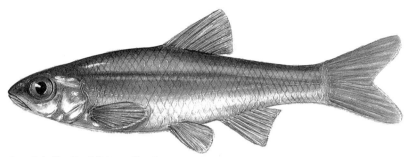

An adult Cardinal Shiner *(Luxilus cardinalis)*. Drawing by Gene Pacheco.

Cardinal Shiner
Luxilus cardinalis (Mayden)

Description: Eye large. Dorsal fin directly above pelvic fins. Bright silvery body that is not at all transparent. Broad stripe on midline of back. A thin, dark line running along upper sides, at boundary of silvery area. Anal fin with nine rays. When spawning, males' fins and lower sides are deep red; and lateral stripe is broad and dark.

Size: Maximum length for an adult of this species is 11 cm (4¼ inches).

Habitat: The Cardinal Shiner (formerly called the Duskystripe Shiner in Kansas) is abundant in Shoal Creek and Spring River in Cherokee County. It occurs as a relict population in the upper Neosho basin, in spring-fed 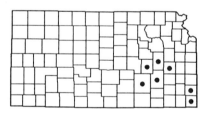 streams of the Flint Hills. This fish requires clear, cool water where the bottom is limestone rubble and gravel. It lives in pools and moderate current.

Reproduction: The Cardinal Shiner spawns during April or May, in or immediately below swift, shallow riffles during daylight.

Food: Food preferences of Cardinal Shiners are not known.

An adult Striped Shiner *(Luxilus chrysocephalus).* Drawing by F. A. Carmichael.

Striped Shiner
Luxilus chrysocephalus Rafinesque (Plate 10)

Description: Resembles the Common Shiner (see next species account), except: scales on back not much smaller than on sides of body; rows of scales accented by zigzag lines. Anal fin with nine rays. Males rose-colored in spring.

Size: Maximum length for an adult of this species is about 18 cm (7 inches).

Habitat: This species inhabits small to medium-size streams having clear, weedless water and moderate to swift current. The Striped Shiner is most common near the margins of riffles with gravel or rubble bottoms. It avoids 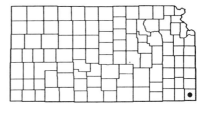 the calm water of large pools. In Kansas, it occurs only in the Spring River drainage (Cherokee County).

Reproduction: The Striped Shiner spawns from late May to early July. Spawning takes place on deep riffles or other clean gravel areas.

Food: The Striped Shiner eats insects.

Subspecies in Kansas: The nominate race, *Luxilus c. chrysocephalus.*

Remarks: The Striped Shiner is rare in Kansas due to its restriction to a single drainage area; listed by Platt et al. (1974) as a peripheral species. Populations in the Spring River vary sporadically from year to year and possibly seasonally.

An adult Common Shiner *(Luxilus cornutus)*. Drawing by F. A. Carmichael.

Common Shiner
Luxilus cornutus (Mitchill) (Plate 10)

Description: Large eye. Bold stripe along midline of back. Sides bright silvery with very high, diamond-shaped scales. Scales along back, in front of dorsal fin, much smaller than scales on sides. Anal fin with nine rays. Males become darker in spring, have rose-colored fins and body, and have large tubercles on head.

Size: Maximum length for the Common Shiner is 18 cm (7 inches).

Habitat: The Common Shiner prefers small to medium-size streams with clear, cool, weedless water, a moderate to swift current, and alternating pools and riffles. It is present only in the Kansas River system, in streams with gravel bottoms.

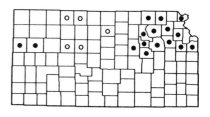

Reproduction: This fish spawns from April to early July at temperatures between 18° and 26°C (64° and 80°F). Breeding sites are always in currents over rubble or gravel bottoms. Common Shiners sometimes use nests of other fishes, especially Creek Chubs or Hornyhead Chubs.

Food: The Common Shiner preys on insects, both aquatic and terrestrial, which it may take from the water surface.

Remarks: The Common Shiner formerly occurred throughout the northern half of the state, in tributaries of the Kansas and Missouri rivers, but the only remaining populations are in the Flint Hills region. This species occasionally hybridizes with the Rosyface Shiner and the Creek Chub.

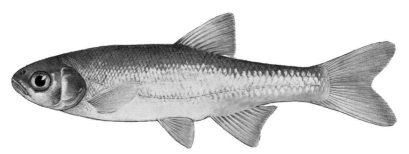

An adult Redfin Shiner *(Lythrurus umbratilis)*. Drawing by Victor Hogg.

Redfin Shiner
Lythrurus umbratilis (Girard)

Description: Dorsal fin arising a little farther back than pelvic fins, not directly above them. Dusky pigment on base of first ray of dorsal fin. Scales small, nearly invisible, along upper sides in front of dorsal fin. Anal fin with ten rays. Color silvery blue, head and fins often dusky gray; fins sometimes reddish near their outer edges.

Size: Maximum length for an adult of this species is 8.5 cm (3½ inches).

Habitat: This fish is abundant in eastern streams south of the Kansas River. The Redfin Shiner prefers small streams with high gradients and rocky riffles, and it avoids waters with heavy siltation or high turbidity. It moves in schools near the surface, mainly in pools.

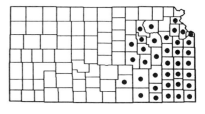

Reproduction: The Redfin Shiner spawns from May to July at water temperatures of 21°C (70°F) or higher, in the nests of sunfish (genus *Lepomis*)—most often the Green Sunfish *(L. cyanellus)*.

Food: Food of the Redfin Shiner consists mostly of animal plankton and small insects.

Subspecies in Kansas: The nominate race, *Lythrurus u. umbratilis.*

Remarks: "Redfin Shiner" is not an apt name for this species because its fins are only faintly red in the Kansas portion of its range, whereas other species that occur with it have bright red fins.

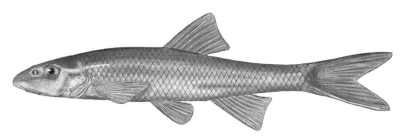

An adult Sturgeon Chub *(Macrhybopsis gelida)*. Drawing by Gene Pacheco.

Sturgeon Chub
Macrhybopsis gelida (Girard)

Description: Body slender; head broad; snout long, wider than high, extending well forward of the ventral mouth. One pair of prominent barbels. Eye very small. Dorsal scales uniformly pigmented (not spotted), each scale with a small, soft keel (not obvious without close scrutiny or magnification). Fins short, not falcate; lower half of caudal fin dark-colored except for its bottom edge, which is creamy white. Most closely resembles Speckled Chub and Sicklefin Chub.

Size: Maximum length for an adult of this species is 8.4 cm (3¼ inches).

Habitat: In Kansas, the Sturgeon Chub has been found only in the Missouri, Kansas, and lower Smoky Hill rivers. It inhabits shallow areas with strong current and bottoms of fine gravel or very coarse sand, often associ-

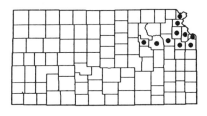

ated with low islands in braided river channels. It may be taken also in small pools, but only in shallow prairie rivers that have loose sand-and-gravel streambeds.

Reproduction: Breeding habits of the Sturgeon Chub are unknown, but presumably spawning occurs in May and June.

Food: The Sturgeon Chub probably eats larval insects.

Remarks: THREATENED SPECIES IN KANSAS. The Sturgeon Chub is well adapted to life in the naturally turbid rivers of the plains. Its depressed head and slender body provide minimal resistance to horizontal flow of water and make use of the downward force of the current to hold the fish on the bottom. Its small eyes are partly shielded from abrasion by water-borne sand. This species has gradually disappeared as impoundments have controlled the flows, water quality, and substrate conditions in the rivers where it originally occurred. It may no longer occur in the Kansas and lower Smoky Hill rivers, but it was recently (1992) found in the Missouri River along the Kansas shoreline.

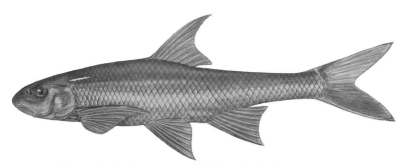

An adult Sicklefin Chub *(Macrhybopsis meeki)*. Drawing by Gene Pacheco.

Sicklefin Chub
Macrhybopsis meeki (Jordan and Evermann)

Description: Sharply pointed, sickle-shaped fins. Mouth beneath rounded snout, with one barbel on each side. Eye very small. Color tawny brown or greenish, sides plain silvery. Scales small (more than 40 in the lateral line). Most resembles Silver Chub and Sturgeon Chub.

Size: The Sicklefin Chub grows to a maximum length of 11 cm (4¼ inches).

Habitat: This species lives on the smooth sand or gravel bottoms of deep water where currents are strong. The Sicklefin Chub is highly adapted to silt-laden large rivers and is found commonly only in the Missouri River.

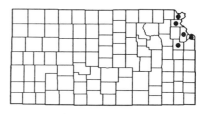

Reproduction: Nothing is known of the breeding habits of the Sicklefin Chub.

Food: The diet of the Sicklefin Chub is unknown.

Remarks: ENDANGERED SPECIES IN KANSAS. The Sicklefin Chub is rare in Kansas because of its restriction to the Missouri River and the lowermost part of the Kansas River, where it has been found on only a few occasions, following floods. Habitat for the Sicklefin Chub has been severely reduced by channel alterations in the Missouri River. Platt et al. (1974) considered this fish a peripheral species on their Kansas rare and endangered list.

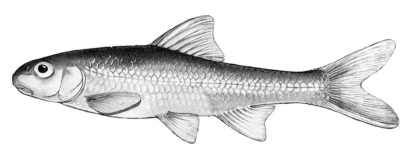

An adult Silver Chub *(Macrhybopsis storeriana)*. Drawing by Victor Hogg.

Silver Chub
Macrhybopsis storeriana (Kirtland) (Plate 10)

Description: Blunt, rounded snout, with small mouth beneath, one barbel on each side. Eye large. Pectoral fins not long or sharply pointed. A bright silvery patch (lacrymal bone) in front of eye. Sides with a narrow, bright silvery streak, translucent dorsally, without dark spots or blotches.

Size: Maximum length for an adult of this species is 23 cm (9 inches).

Habitat: This species lives in large, sandy rivers. It is common only in the Missouri and Kansas rivers. During summer, the Silver Chub prefers the deeper parts of the mainstream, where it is difficult to capture, but many can be caught in shallow currents along sandbars in spring and fall.

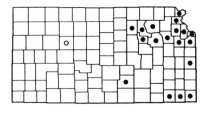

Reproduction: The Silver Chub spawns in April or May. Little else is known of its breeding habits.

Food: Food preferences of the Silver Chub are not known, but they probably consist of larval insects and other small invertebrates living on the riverbed.

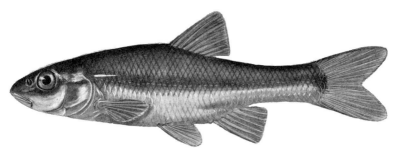

An adult Hornyhead Chub *(Nocomis biguttatus)*. Drawing by Gene Pacheco.

Hornyhead Chub
Nocomis biguttatus (Kirtland) (Plate 11)

Redspot Chub
Nocomis asper Lachner and Jenkins (Plate 11)

These two species are discussed together for several reasons. They differ so little that only large males are easily distinguished. Their habitats are similar so far as is known, but they occupy different parts of the state. People's effect on their habitat has reduced their numbers, eliminating them from many places where they occurred years ago. They are examples of species that are now endangered in Kansas, and we have chosen them for explanation of why and how this depletion occurred. For a contrasting example of a species that has increased because of people's effects on stream habitats, see the account of the Red Shiner.

Description: Head large, mouth large and nearly terminal. Small barbel on each side of mouth, projecting from groove behind lips. Eye larger than in most minnows with barbels. Fins small and rounded, anal fin with seven rays. Scales moderately large, about 42 in the lateral-line row along the middle of the side. Back greenish, sides and fins often yellowish, belly white; body never straw-colored, transparent, or bright silvery as in most other minnows with barbels. Young and some adults with a dusky streak along sides, ending in a black spot at base of tail fin. Young with orange fins.

The Hornyhead Chub and the Redspot Chub most resemble the Creek Chub, which has much smaller scales and a small brown spot at the front of the dorsal fin. The Redspot Chub differs from the Hornyhead Chub in having a longer snout, and tubercles on the body as well as on the head in breeding males. Males of both species share the characters that give them their common names: a patch of large thornlike structures (tubercles) on the top of the head, and a red spot on the gill cover behind the eye.

Size: Maximum length for the Redspot Chub is 22 cm (8½ inches); for the Hornyhead Chub 26 cm (10¼ inches). Neither ordinarily grows more than 15 cm (6 inches) long. They are the largest of the native minnows except for the Creek Chub.

Habitat: The Hornyhead Chub inhabits streams in the Kansas and Marais des Cygnes river basins. A century ago it occurred over most of northern Kansas, but it is found now in only a few streams in the eastern part of the state. The Redspot Chub inhabits streams that flow into the Arkansas River (Neosho and Spring rivers). Within each basin, the two species live only in streams that have a fairly steady flow of clear, cool water in deep "runs" and pools. These chubs are most common in small streams that have aquatic plants along their margins.

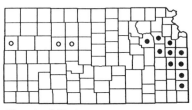

Hornyhead Chub

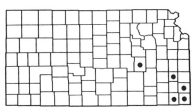

Redspot Chub

Reproduction: Hornyhead and Redspot Chubs spawn in May or June. Water temperature, the volume of flow, and the muddiness of the water influence the time of spawning; but once breeding has begun, it probably lasts only two or three weeks each year. Gravel areas are used for spawning, and the male builds the nest. Rather than excavating a shallow pit as many fishes do, removing sediment in the process, they build a mound of gravel and excavate temporary pits. The bottom must be free of silt, with small stones that the male can lift with his mouth and arrange in a pile. Clear water flowing gently through the nest cleans the gravel and supplies oxygen to the eggs.

Normally each male has a separate nest, although several fish may cooperate in the early stages of its construction. Actual spawning takes place above the nest; the fertilized eggs fall onto its surface. Then the female leaves the nest area, while the male remains to cover the eggs with another layer of gravel. The nest may grow to a height of several inches and a diameter of two to three feet. Other kinds of minnows, such as the Common Shiner, Rosyface Shiner, and Southern Redbelly Dace sometimes use chub nests as spawning sites. The male chub abandons the nest only after the young have hatched, wriggled free of the gravel, and left the area. The young move to the shallow edges of pools, where they feed on microscopic animals and plants.

These chubs become sexually mature in the third spring after they hatch. Their streams must remain constantly favorable for that long, at least, in order for another generation to be produced. Nest sites are limited, and each one takes considerable space, so there can never be many nests. If high water washes out the nests or covers them with silt, that year's production is lost. The adults cannot withstand long periods when the water is muddy, or dry periods when flow stops and they are forced into a few small, warm pools.

Food: Adults of these two species feed on mayflies, crayfishes, snails, and other small invertebrates.

Remarks: THREATENED SPECIES IN KANSAS. Intensive use of the land by people has changed many small streams in ways harmful to chubs. Runoff from fields, roads, and barn lots after spring rains puts more water into the streams than their channels can carry. Mud and polluting wastes ride with the surge of water, then settle to the bottom of the stream as the flow subsides. Failure of that water to soak into the ground may cause springs to dry later in the year. If the streams dry also, chubs disappear. The streams are never without any fishes, because species tolerant of the new conditions, such as Red Shiners, compete with the chubs and take their place. Only a few species withstand the conditions described, however. Thus, if chubs die out several other species are likely to follow. One or two dominant fishes substitute for a larger and more valuable group of species. Because chubs are especially sensitive to change, they are useful indicators of change, a kind of yardstick that tells us how much our streams have deteriorated over long periods of time. Attention to this sign of deterioration can give us time to correct the situation before it worsens further—by protecting the land and water supplies through grassland restoration, terracing where it is needed to reduce erosion from croplands, and other measures to restore flows of clean water in our streams. Occasional high flows are important also, to scour sediments that accumulate in the gravel riffles and pools, to the detriment of these species.

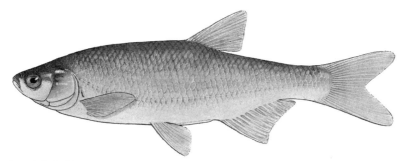

An adult Golden Shiner *(Notemigonus crysoleucas)*. Drawing by Victor Hogg.

Golden Shiner
Notemigonus crysoleucas (Mitchill) (Plate 11)

Description: Small mouth. Thin, fleshy keel on belly behind pelvic fins. Long anal fin (11–15 rays). Lateral line very low on side, with about fifty scales from head to base of tail fin. Color greenish yellow, without dark bands or spots on body or fins.

Size: The Golden Shiner grows to a maximum length of 30 cm (12 inches).

Habitat: This species prefers deep pools and lakes with aquatic vegetation. Its use as fishing bait has established it in many impoundments in Kansas. The Golden Shiner occurs also in pools below dams and in oxbows with reasonably clear water.

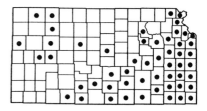

Reproduction: The Golden Shiner spawns in late spring and summer. The eggs are scattered in weed beds where they stick to stems and finely divided leaves. The parents do not prepare a nest, and they ignore the eggs and young.

Food: Microscopic animals (zooplankton) and some aquatic insects are eaten by this fish.

Remarks: This species is produced in ponds for sale as bait minnows, in Kansas and elsewhere. Through such use, it is probably distributed more widely than any other fish in Kansas apart from Largemouth Bass, Bluegill, crappies, and Channel Catfish, which are stocked in ponds as game fishes. Golden Shiners occurred naturally in streams of eastern Kansas, and their range has expanded into many western streams during the past forty years. In some lakes, Golden Shiners grow large enough to be caught on hook and line.

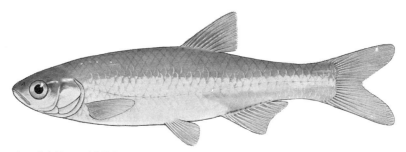

An adult Emerald Shiner *(Notropis atherinoides)*. Drawing by Victor Hogg.

Emerald Shiner
Notropis atherinoides Rafinesque (Plate 11)

Description: Dorsal fin arising farther back than pelvic fins, rather than directly above them. Body slender, nearly transparent, with narrow silver streak on sides; otherwise colorless. Mouth at front of head, no barbels. Resembles Rosyface Shiner but snout is shorter. Anal fin with 10–11 rays.

Size: Maximum length for an adult of this species is 13 cm (5 inches).

Habitat: This fish inhabits large sandy rivers in Kansas. It moves in schools above the bottom, often rising to the surface. Although Emerald Shiners live in rather strong currents of rivers, they also occupy reservoirs.

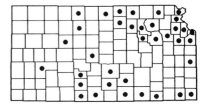

Reproduction: The Emerald Shiner spawns from May to July. Little else is known of its reproductive habits in Kansas.

Food: The Emerald Shiner feeds mainly on animal plankton (micro-crustaceans).

Remarks: Emerald Shiners seem to be declining in abundance, presumably due to dewatering in the Arkansas River and the effects of regulated flow in the Kansas River.

Red River Shiner
Notropis bairdi Hubbs and Ortenburger

Description: Breast and nape partly unscaled; head broad and flat; mouth large, nearly terminal (ending behind front of eye); eye small and high on head; dorsal fin low, its origin in front of pelvic fin origin; robust body; usually seven anal fin rays, fifteen pectoral fin rays, falcate in adult males.

Size: Maximum length for an adult of this species is 8 cm (3¼ inches).

Habitat: The Red River Shiner prefers the sandy, turbid channels of shallow plains rivers.

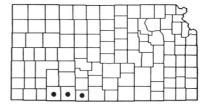

Reproduction: Red River Shiners spawn in summer, scattering their eggs to drift downstream during development.

Food: This species feeds on insects that fall into the stream, and on organisms exposed by movement of the sand or washed downstream.

Remarks: INTRODUCED SPECIES. The Red River Shiner is now established in the Cimarron River in southwestern Kansas, where it has replaced the Arkansas River Shiner.

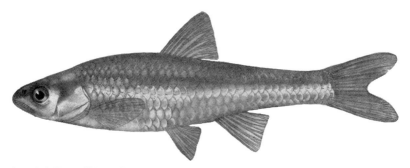

An adult River Shiner *(Notropis blennius).* Drawing by F. A. Carmichael.

River Shiner
Notropis blennius (Girard)

Description: Head large and broad, nearly as wide as high. Mouth and eye large. Stripe along midline of back well developed, continuous around dorsal fin base. Scales rounded, not diamond-shaped. Anal fin with seven rays. Color pale, silvery stripe along middle of sides, little or no dark pigment and no distinctive breeding coloration.

Size: The River Shiner grows to a length of 13 cm (5¼ inches).

Habitat: This species is common in the Missouri River and the lower Arkansas River. It has been found rarely in the lower Kansas, Ninnescah, and Cimarron rivers. Formerly, it occurred in northwestern Kansas in the

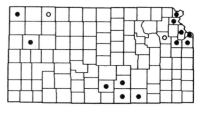

Smoky Hill and Republican drainages. The River Shiner prefers flowing water over sand bottom in large streams having broad, exposed channels.

Reproduction: River Shiners spawn from mid-June to mid-July. Little else is known of their reproductive habits in Kansas.

Food: The food of River Shiners consists mainly of small larval insects and microcrustacea.

Remarks: SINC SPECIES.

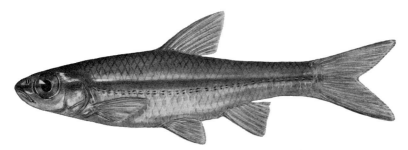

An adult Bigeye Shiner *(Notropis boops)*. Drawing by Gene Pacheco.

Bigeye Shiner
Notropis boops Gilbert (Plate 12)

Description: Large eye. High, sharply pointed dorsal fin. Dark band around snout, from eye to eye, crossing lips. Dusky streak along middle of sides, ending in small spot at base of tail fin. Scales on back large and sharply outlined, no streak along midline of back. No bright breeding colors. Anal fin with eight rays.

Size: The Bigeye Shiner grows to a length of 9 cm (3½ inches).

Habitat: In Kansas, this fish is common in the Spring River system in Cherokee County, and in the Verdigris and Caney rivers in the southern Flint Hills. It is absent from the Neosho. The Bigeye Shiner prefers clear upland streams with high gradients and rocky bottoms.

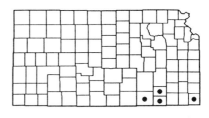

Reproduction: This species spawns from June through August at water temperatures of 26°C (80°F) or higher.

Food: The Bigeye Shiner eats small insects.

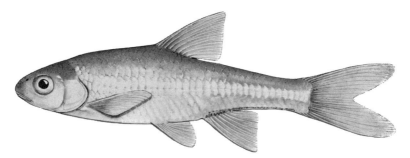

An adult Ghost Shiner *(Notropis buchanani)*. Drawing by Victor Hogg.

Ghost Shiner
Notropis buchanani (Meek)

Description: Scales in one row on sides (lateral-line row) obviously higher than other scales. Dorsal fin high, acutely pointed. Anal fin with eight rays. Color transparent with silver lateral stripe, almost without dark pigment except in base of dorsal and anal fins.

Size: Maximum length for an adult of this species is 6.4 cm (2½ inches).

Habitat: This species inhabits the larger streams of eastern Kansas, reaching its greatest abundance in the Neosho, Verdigris, and Marais des Cygnes rivers. The Ghost Shiner prefers gentle eddies adjacent to strong currents

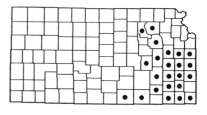

in the main channels of rivers. It is found in pools where small, intermittent creeks join rivers, and alongside the lower part of gravel bars in the mainstream of rivers where the direction of flow is reversed.

Reproduction: The Ghost Shiner spawns from May to mid-August.

Food: The diet of the Ghost Shiner is not known.

Remarks: The Ghost Shiner is so small that it will escape through the meshes of most seines. The adults are no larger than the "fry" of other fishes, and are often mistaken for them.

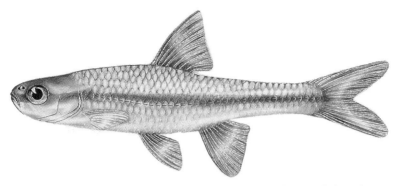

An adult Pugnose Minnow *(Notropis emiliae)*. Drawing by Thomas H. Swearingen.

Pugnose Minnow
Notropis emiliae (Hay) (Plate 12)

Description: Short head and moderately compressed, elongate body; short, blunt snout; small, sharply upturned, vertical mouth; length of upper jaw less than diameter of eye; dorsal fin rays nine; anal fin rays eight; narrow, dark lateral band may be present; lateral line incomplete.

Size: Maximum length for an adult of this species is 6.4 cm (2½ inches).

Habitat: The Pugnose Minnow inhabits low gradient upland streams, lowland streams, lakes, and swamps. It prefers clear sandy areas with heavy vegetation.

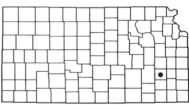

Reproduction: Spawning by Pugnose Minnows probably occurs in early summer.

Food: Pugnose Minnows feed primarily on insect larvae and microcrustaceans.

Subspecies in Kansas: The nominate race, *Notropis e. emiliae.*

Remarks: This species is included as part of the Kansas fish fauna on the basis of four specimens obtained in 1931 from Big Sandy Creek, a tributary to the Verdigris River in Woodson County. No other occurrences in the state have been recorded.

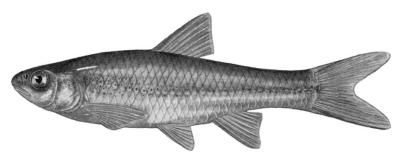

An adult Arkansas River Shiner *(Notropis girardi)*. Drawing by Gene Pacheco.

Arkansas River Shiner
Notropis girardi Hubbs and Ortenburger (Plate 12)

Description: Small size, very small head and eye. Mouth beneath tip of snout, not quite terminal. Straw-colored with silvery sides and scattered brown flecks on sides behind head. Nape fully scaled, without a distinct mid-dorsal stripe. Resembles Sand Shiner, but pectoral and dorsal fins higher, with pointed tips. Anal fin with eight rays. See also Red River Shiner.

Size: Maximum length for an adult of this species is 8 cm (3¼ inches).

Habitat: This species is restricted to the broad, sandy channels of the major western tributaries of the Arkansas River system, where it used to be abundant. In those streams, the Arkansas River Shiner inhabits the "lee" of sand ridges which are formed by steady, shallow waterflow.

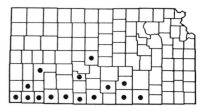

Reproduction: The Arkansas River Shiner spawns from June to August when stream flow increases abruptly. The eggs drift near the surface in the swift currents of open channels. Development is rapid and the hatchlings swim to sheltered areas three or four days after the eggs are deposited.

Food: The Arkansas River Shiner faces into the current and feeds on organisms exposed by movement of the sand or washed downstream.

Remarks: ENDANGERED SPECIES IN KANSAS; proposed for federal listing as endangered in 1994. Since the 1960s, the Arkansas River Shiner has disappeared from the Arkansas River mainstream and from most of the rest of its original range.

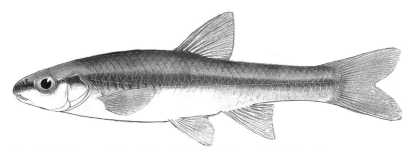

An adult Blacknose Shiner *(Notropis heterolepis)*. Drawing by Victor Hogg.

Blacknose Shiner
Notropis heterolepis Eigenmann and Eigenmann

Description: Dark stripe along sides of body extends anteriorly across snout, but barely onto upper lip and absent from chin; black crescents within stripe; snout round, somewhat elongate; subterminal mouth small, nearly horizontal; dorsal fin origin slightly behind pelvic fin origin; olive to straw-colored above; darkly outlined scales, except those above dark stripe along silvery side; fourteen pectoral fin rays; eight anal fin rays.

Size: Maximum length for an adult of this species is 9.8 cm (3¾ inches).

Habitat: The Blacknose Shiner inhabits the bottoms of clear vegetated lakes and quiet pools of prairie streams and small rivers. Bottoms with muck or organic debris, often overlaying sand, gravel, or rock, are preferred.

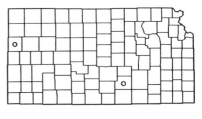

This species is intolerant of continuously turbid water.

Reproduction: Blacknose Shiners are reported to spawn in June or July.

Food: The food habits of the Blacknose Shiner in Kansas are unknown.

Remarks: The Blacknose Shiner is included in this book as a part of the fish fauna of Kansas on the basis of two records, the first in 1885 from the Smoky Hill River in Wallace County, and the second in 1891 from near Wichita, Sedgwick County. Pleistocene fossils of this species were found in Meade County, in southwestern Kansas. Isolated populations of this fish still occur in central Missouri.

An adult Sand Shiner *(Notropis ludibundus)*. Drawing by Gene Pacheco.

Sand Shiner
Notropis ludibundus (Cope) (Plate 12)

Description: Body stout, not compressed. Dorsal fin with a short black line in its base. Sides plain silvery but with the lateral line prominent because of pigment alongside the pores. Small dusky spot at base of tail often present. Resembles Bigmouth Shiner but mouth smaller, and Topeka Shiner but fins never colored. Usually seven anal fin rays. Pectoral fins rounded.

Size: Maximum length for the Sand Shiner is 8.1 cm (3¼ inches).

Habitat: Two subspecies of this fish occupy different habitats in Kansas (as discussed below). One occurs in nearly all shallow, sandy streams, where it is one of the most abundant minnows. This race invades rocky upland tributaries of the Kansas River but is rare there. It lives mainly in slowly flowing or quiet water, either in shallow pools of small western streams or along sandbars in rivers such as the Kansas River. The other subspecies inhabits the Neosho and Osage rivers and their tributaries. It is less abundant than the sandy-river form in Kansas. It lives in shallow pools or moderate currents where the bottom consists of coarse sand, fine gravel, or silt.

Reproduction: The Sand Shiner spawns from April through August, a long reproductive season that may be an important adaptation to life in plains rivers whose volume of flow fluctuates widely and irregularly.

Food: Sand Shiners eat small insects and microscopic animals associated with the stream bottom.

Subspecies in Kansas: The Sand Shiner is represented by two subspecies in Kansas: *Notropis l. ludibundus* in the Osage and Neosho river drainages; and *N. ludibundus missuriensis* in the Kansas and Arkansas river systems and in small, direct tributaries of the Missouri River in Atchison and Doniphan counties in northeastern Kansas. Recently, the specific name *stramineus* was shown to be a junior synonym of *N. ludibundus.*

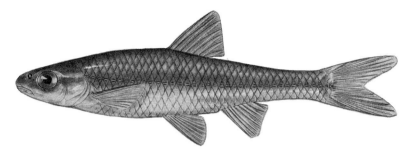

An adult Ozark Minnow *(Notropis nubilus).* Drawing by Gene Pacheco.

Ozark Minnow
Notropis nubilus (Forbes) (Plate 13)

Description: Slender, greenish body with line of dark dots on sides, or a narrow black stripe around snout, through center of eye, and full length of sides. Snout rounded, protruding slightly above mouth. Gut long and coiled; lining of body cavity black. Anal fin with eight rays. Breeding males with pink or orange belly and fins.

Size: Maximum length for an adult of this species is 9.3 cm (3¾ inches).

Habitat: The Ozark Minnow is found in Shoal Creek, Cherokee County, in extreme southeastern Kansas. It prefers high-gradient, clear, strongly flowing streams.

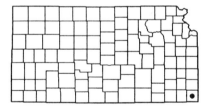

Reproduction: Ozark Minnows spawn in May and June.

Food: Algae and microscopic animals that grow as a film on rocks along the bottom are the preferred food of the Ozark Minnow.

Remarks: SINC SPECIES. The Ozark Minnow was listed as a peripheral species by Platt et al. (1974), meaning that its population is so localized in Kansas that it could easily be lost to our fauna. The Ozark Minnow probably cannot occur much more widely in Kansas under present climatic conditions, but fossils prove its existence in the southwestern part of our state during an earlier, glacial period.

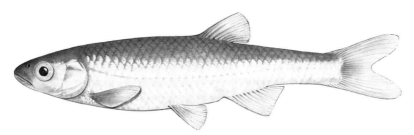

An adult Rosyface Shiner *(Notropis rubellus)*. Drawing by Victor Hogg.

Rosyface Shiner
Notropis rubellus (Agassiz) (Plate 2)

Description: Dorsal fin arising farther back than pelvic fins, rather than directly above them. Body slender, not transparent, green above and silvery white below. Pale pink pigment in base of dorsal fin always evident in life. Snout sharper than Emerald Shiner, and dorsal fin rounded at distal tip, rather than high and pointed as in the Emerald Shiner. Anal fin with ten rays.

Size: Maximum length for an adult of this species is 9 cm (3½ inches).

Habitat: The Rosyface Shiner inhabits clear, upland streams in the Kansas, Osage, and Arkansas river systems. It prefers streambeds of limestone with steep gradients. Schools of this fish move in the open water of pools, well

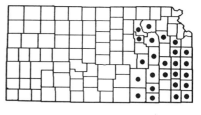

above the stream bottom, but they are not found in lakes. Neither are they found in the sandy rivers occupied by Emerald Shiners, except as noted in the Remarks below.

Reproduction: This species spawns from late April to early June, rarely as late as July. Schools of Rosyface Shiners congregate for spawning in riffles or eddies adjacent to gravel bars. Eggs are deposited in coarse gravel that is free of silt.

Food: Aquatic insects are the main diet of the Rosyface Shiner.

Remarks: In the drought of 1952–1957, Rosyface Shiners occupied the Neosho River in Lyon, Coffey, Woodson, Allen, Neosho, and Labette counties. The extremely low water flow across the gravel bars and into pools along the Neosho mainstream better satisfied the needs of this species in drought than did the drying Flint Hills tributaries, its main habitat in more favorable climatic cycles. Formerly, populations of this species expanded and contracted, and shifted upstream and downstream in the Neosho Basin with long-term wet and dry cycles that characterize the Plains region. Rosyface Shiners persisted in the Neosho Basin so long as they were able to "follow" favorable environments along unobstructed stream channels. In the 1960s, impoundment of the Neosho River by construction of John Redmond Reservoir, coupled with pollution from new large livestock feedlots upstream, eliminated the riverine refuges of the Rosyface Shiner, and it disappeared from the Neosho Basin in Kansas.

Dams had a different effect on Rosyface Shiners in the Kansas River, where muddy waters and shifting sand bottoms afforded little if any mainstream habitat suitable to it. The Rosyface Shiner was never found in the Kansas River until the 1980s, after reservoirs on all its major western tributaries altered flows in ways that made the lower mainstream less inhospitable to this fish, especially in winter. Since 1983, a few Rosyface Shiners have been taken in fall and winter from the Kansas River at Lawrence, alongside a rocky island formed by continuous turbulent flow over the Bowersock Dam. The river is usually low and relatively clear at this site in winter, and water depths, currents, and the rocky substrate beside the island provide a patch of habitat somewhat like that in the upland streams preferred by this species. Similar sites probably exist elsewhere in the Kansas River at present. Thus, in contrast with the Neosho River, the Kansas River may now offer more favorable temporary refuge for tributary species than it did in its natural state. No large reservoirs intercept its movement into the lower mainstream from upland tributaries such as Mill Creek in Wabaunsee County, where Rosyface Shiners remain abundant.

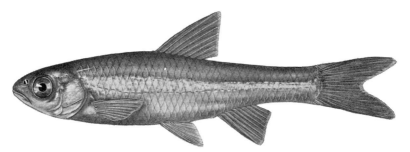

An adult Silverband Shiner *(Notropis shumardi)*. Drawing by Gene Pacheco.

Silverband Shiner
Notropis shumardi (Girard)

Description: Dorsal fin high, sharply pointed, directly above pelvic fins. Body compressed, moderately deep. Color pale green, transparent with narrow silvery lateral stripe. Anal fin with 8–9 rays.

Size: Maximum length for an adult of this species is 10 cm (4 inches).

Habitat: This species was found only in the lower Kansas River and the Missouri River in Kansas. Confined to large rivers throughout its range, the Silverband Shiner prefers moderately deep, flowing water along sand or gravel bars.

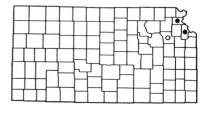

Reproduction: Nothing is known of the breeding habits of the Silverband Shiner.

Food: The diet of the Silverband Shiner is not known.

Remarks: THREATENED SPECIES IN KANSAS. This species was listed along with threatened species by Platt et al. (1974), because it had only limited, peripheral populations in Kansas. The Silverband Shiner has not occurred in recent collections from the lower Kansas River or the Missouri River along our border; it may have been extirpated from the state. Extensive modification of the Missouri River for navigation has eliminated most sandbar habitat, probably explaining the decline of this fish in that waterway.

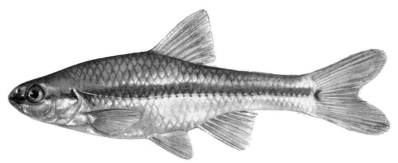

An adult Topeka Shiner *(Notropis topeka).* Drawing by F. A. Carmichael.

Topeka Shiner
Notropis topeka (Gilbert)

Description: Body stout, slightly compressed (nearly as wide as high). Dorsal fin rather high and acutely pointed, often reddish. Eye small but nearly as long as snout. Mouth small and terminal. Tail fin with a tiny, chevronlike spot at its base. Most resembles Sand Shiner, but differs from that species in having a dusky streak along sides, and red fins in summer (when spawning). Anal fin with seven rays.

Size: Maximum length for an adult of this species is 7.6 cm (3 inches).

Habitat: Although formerly widespread in Kansas, this species is now restricted to small streams in the Flint Hills (both Kansas and Neosho drainages) plus a very few streams elsewhere in the state (Willow Creek, Wallace County; Cherry Creek, Cheyenne County; and single streams in Jefferson and Johnson counties). Topeka Shiners prefer open pools near the headwaters of streams that maintain a stable water level due to weak springs or percolation through riffles. The water in these pools is usually clear, except as plankton blooms develop in summer.

Reproduction: The Topeka Shiner spawns from late June to August, and the young mature in one year. The maximum life span is two or three years.

Food: The diet of the Topeka Shiner consists of midge larvae and other aquatic insects, plus other small organisms, most of which are found on stream bottoms.

Remarks: SINC SPECIES. The Topeka Shiner is currently a candidate for federal listing as a threatened species. Its status requires attention because of a general reduction in its range. Most of its remaining populations are in Kansas; it formerly occurred in at least twelve counties in central and western Kansas where it has not been found recently.

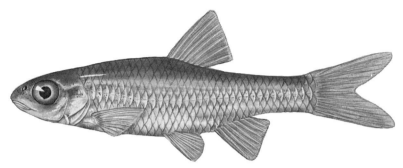

An adult Mimic Shiner *(Notropis volucellus).* Drawing by Gene Pacheco.

Mimic Shiner
Notropis volucellus (Cope) (Plate 13)

Description: Scales in one row on sides (lateral-line row) obviously higher than other scales. Back with scales outlined but without a dark stripe on midline. Eye large. Color greenish, silvery below. Anal fin with eight rays. Resembles the Ghost Shiner, but has more dark pigment and a complete sensory canal along the lower rim of the orbit.

Size: Maximum length for an adult of this species is 7.6 cm (3 inches).

Habitat: This species is restricted to the eastern part of the Arkansas River system in southeastern Kansas. The Mimic Shiner is most common in upland streams that have rocky bottoms and permanent flow (Caney, Elk, Fall, Verdigris, and South Fork of Cottonwood rivers).

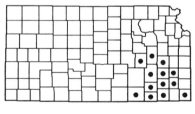

Reproduction: The Mimic Shiner spawns in July and August, later than most Kansas fishes. Spawning takes place on broad riffles with moderate current.

Food: Food of the Mimic Shiner is not known. Elsewhere in its range, it is reported to eat midge larvae, other aquatic insects, microcrustaceans, and algae.

Subspecies in Kansas: The highly variable populations of this fish are much in need of study; for this reason, we do not use a subspecific designation for the Kansas portion of the range.

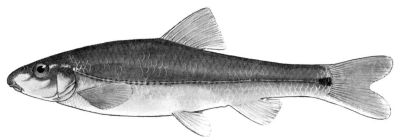

An adult Suckermouth Minnow *(Phenacobius mirabilis)*. Drawing by Victor Hogg.

Suckermouth Minnow
Phenacobius mirabilis (Girard) (Plate 13)

Description: Small mouth with lobed lips beneath fleshy snout. No barbels. Body slender, greenish, with dusky lengthwise streak and dark spot at base of tail fin.

Size: Maximum length for an adult of this species is 12 cm (4¾ inches).

Habitat: This fish is widespread in Kansas. It is most abundant in tributary streams having permanent flow, moderate gradient, and bottoms of mixed sand and small gravel. The Suckermouth Minnow is adapted for existence in riffles, but seems more tolerant of fluctuating water levels and high turbidity than other species that live in riffles.

Reproduction: The Suckermouth Minnow has a long reproductive period, from April through August, probably as an adaptation to the erratic flow of rivers in the plains region.

Food: Larval insects and microscopic organisms gleaned from coarse sand or gravel bottoms are the preferred food of the Suckermouth Minnow.

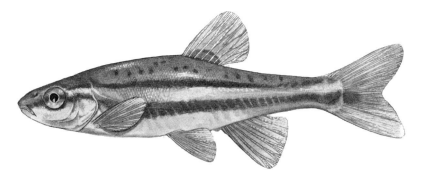

An adult Southern Redbelly Dace *(Phoxinus erythrogaster)*. Drawing by F. A. Carmichael.

Southern Redbelly Dace
Phoxinus erythrogaster (Rafinesque) (Plates 2, 13)

Description: Two dark stripes on sides, with pale area between them. Scales extremely small, nearly invisible. Gut long, lining of body cavity black. In spring, males have bright yellow fins and the lower sides are red.

Size: The Southern Redbelly Dace grows to a maximum length of 9.1 cm (3½ inches).

Habitat: The Southern Redbelly Dace prefers small, clear streams and is most common near the sources of springs. Watercress or other vegetation often is present.

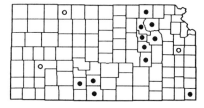

Reproduction: The Southern Redbelly Dace spawns from late March to May, when water temperatures are 10° to 15°C (50° to 60°F). The eggs are deposited in swift, shallow water over gravel or in the gravel nests of other fishes, such as the Central Stoneroller or the Creek Chub.

Food: This fish feeds on micro-organisms, including algae that grow on plant stems and the stream bottom.

Remarks: The Southern Redbelly Dace now occurs in three widely separated areas in Kansas: (1) Spring River drainage in Cherokee

County; (2) streams of the northern Flint Hills, from the Cottonwood
River in Chase County northward to Marshall County; (3) headwaters of the Medicine Lodge and Ninnescah rivers in Kiowa and Pratt
counties. Streams in the latter two areas drain extensive rangeland
with little cultivation. The Southern Redbelly Dace was much more
widely distributed in Kansas prior to European settlement, based on
nineteenth-century records in Finney and Norton counties.

An adult Bluntnose Minnow *(Pimephales notatus)*. Drawing by Victor Hogg.

Bluntnose Minnow
Pimephales notatus (Rafinesque) (Plates 2, 14)

Description: Slender body with broad back. Scales small and crowded on back. Dark streak along side, black spot at base of tail fin. Spot in dorsal fin diffuse or absent. Snout blunt, extending beyond mouth; upper lip not wider at center. Fins rounded. Anal fin with seven rays. Gut long, lining of body cavity black.

Size: Maximum length for an adult of this species is 11 cm (4¼ inches).

Habitat: The Bluntnose Minnow occurs principally in the clear pools of small streams.

Reproduction: This fish spawns from late May to early July at water temperatures of 21°C (70°F) or higher. It attaches its eggs to the undersides of stones (limestone or shale) or debris such as clamshells, boards, or scrap metal. Male Bluntnose Minnows prepare nest sites by cleaning a small cavity beneath the covering object selected, and guard the eggs and young fishes until they disperse from the nest.

Food: The diet of the Bluntnose Minnow is mainly organic detritus and midge larvae.

An adult Fathead Minnow *(Pimephales promelas)*. Drawing by Gene Pacheco.

Fathead Minnow
Pimephales promelas (Rafinesque) (Plate 14)

Description: Chunky body and round head. Scales small, not clearly evident. Mouth small, nearly terminal. Fins low and rounded. Anal fin with seven rays. Gut long and coiled, lining of body cavity black. Color greenish or brownish, not silvery, becoming nearly black in breeding season.

Size: Maximum length for an adult of this species is 10 cm (4 inches).

Habitat: This is one of the most widespread fishes in Kansas. Its abundance is greatest in pools of intermittent creeks that have bottoms of mud or firm clay. It is least common in the sandy mainstream of rivers. The Fathead Minnow is like a hardy pioneer—among the first fishes to invade intermittent drainages after rains, and the last fish to disappear from small, muddy, isolated pools during drought. Another aspect of its hardiness, which enables it to flourish where other fishes perish, is its high tolerance of pollution.

Reproduction: The Fathead Minnow spawns from April through August. The eggs are attached to the underside of a stone, piece of bark, or other debris in the water. The male rests just beneath the eggs throughout their development, brushing them with his dorsal fin and a fleshy pad on his back. The young sometimes mature and spawn during the same summer in which they hatch.

Food: This fish is omnivorous, consuming small animals, plants, and organic detritus.

Remarks: The Fathead Minnow is widely cultivated in ponds as a bait fish.

An adult Slim Minnow *(Pimephales tenellus)*. Drawing by Victor Hogg.

Slim Minnow
Pimephales tenellus (Girard)

Description: Slender body with broad back; scales on back small and crowded but dark-outlined (cross-hatched). Distinct spots on both the dorsal and tail fins, and narrow dark stripe along middle of sides. Mouth small, upper lip expanded at its center (wider in front), not overhung by snout. Fins rounded. Anal fin with seven rays. Gut short, lining of body cavity silvery.

Size: Maximum length for an adult of this species is 7 cm (2¾ inches).

Habitat: The Slim Minnow occurs in streams with clear, flowing water over rocky bottoms, in the eastern part of the Arkansas River system.

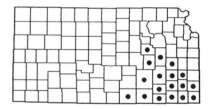

Reproduction: The Slim Minnow spawns from May to July at water temperatures ranging from 24° to 29°C (75° to 85°F). Nest sites are under rocks in fast water. See accounts of Fathead Minnow and Bluntnose Minnow.

Food: Food preferences of the Slim Minnow are not known.

Subspecies in Kansas: The nominate race, *Pimephales t. tenellus.*

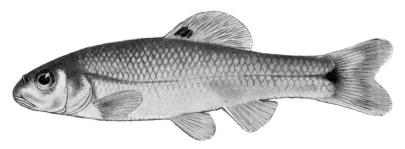

An adult Bullhead Minnow *(Pimephales vigilax).* Drawing by Victor Hogg.

Bullhead Minnow
Pimephales vigilax (Baird and Girard) (Plate 14)

Description: Body stout, head large, snout blunt. Mouth subterminal, upper lip expanded at its center. Fins rounded. Anal fin with seven rays. Dorsal and tail fin with a black spot, rest of fish pale, without dark lateral streak. Gut short, lining of body cavity silvery. Males become dark, their heads almost black, when spawning.

Size: Maximum length for an adult of this species is 8.9 cm (3½ inches).

Habitat: The Bullhead Minnow is native to the Arkansas River system in Kansas, and, following its introduction, became common in the Kansas River as far west as Saline County. It occurs chiefly in the mainstreams of rivers and 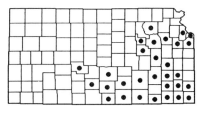 in the lower parts of their largest tributaries. It prefers pools or backwaters that have sandy or silted bottoms, and the lower ends of large gravel and sandbars where eddies deposit silt.

Reproduction: The Bullhead Minnow spawns in June and July, beneath flat stones or debris in shallow pools or slowly flowing water. The eggs are suspended from the roof of the nest, and the male Bullhead Minnow lies below them. He rubs the eggs occasionally with his dorsal fin and a fleshy pad on his back.

Food: Larval insects and small crustaceans make up the diet of the Bullhead Minnow.

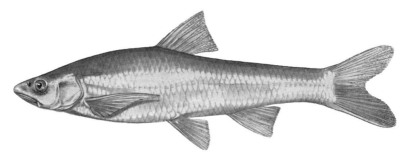

An adult Flathead Chub *(Platygobio gracilis)*. Drawing by F. A. Carmichael.

Flathead Chub
Platygobio gracilis (Richardson) (Plate 15)

Description: Broad, wedge-shaped head. Mouth large, with one small barbel on each side. Pectoral fins long and sickle-shaped. Back light greenish or brown, sides plain silvery without spots.

Size: The Flathead Chub grows to a maximum length of 32 cm (12½ inches).

Habitat: In Kansas, this species has occurred in the mainstream of the Missouri and Kansas rivers and in parts of the Nemaha, Republican, Arkansas, and Cimarron rivers. The Flathead Chub usually occupies shallow pools, but it is found also in strong currents over clean sand bottoms.

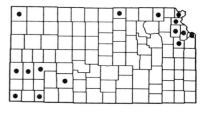

Reproduction: Reproductive habits of the Flathead Chub are unknown, but spawning probably occurs in July and August.

Food: The Flathead Chub feeds on terrestrial insects that fall in the water, and on larval aquatic insects.

Subspecies in Kansas: Two subspecies of *Platygobio gracilis* occur in Kansas. These are *Platygobio g. gracilis* in the Missouri River system, and *Platygobio gracilis gulonella* in the Arkansas River drainage.

Remarks: THREATENED SPECIES IN KANSAS. Populations of Flathead Chubs declined precipitously in Kansas in the latter half of this century, following reservoir construction and/or drying of the plains rivers where it occurred.

An adult Blacknose Dace *(Rhinichthys atratulus)*. Drawing by Joseph R. Tomelleri.

Blacknose Dace
Rhinichthys atratulus (Hermann) (Plate 15)

Description: Barbel in corner of mouth; groove above upper lip not continuous across tip of snout; snout pointed, overhanging mouth; caudal peduncle deep; back and sides covered with many brown-black specks; light brown above; black spot followed by silver spot on dorsal fin base; seven anal fin rays.

Size: Maximum length for an adult of this species is 10 cm (4 inches).

Habitat: The Blacknose Dace prefers clear headwater creeks and small rivers with gravel bottoms. In Kansas, it is restricted to Pole Creek, Manley Creek, and Clear Creek, all spring-fed brooks in the upper Nemaha River drainage.

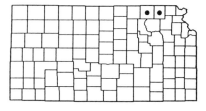

Reproduction: The Blacknose Dace breeds in May and early June. Breeding males develop dull red pigment on their heads and a reddish stripe along their sides.

Food: The Blacknose Dace eats small insects, darting from beneath rocks to snare them as they drift past.

Subspecies in Kansas: A western race, *Rhinichthys atratulus meleagris.*

Remarks: SINC SPECIES. Isolated populations of the Blacknose Dace in the Nemaha River basin of Kansas and Nebraska may be relictual, from widespread southwestward distribution during glacial times.

Rudd
Scardinius erythrophthalmus (Linnaeus)

Description: Dorsal fin with 9–11 rays; scaled bony keel along belly from pelvic to anal fin; body deep and compressed; head small; mouth oblique and terminal; lateral line low on side, with 37–47 scales; dorsal fin origin behind pelvic fin origin; anal, pelvic, and pectoral fins bright red; eye gold with red spot at top; 10–11 anal fin rays.

Size: Maximum length for an adult of this species is 48 cm (19 inches).

Habitat: In its native range in Eurasia, the Rudd inhabits lakes and the sluggish pools of medium to large rivers, as well as large reservoirs.

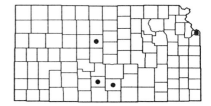

Reproduction: The Rudd lives for up to seventeen years, and matures in its second or third year. Females are reported to lay as many as 232,000 eggs.

Food: Nothing is known of the food habits of the Rudd in Kansas, but they may closely parallel those of the Golden Shiner.

Remarks: INTRODUCED SPECIES. After repeated but unsuccessful attempts at introduction in the late 1800s and early 1900s, the Rudd was successfully bred and distributed as a bait fish in Arkansas in the early 1980s, and was sold by many Kansas bait shops. This species is known to hybridize with the Golden Shiner, the native species that it most closely resembles.

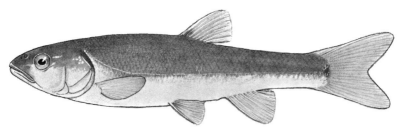

An adult Creek Chub *(Semotilus atromaculatus)*. Drawing by Victor Hogg.

Creek Chub
Semotilus atromaculatus (Mitchill) (Plate 15)

Description: Large, terminal mouth. Large head, about as broad as high. Small brownish or black spot at base of dorsal fin and tail fin. About sixty scales in lateral-line row. Anal fin with eight rays. Color dull gray to green.

Size: The Creek Chub grows to a maximum length of 30 cm (12 inches).

Habitat: The Creek Chub is common throughout the Kansas River system, but occurs at only a few localities in the Arkansas River drainage. As its name implies, the species frequents small tributaries, where it lives in pools. However, occasional individuals are taken in the mainstream of rivers. In the Kansas River drainage, the Creek Chub inhabits intermittent streams; but in the Arkansas River system, it lives only in clear, permanently flowing streams.

Reproduction: The Creek Chub spawns in April. Males construct nests and guard the eggs. Generally, the nests are formed as gravel ridges. Eggs are deposited in batches at the downstream end of the ridge and are covered by small stones.

Food: This species is an opportunistic carnivore, feeding on other fishes, worms, crayfishes, mollusks, and an assortment of insects.

Remarks: The Creek Chub is easily captured on hook and line. It is sporty for its size, making fast runs and occasional jumps, but it lacks endurance.

Suckers (Family Catostomidae)

Suckers would win few beauty contests among fishes or popularity contests if judged by anglers. Some kinds of suckers grow very large, but they seldom take an angler's bait and their meat is full of bones. Furthermore, they are suspected of competing with game fish. Generations of anglers have learned that suckers are "rough" fishes, bad company to keep. You are less likely to have your picture taken with a five-pound buffalofish than with a five-pound bass.

This is not the reputation suckers should have. As for their looks, suckers are beautifully constructed for the job they do—a job quite different from that of game fish. Their job is to make use of the abundance of small organisms and detritus that accumulate on the bottoms of rivers and lakes. To do this job, a sucker moves over the bottom like a busy vacuum cleaner: its protrusible mouth is the nozzle; its fleshy lips, the brushes. This living vacuum cleaner is selective in its "lint-gathering," of course, swallowing organisms that are useful to it as food and discarding the rest. Some of these organisms might otherwise become food for small game fish, but most would not because they are items that game fish never eat. If game fish could eat them, they would be as abundant as suckers—but much less inclined to bite a hook.

Out of water, suckers do not look shapely or streamlined. Actually they are perfectly formed for easy movement along the bottom of streams. Most suckers have one of two body forms: slender and rounded in cross-section, or with the back arched highly so the body is wedge-shaped in cross-section. In both cases the body tapers to a narrow tail, and the belly is flattened for "hugging the bottom." The slender species live mostly in small rivers, where the water is shallow and tends to tumble as it flows across the bottom. Most deep-bodied suckers (those with arched backs), live in larger rivers where the water is deep. The ridge of the back splits the current, so it passes along the sides of the fish with the least drag. Such force as the current exerts against the fish's body is mostly downward, holding it against the bottom. The pectoral fins of a sucker stick out horizontally like wings, rather than vertically like paddles. Since the pectorals are in contact with the bottom, the force of flowing water is mostly against the upper surface, which helps to hold the fish on the bottom. Thus a Northern Hogsucker, Blue Sucker, or a Smallmouth Buffalo can hold its position in fast water more easily than a bass or a trout.

Like catfish and minnows, suckers have a thick-skinned air bladder in the body cavity that can be removed as an intact balloon if it is very carefully released from its moorings at the front end. Small bones there hook into the skin of the balloon and usually deflate it when it is torn free. These bones are part of a chain that connects the air bladder to the ear of the fish, buried within the bones of its head. The air bladder in suckers (and minnows and catfish) serves as a kind of sounding board; these fishes are sensitive to a greater range of vibrations in the water around them than are other fishes. The air bladders of suckers (and minnows and catfish) divided into two or three chambers, which aids them in adjusting to the great changes in pressure that occur as a fish changes its depth. No other groups have the air bladder quite so well developed for hearing as do the suckers, minnows, and catfish.

Suckers reproduce by scattering large numbers of eggs in shallow water during the spring. The spawning sites differ with the species, but the places most often used for deposition of the eggs are either clean rocky bottoms in or near riffles or vegetation and debris in calm water. No nests are built for the eggs, nor is any attention given to them after they are laid. However, some suckers do bury their eggs slightly in fine gravel. In many kinds of suckers, spawning activity is greatest when the water level is high, following runoff from spring rains.

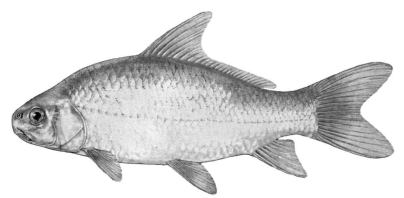

An adult River Carpsucker *(Carpiodes carpio)*. Drawing by F. A. Carmichael.

River Carpsucker
Carpiodes carpio (Rafinesque) (Plate 16)

Description: Sides plain silvery or white. Lower fins (pectorals, pelvics, anal) colorless or pale pinkish yellow. Gill cover angular in front of pectoral fin. Snout very short, firm and rounded. Mouth small, ventral, directly below nostrils. Lips thin, the lower lip with a sharp angle or "nipple" at its center.

Size: Mostly less than 40.5 cm (16 inches) long and weighing less than 0.9 kg (2 pounds); rarely 51 cm (20 inches) and 2.8–3.7 kg (6–8 pounds) in Kansas. Elsewhere in its range, this fish attains a maximum length of 64 cm (25 inches).

Habitat: This is the most common sucker in Kansas, occurring in streams in all parts of the state, and in many reservoirs also. The River Carpsucker is most abundant in large, sandy streams, but it lives in creeks as well, including mud-bottomed streams that flow only part of the year. Pools, backwaters in creek mouths and along mudbars, and deep channels along the banks are its primary habitat—anyplace where the current is slack and its microscopic food accumulates on sand, clay, or gravel stream bottoms.

Reproduction: River Carpsuckers mature at a length of 25 to 28 cm (10 to 11 inches) and spawn from May to July, when the water is warm (about 26°C [80°F]). They deposit their eggs on plant debris lodged in the stream, or on fibrous roots hanging downward from undercut banks. There is no true nest.

Food: River Carpsuckers feed entirely on tiny organisms sorted from the bottom ooze—mainly diatoms, desmids, and filamentous algae, along with some insect larvae (mostly bloodworms).

Remarks: Despite their abundance, River Carpsuckers are seldom caught on hook and line, other than accidentally, as by snagging. They are called "white carp" by many anglers. They have some commercial importance but are not considered a good food fish because of their small size and extremely bony flesh.

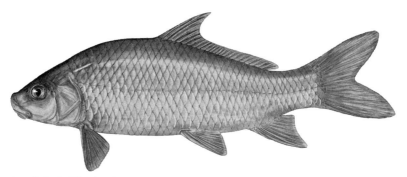

An adult Quillback *(Carpiodes cyprinus)*. Drawing by Gene Pacheco.

Quillback
Carpiodes cyprinus (Le Sueur) (Plate 16)

Description: Sides of body plain white. Pectoral, pelvic, and anal fins with little or no dark pigment. Gill cover angular in front of pectoral fin. Snout larger than in other carpsuckers, mouth small and ventral but farther forward than nostrils (rather than directly below them). Lips thin but lower lip without a sharp angle or "nipple" at its center.

Size: Quillbacks that we have seen in Kansas are 45.5 cm (18 inches) or less in length, but elsewhere the species grows as large as 66 cm (26 inches) long and weighs up to 4.5 kg (10 pounds).

Habitat: Quillbacks inhabit sandy bottoms of mainstem rivers and the lower parts of their tributaries in Kansas. They are now known from the Missouri, Kansas, Nemaha, Blue, Republican, Arkansas, Ninnescah, and Chikaskia rivers in our state. Their numbers seem to be increasing. In the 1950s and 1960s, we found Quillbacks commonly only in the Ninnescah River, downstream from the state fish hatchery.

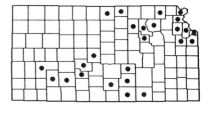

Reproduction: There is no information on the breeding habits of the Quillback in Kansas. In Iowa, Quillbacks scatter eggs over sand or mud bottom, in quiet parts of streams or in overflow ponds, mostly in May.

Food: The Quillback dines on organic matter that accumulates as a film of "ooze" where the current slackens in sandy rivers (pools and shallow embayments at the lower ends of sandbars). Nearly all of its food is microscopic—diatoms and other algae, and small blood-worms.

Remarks: There were no records of the Quillback in Kansas prior to 1950. Its presence may be due to extensions of its range after con-struction of reservoirs, or it may be due to introductions.

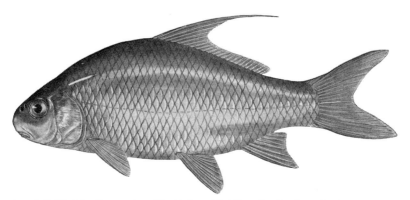

An adult Highfin Carpsucker *(Carpiodes velifer)*. Drawing by Gene Pacheco.

Highfin Carpsucker
Carpiodes velifer (Rafinesque) (Plate 16)

Description: Rays at front of dorsal fin very long, whiplike. Body deeper than that of any other sucker except the Smallmouth Buffalo. Sides silvery or slightly brassy. Ventral fins colorless. Snout short, firm, and rounded. Mouth often behind a vertical line from nostrils. Lips thin and angular, the lower lip with a sharp angle or "nipple" at its center.

Size: Maximum length for an adult of this species is 50 cm (19½ inches); weight less than 0.9 kg (2 pounds).

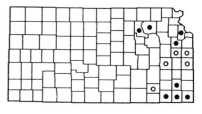

Habitat: To our knowledge, the Highfin Carpsucker has recently been caught only in the Elk, Neosho, and Spring rivers in southeastern Kansas. Much earlier in this century, Highfin Carpsuckers were reported from the Kansas, Blue, Wakarusa, and Marais des Cygnes rivers. This species likes clean streams, with clear water and rocky bottoms.

Reproduction: Breeding habits of the Highfin Carpsucker in Kansas are unknown. See the family account for suckers.

Food: Micro-organisms that settle on stream bottoms, including algae, are the preferred foods of the Highfin Carpsucker.

Remarks: SINC SPECIES. The Highfin Carpsucker is rare in Kansas and is declining in several other parts of its range.

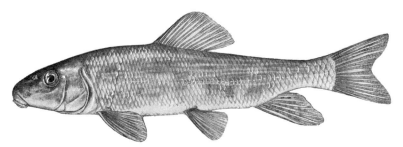

An adult White Sucker *(Catostomus commersonii)*. Drawing by F. A. Carmichael.

White Sucker
Catostomus commersonii (Lacépède) (Plates 2, 17)

Description: Short dorsal fin (11–13 rays). Slender, plain greenish or yellowish body. Scales on back, in front of dorsal fin, much smaller than scales on sides in front of tail fin. Top of head rounded rather than flat between eyes. Lips papillose (bumpy rather than grooved). Young with three dark spots on each side.

Size: Maximum length for an adult of this species is rarely more than 38 cm (15 inches) in streams; attains a weight of 1.4 kg (3 pounds) in lakes. Elsewhere in its range, this fish attains a maximum length of 64 cm (25 inches).

Habitat: White Suckers occur in most small streams that have some areas of rocky bottom (riffles) in the Kansas and Osage river basins. In the Arkansas River basin, White Suckers are known only from the Arkansas River in Hamilton and Kearny counties; specimens caught there probably had drifted downstream from cooler, clearer waters in Colorado. The species may occur in Spring River or Shoal Creek in Cherokee County. White Suckers live in clear lakes in limestone uplands (Lone Star, Douglas County State Lake, Lake Wabaunsee, Crawford County State Lake) and in small, clear, rocky streams. They normally occupy pools but move into riffles for feeding and spawning.

Reproduction: The White Sucker breeds in late March to early May over clean rocky bottoms. See the family account for suckers.

Food: In streams, White Suckers feed on larval insects and algae attached to stones; in lakes, they relish burrowing mayflies.

An adult Blue Sucker *(Cycleptus elongatus).* Drawing by F. A. Carmichael.

Blue Sucker
Cycleptus elongatus (Le Sueur) (Plate 17)

Description: The only sucker with a long, sickle-shaped dorsal fin on a slender body. Head small, snout long and pointed, eye in back half of head. Mouth small but lips full and papillose (bumpy rather than grooved). Color blue-gray; young with lower half of tail fin dark, upper half pale.

Size: Most adults are 38–63.5 cm (15–25 inches). The largest specimen from Kansas was 76.3 cm (30 inches) in length; heaviest example from Kansas weighed 4.1 kg (8.9 pounds). Maximum size reported elsewhere is 101 cm (40 inches) and 6.9 kg (15 pounds).

Habitat: Blue Suckers occur in the Missouri, Kansas, and Neosho rivers, where they occupy swift currents in the main channels. In the Neosho River, they concentrate in "chutes" or rapids where the water is deep and the bottom is rocky, wholly free of silt.

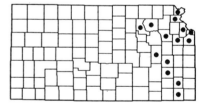

They are also found in stilling basins, where water is discharged into the river from reservoirs such as John Redmond, Tuttle Creek, and Perry.

Reproduction: This species probably spawns in spring, scattering its eggs on rocky bottoms in the current after migrating upstream. In summer, young Blue Suckers are found along gravel bars in slightly shallower water and less swift currents than adults.

Food: The Blue Sucker eats insects; probably also micro-organisms including algae attached to stones on the bottom.

Remarks: SINC SPECIES. The Blue Sucker is a good food fish, among the most valuable of the suckers. Once taken commercially in significant numbers, the species declined long ago over much of its range. Fairly large numbers remain in the Neosho River.

An adult Northern Hogsucker *(Hypentelium nigricans)*. Drawing by F. A. Carmichael.

Northern Hogsucker
Hypentelium nigricans (Le Sueur) (Plate 17)

Description: Short dorsal fin (10–12 rays). Slender body, marked by dark "saddles" that angle forward on the sides. Broad head, flattened between eyes. Long, slender snout, lips full and papillose (bumpy rather than grooved).

Size: Adults of the Northern Hogsucker are usually less than 38 cm (15 inches) in length and 0.4 kg (1 pound) in weight. Elsewhere in their range, they have been known to attain 61 cm (24 inches) in length.

Habitat: Northern Hogsuckers now occur only in the Spring River drainage of Crawford and Cherokee counties. A century ago, they were reported from the Neosho River and the Osage River in Kansas. Northern Hog-

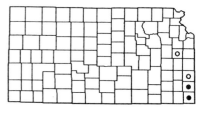

suckers live in deep riffles of small to medium-size streams that have a permanent flow of clear, cool water over rocky bottoms.

Reproduction: The Northern Hogsucker spawns in April or May, at water temperatures of 15° to 21°C (60° to 70°F).

Food: Northern Hogsuckers forage by sucking small organisms off the exposed surfaces of stones or by overturning rocks to obtain insect larvae that lie in crevices within the loose rubble.

Remarks: SINC SPECIES. Northern Hogsuckers have become rare because only Shoal Creek has maintained the permanent flow of clear water and deep gravel riffles that this species must have to survive in Kansas.

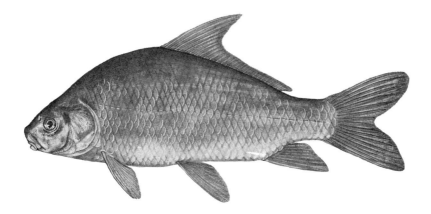

An adult Smallmouth Buffalo *(Ictiobus bubalus)*. Drawing by F. A. Carmichael.

Smallmouth Buffalo
Ictiobus bubalus (Rafinesque) (Plate 18)

Description: A pale gray sucker with dusky pectoral, pelvic, and anal fins and highly arched back (therefore, deep-bodied and slab-sided). Head small and roughly triangular, mouth ventral and small, often smaller than eye.

Size: The largest Smallmouth Buffalo caught in Kansas weighed 23.1 kg (51 pounds) and measured 104 cm (41 inches) in total length. It was taken on rod and reel by Scott Butler of Lawrence from an urban impoundment in Douglas County on 2 May 1979, and was then the world record weight and length for this fish.

Habitat: The Smallmouth Buffalo occurs in all large streams of eastern Kansas. It is most abundant in the current over rocky bottoms, but is also found in pools, oxbow lakes, and backwaters in the mouths of tributaries. "Deadfalls" or log drifts commonly attract Smallmouth Buffalo. This species may be extending its range westward along the major tributaries of the Kansas River, due to the clearer, more stable flows now emanating from reservoirs.

Reproduction: Smallmouth Buffalo breed in spring, most often in May. See the family account for suckers.

Food: Larval insects make up much of the diet of the Smallmouth Buffalo, plus smaller organisms living as a thin layer on stones or other firm bottom material—probably including log drifts.

Remarks: A good food fish, the Smallmouth Buffalo was taken commercially in the lower Kansas River until the 1920s. A few are caught on hook and line. In Kansas, the species now seems most abundant in the Neosho River.

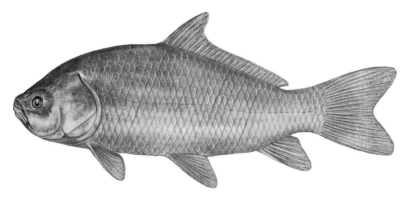

An adult Bigmouth Buffalo *(Ictiobus cyprinellus)*. Drawing by F. A. Carmichael.

Bigmouth Buffalo
Ictiobus cyprinellus (Valenciennes) (Plate 18)

Description: The only sucker with a large, thin-lipped mouth that opens nearly straight forward from the front of the head.

Size: The largest Bigmouth Buffalo from Kansas weighed 25 kg (54.25 pounds) and measured 115 cm (45 inches) in length. It was taken with a bankline from a farm pond by Randy Lee of Minneapolis on 24 May 1971.

Habitat: The Bigmouth Buffalo lives in all large rivers of the eastern half of the state, but is most abundant in lakes. It inhabits large, deep pools of rivers, cutoff lakes or oxbows, and reservoirs. Bigmouth Buffalo prefer areas with silt or sand bottom. Large poundages of this fish are sometimes found in oxbow lakes and impoundments—up to 1,000 pounds per acre, but more often a few hundred pounds per acre of lake.

Reproduction: Bigmouth Buffalo spawn in spring, during high water. They move into shallow weedy areas or mudflats to scatter their small eggs on plant stems or debris. No nest is made, and no parental attention is given to eggs or young after spawning.

Food: To a greater extent than any other sucker, the Bigmouth Buffalo feeds above the bottom on tiny, free-floating animals and plants called plankton. Water fleas (cladocerans) and copepods predominate in their diet, but some algae are eaten also. Bottom-dwelling organisms, mainly insects, are taken in lesser amounts.

Remarks: Formerly an important commercial food fish, Bigmouth Buffalo have again become a commercial species, especially in reservoirs, because of their high productivity. They can also be raised in ponds. This species has a low value as food, however, and it is almost never caught on hook and line.

An adult Black Buffalo *(Ictiobus niger)*. Drawing by F. A. Carmichael.

Black Buffalo
Ictiobus niger (Rafinesque) (Plate 18)

Description: A steely blue or gray sucker with a thick body, not highly arched or slab-sided. Head bulky, eye smaller than mouth, which is ventral and thick-lipped. All fins dusky.

Size: This species commonly attains a weight of 2.3–4.6 kg (5–10 pounds). The largest example reported from Kansas was 104 cm (41 inches) long and weighed 13 kg (28 pounds).

Habitat: Black Buffalo inhabit most rivers in eastern Kansas. They are found together with larger numbers of either the Smallmouth Buffalo or the Bigmouth Buffalo. We have caught large Black Buffalo most often 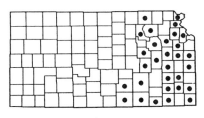 in deep, fast riffles where the channel narrows. At other times we have found them in shallow riffles, where currents sweep across bedrock bottoms or gravel bars. This species, like other buffalofish, occupies reservoirs as well as flowing water.

Reproduction: The place and mode of spawning for the Black Buffalo in Kansas are unknown.

Food: The diet of this species consists mainly of animal matter, including aquatic insects, small clams, and crayfishes. Although most of its food is taken from the bottom, the Black Buffalo consumes some plankton in reservoirs, and limited amounts of vegetation.

Remarks: The Black Buffalo is sometimes caught on hook and line, using worms or doughballs as bait.

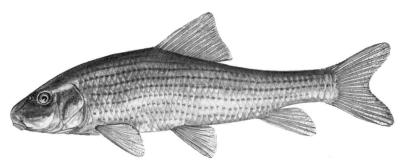

An adult Spotted Sucker *(Minytrema melanops)*. Drawing by F. A. Carmichael.

Spotted Sucker
Minytrema melanops (Rafinesque) (Plate 18)

Description: Short dorsal fin (11–13 rays), 9–10 rays in pelvic fin. Dorsal and caudal fins never red. Dark dots, one on each scale, line sides. Both lips thin and grooved. Air bladder with two chambers.

Size: Maximum length for an adult of this species is 50 cm (19½ inches).

Habitat: Spotted Suckers are relatively rare in Kansas, in the Arkansas and Osage river systems, including the Spring River in Cherokee County. This fish avoids currents, living in pools of small streams and overflow

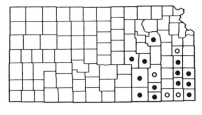

ponds in the flood plain of rivers. The pools occupied usually have firm bottoms and aquatic vegetation or other plant debris. Spotted Suckers seem to require clear, relatively soft water.

Reproduction: Spotted Suckers spawn in late spring or summer. See the family account for suckers.

Food: The Spotted Sucker mainly eats small insects and crustaceans.

Remarks: SINC SPECIES.

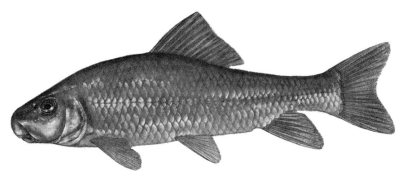

An adult River Redhorse *(Moxostoma carinatum).* Drawing by F. A. Carmichael.

River Redhorse
Moxostoma carinatum (Cope) (Plate 19)

Description: Resembles the Golden Redhorse except that the dorsal and tail fins are red. Lower lip very full, nearly straight along its hind edge. The principal character separating this species from other redhorses is an internal one: the pharyngeal (throat) teeth are stubby rather than comblike. The teeth are embedded in flesh behind the gills, and their removal requires dissection.

Size: Seldom more than 45.5 cm (18 inches) long in Kansas, but potentially larger than other redhorses. Maximum weight of 4.5 kg (10 pounds) reported. Elsewhere in its range, this fish attains a maximum length of 77 cm (30 inches).

Habitat: The River Redhorse has been taken recently in the Spring, Neosho, and Verdigris rivers, where it is rare. Formerly, it inhabited the Kansas and Osage rivers also. The species lives in pools and in deep, flowing water. The water must be clear and unpolluted.

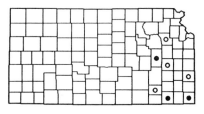

Reproduction: Spawning in this species occurs on gravel shoals, usually in May. Shallow nests are prepared and the eggs are covered with gravel after being released and fertilized.

Food: The diet of the River Redhorse is mainly mollusks (small clams), but also several kinds of larval insects that cling to the bottom or burrow into it.

Remarks: SINC SPECIES. Only a few River Redhorse have been seen in the past forty years in Kansas. Early records indicate that this species may have been common in the larger rivers of the eastern third of the state. It has declined throughout its range in the Mississippi River valley.

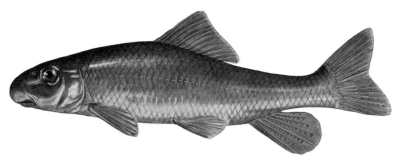

An adult Black Redhorse *(Moxostoma duquesnii)*. Drawing by Gene Pacheco.

Black Redhorse
Moxostoma duquesnii (Le Sueur) (Plate 19)

Description: Slender body, short dorsal fin (13–14 rays); ten rays in pelvic fin. Dorsal and tail fins dusky, never red. Sides plain, unspotted. Snout large, firm, and rounded; upper lip nearly hidden by fold of skin on snout. Lower lip deeply grooved, much thicker than upper lip. Air bladder with three chambers.

Size: Maximum size for an adult of this species is usually 40.5 cm (16 inches) or less in length and 0.4–0.9 kg (1–2 pounds) in weight. Elsewhere in its range, this fish attains a maximum length of 51 cm (20 inches).

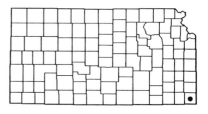

Habitat: The Black Redhorse is now confined to Spring River and Shoal Creek (Cherokee County), although nineteenth-century reports suggest that it occurred more widely in the Arkansas basin and possibly in the Marais des Cygnes. Black Redhorses live in streams that have gravel bottom and permanent flow of clear, cool water. Usually they are found in the deeper "runs" (places where the water flows fairly rapidly but smoothly) rather than in quiet pools or turbulent riffles.

Reproduction: Spawning in this species occurs in April or May, when water temperatures are above 15°C (60°F). Black Redhorses deposit their eggs on clean gravel bottoms in the current, just upstream from riffles.

Food: Aquatic insects, mainly fly larvae, are removed from stones on the stream bottom and eaten by the Black Redhorse.

Remarks: SINC SPECIES. The Black Redhorse was mentioned along with threatened species by Platt et al. (1974) because its range and abundance in Kansas are so limited that the species could easily be lost to our fauna.

An adult Golden Redhorse *(Moxostoma erythrurum)*. Drawing by F. A. Carmichael.

Golden Redhorse
Moxostoma erythrurum (Rafinesque) (Plate 19)

Description: Short dorsal fin (12–14 rays); nine rays in pelvic fin. Dorsal and tail fins dusky, never red. Sides plain, not lined. Snout blunt and moderately heavy but not concealing upper lip. Lower lip thicker than upper lip, both grooved; air bladder with three chambers.

Size: Maximum length for an adult of this species is 45.5 cm (18 inches) in Kansas, but elsewhere as large as 78 cm (30½ inches) and 2 kg (4½ pounds).

Habitat: This is the most common redhorse in the Arkansas River system in Kansas. It occurs also in many streams of the Osage River system, but in the Kansas River basin it has been found only in Mill Creek, Wabaunsee County.

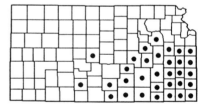

The Golden Redhorse is most abundant in streams smaller than those preferred by other species of redhorses, but larger than those occupied by White Suckers. Golden Redhorses usually occupy clear pools with firm bottoms of bedrock, gravel, or clay.

Reproduction: Golden Redhorse are mature at a length of 25 to 30 cm (10 to 12 inches). They move upstream, usually in May, to spawn in shallow pools having rocky bottoms or in areas with smooth streaming flow near riffles. See family account.

Food: Larval insects attached to the stream bottom are eaten by Golden Redhorses.

An adult Shorthead Redhorse *(Moxostoma macrolepidotum).* Drawing by F. A. Carmichael.

Shorthead Redhorse
Moxostoma macrolepidotum (Le Sueur) (Plate 19)

Description: Fins red. Head small, snout tapering, less massive than in River Redhorse. Mouth small, lower lip oval in shape, upper lip often with a slightly swollen, callouslike knob at its center. Air bladder three-chambered. Pharyngeal teeth comblike (see account of River Redhorse).

Size: Maximum length for an adult of this species is 45.5 cm (18 inches) in Kansas. Elsewhere, the maximum reported size is 75 cm (29½ inches) and 1.8–2.8 kg (4–6 pounds).

Habitat: Shorthead Redhorses occur in all major drainages of eastern Kansas, mostly in large streams (Kansas, Blue, Marais des Cygnes, Neosho, and Verdigris rivers). This is the only redhorse likely to be caught in the Kansas

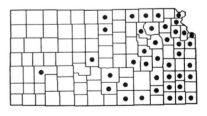

River system. It has recently inhabited the Arkansas River mainstream wherever continuous, moderately clear flow exists, as far west as Finney County. The species lives in moderate currents over rocky bottoms or a mixture of sand and gravel, often just upstream from riffles.

Reproduction: The Shorthead Redhorse breeds in April or May, usually over gravel in currents. See the family account for suckers.

Food: Larval insects gleaned from rocks make up the main diet of the Shorthead Redhorse; some small mollusks and plant material are also eaten.

Subspecies in Kansas: The Shorthead Redhorse is represented in Kansas by two subspecies, an Ozarkian race *(Moxostoma macrolepidotum pisolabrum)* from the southeastern and south-central rivers of the state, and intergrades between it and the nominate race *(Moxostoma m. macrolepidotum)* in the Kansas River basin to the north.

ORDER SILURIFORMES

CATFISHES (Family Ictaluridae)

Twelve kinds of catfish occur in Kansas. Some are important food and game fish—the Channel Catfish, the Blue Catfish, three kinds of bullheads, and the Flathead Catfish. Except for the Blue Catfish, these species may be caught in rivers, reservoirs, or ponds almost anywhere in the state. Blue Catfish are found naturally only in the largest rivers of northeastern Kansas, but they have been stocked elsewhere. Some Channel Catfish are mistakenly called "blue catfish" by anglers. A species not native to Kansas, the Brown Bullhead, has been brought into the state for use in private ponds. It does not seem to have reproduced abundantly or spread far beyond the places where it was stocked, but an account of the Brown Bullhead is included in this book because it is occasionally caught in our state.

Six of the native catfish, nearly half of the species known from Kansas, are so small and secretive that they are never seen by many people other than biologists whose job it is to know about such animals. A few curious anglers do know about them, and probably gave them their common name, "madtoms." The stiff, sharp spines in the fins of these little fishes can cause a painful injury if they are handled carelessly. The effect is about like that of an ant bite, or perhaps a bee sting. Very small bullheads and Channel Catfish can cause similarly unpleasant stab wounds, but none of the catfish is poisonous enough to be truly dangerous. The function of the fin spines may be to discourage predators. They are not totally effective, however, because carnivorous fishes sometimes eat madtoms. More effective protection against predators is afforded by the habits of madtoms and other small catfish. They hide most of the time in crevices between rocks on the stream bottom, or beneath leaves and trash that fall into the water and settle to the bottoms of pools.

The "whiskers" of catfish have a sensory function—touch, of course, but more importantly taste. The whiskers are more properly termed *barbels*. Each barbel carries hundreds of taste buds, and taste buds are also scattered over the fins and the smooth, scaleless skin of the catfish body. Fishes can afford to let these structures all hang out, because they are constantly bathed in water and are not subject to drying as in land animals. Catfish have a keen sense of smell also, but that sense is limited to the nostrils, small pits near the pair of barbels atop the head.

Because catfish are most active at night, they must depend more on their chemical senses—taste and smell—than on sight to find their food. Catfish, as well as several other kinds of fishes, can locate a food item and decide whether it is desirable without first seeing the food or taking it into the mouth. In muddy water, catfish are better able to find food than are fishes that feed by sight, so catfish usually are the dominant sport fishes in muddy streams and lakes.

Catfish whose spawning habits are known deposit eggs in darkened nest-cavities, or at least in places that are partly concealed by overhead shade or cover. Discarded beverage cans are sometimes used as nests by madtoms. Before such litter became available, catfish managed very well in cavities beneath stones or in hollows in the bank or beneath fallen trees lodged in the stream.

Catfish spawning takes place once each year, in late spring or early summer, May to July. The male (often the female, in the case of bullheads) selects the spot and enlarges the cavity or cleans the nest of silt as necessary. The female enters and drops her eggs, which stick together in a firm jellylike mass. The eggs are fertilized as laid. Thereafter, the male (or sometimes both parents) remains with the eggs, "fluffing" them with his pelvic fins, swimming in circles above them and otherwise maintaining the slight movement of water around the eggs that seems necessary for their healthy development. After hatching, the young remain tightly schooled for days or weeks, often attended by one or both parents (except young-of-the-year Channel Catfish, which are ignored by their parents). Later they spread out over the bottom, seek cover in which they can hide, and dart out to intercept passing food detected by their sensitive barbels.

Some catfish, especially Channel Catfish, can be fed in ponds or cages like farm animals, as valuable livestock. Small catfish, especially the Slender Madtom, make interesting aquarium pets.

Plate 1

Eight views of Kansas streams and rivers, showing their diversity. From top to bottom (left column): Arikaree River, Cheyenne County; Cimarron River, Meade County; Chikaskia River, Sumner County; Little Arkansas River, Sedgwick County. From top to bottom (right column): Elk River, Elk County; Independence Creek, Atchison County; Wildcat Creek, Nemaha County; Neosho River, Neosho County.

Plate 2

All photographs taken in Kansas and © by Garold Sneegas.

Underwater images of live examples of eight species of Kansas fishes. From top to bottom (left column): tuberculate male Central Stoneroller (*Campostoma anomalum*) from Illinois Creek, Wabaunsee County; spawning Rosyface Shiners (*Notropis rubellus*) from Verdigris River, Chase County; spawning male and female Southern Redbelly Dace (*Phoxinus erythrogaster*) from Illinois Creek, Wabaunsee County; male Bluntnose Minnow (*Pimephales notatus*) fanning fry on underside of rock, Illinois Creek, Wabaunsee County. From top to bottom (right column): male White Sucker (*Catostomus commersonii*) in spawning color, Illinois Creek, Wabaunsee County; Slender Madtom (*Noturus exilis*) from Illinois Creek, Wabaunsee County; Blackstripe Topminnow (*Fundulus notatus*) from South Fork Cottonwood River, Greenwood County; Green Sunfish (*Lepomis cyanellus*) from Illinois Creek, Wabaunsee County.

Plate 3

Adult (top) and immature (ammocoete) (bottom) Chestnut Lamprey
(*Ichthyomyzon castaneus*).

Adult Lake Sturgeon (*Acipenser fulvescens*).

Adult Pallid Sturgeon (*Scaphirhynchus albus*).

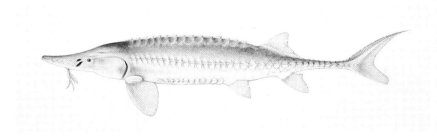

Adult Shovelnose Sturgeon (*Scaphirhynchus platorynchus*).

Plate 4

Adult Paddlefish (*Polyodon spathula*).

Adult Longnose Gar (*Lepisosteus osseus*).

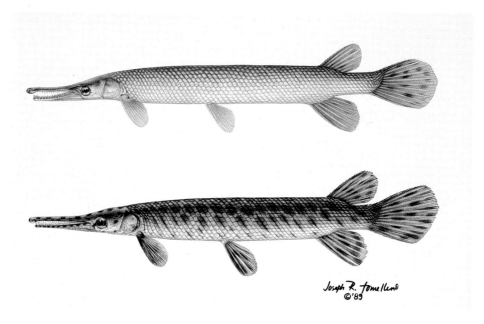

Adult Shortnose Gar (*Lepisosteus platostomus*, top) and adult Spotted Gar (*Lepisosteus oculatus*, bottom).

Plate 5

Adult female Bowfin (*Amia calva*).

Juvenile male Bowfin (*Amia calva*).

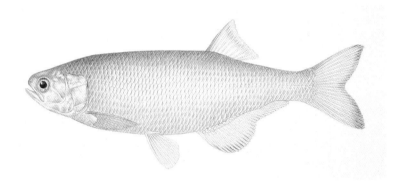

Adult Goldeye (*Hiodon alosoides*).

Adult American Eel (*Anguilla rostrata*).

Plate 6

Adult Skipjack Herring (*Alosa chrysochloris*).

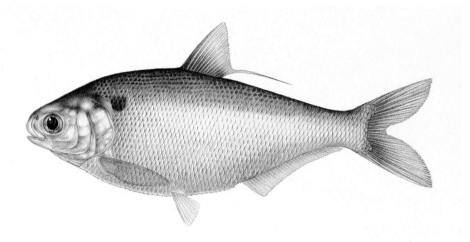

Adult Gizzard Shad (*Dorosoma cepedianum*).

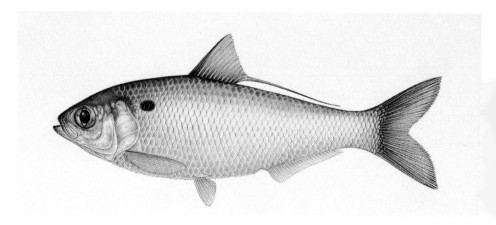

Adult Threadfin Shad (*Dorosoma petenense*).

Plate 7

Breeding male (top) and adult female (bottom) Central Stoneroller
(*Campostoma anomalum*).

Adult Goldfish (*Carassius auratus*).

Adult Grass Carp (*Ctenopharyngodon idella*).

All drawings © by Joseph R. Tomelleri.

Plate 8

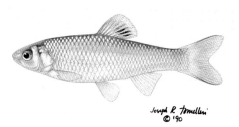

Adult Bluntface Shiner (*Cyprinella camura*).

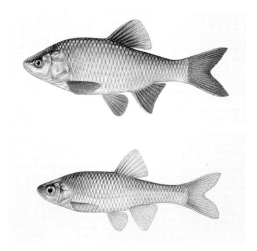

Breeding male (top) and adult female
(bottom) Red Shiner (*Cyprinella lutrensis*).

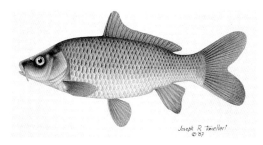

Adult Common Carp (*Cyprinus carpio*).

Adult variant of Common Carp (*Cyprinus carpio*).

Plate 9

Adult Gravel Chub (*Erimystax x-punctatus*).

Adult Speckled Chub (*Extrarius aestivalis*): two barbels (top); four barbels (bottom).

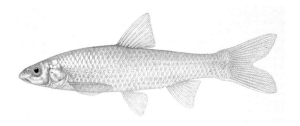

Adult Plains Minnow (*Hybognathus placitus*).

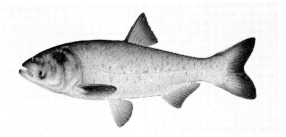

Adult Bighead Carp (*Hypophthalmichthys nobilis*).

Plate 10

Large male Striped Shiner (*Luxilus chrysocephalus*, top); adult female Common Shiner (*Luxilus cornutus*, middle); breeding male Common Shiner (*Luxilus cornutus*, bottom).

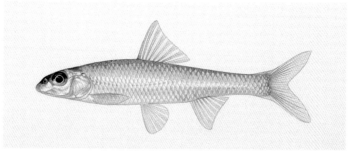

Adult Silver Chub (*Macrhybopsis storeriana*).

All drawings © by Joseph R. Tomelleri.

Plate 11

Adult postnuptial male Redspot Chub (*Nocomis asper*, top); adult Hornyhead Chub (*Nocomis biguttatus*, bottom).

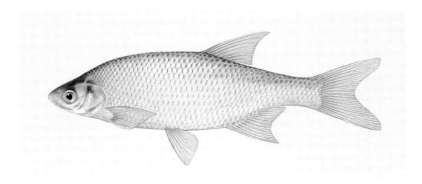

Adult Golden Shiner (*Notemigonus crysoleucas*).

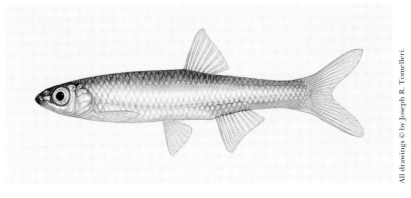

Adult Emerald Shiner (*Notropis atherinoides*).

Plate 12

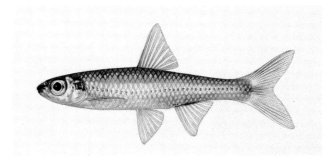

Adult Bigeye Shiner (*Notropis boops*).

Adult Pugnose Minnow (*Notropis emiliae*).

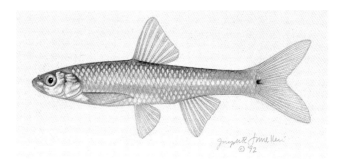

Adult Arkansas River Shiner (*Notropis girardi*).

Adult Sand Shiner (*Notropis ludibundus*).

Plate 13

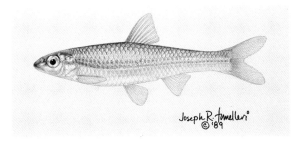

Adult Ozark Minnow (*Notropis nubilus*).

Adult Mimic Shiner (*Notropis volucellus*).

Adult Suckermouth Minnow (*Phenacobius mirabilis*).

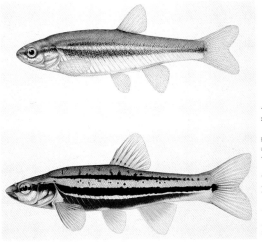

Adult female (top) and breeding male (bottom)
Southern Redbelly Dace (*Phoxinus erythrogaster*).

Plate 14

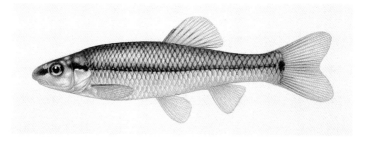

Adult Bluntnose Minnow (*Pimephales notatus*).

Adult female (top) and breeding male (bottom) Fathead Minnow
(*Pimephales promelas*).

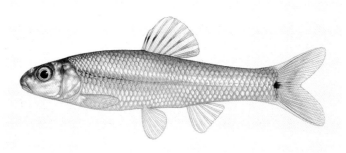

Adult Bullhead Minnow (*Pimephales vigilax*).

Plate 15

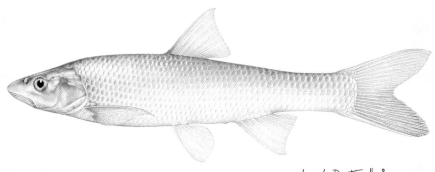

Adult Flathead Chub (*Platygobio gracilis*).

Breeding male Blacknose Dace (*Rhinichthys atratulus*).

Adult Creek Chub (*Semotilus atromaculatus*).

Plate 16

Adult River Carpsucker (*Carpiodes carpio*).

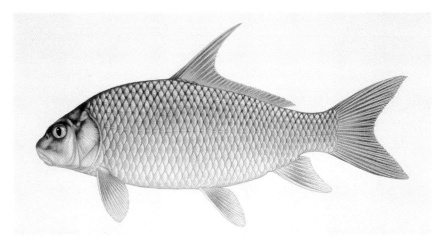

Adult Quillback (*Carpiodes cyprinus*).

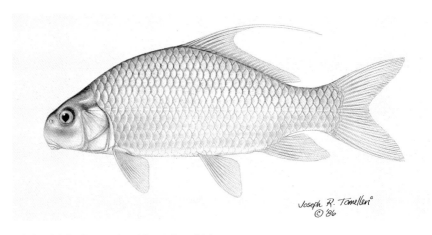

Adult Highfin Carpsucker (*Carpiodes velifer*).

Plate 17

Adult White Sucker (*Catostomus commersonii*).

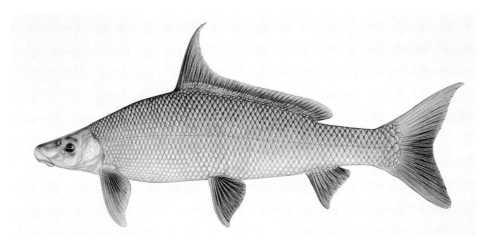

Adult Blue Sucker (*Cycleptus elongatus*).

Adult Northern Hogsucker (*Hypentelium nigricans*).

All drawings © by Joseph R. Tomelleri.

Plate 18

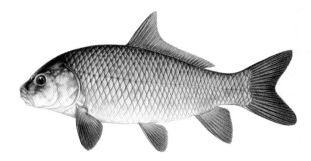

Adult Black Buffalo (*Ictiobus niger*).

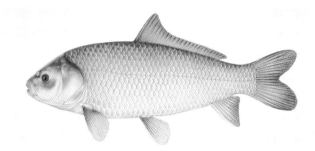

Adult Bigmouth Buffalo (*Ictiobus cyprinellus*).

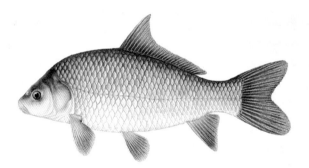

Adult Smallmouth Buffalo (*Ictiobus bubalus*).

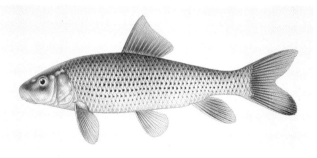

Adult Spotted Sucker (*Minytrema melanops*).

All drawings © by Joseph R. Tomelleri.

Plate 19

Adult River Redhorse (*Moxostoma carinatum*).

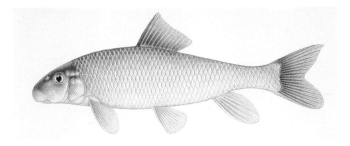

Adult Black Redhorse (*Moxostoma duquesnii*).

Adult Golden Redhorse (*Moxostoma erythrurum*).

Adult Shorthead Redhorse (*Moxostoma macrolepidotum*).

All drawings © by Joseph R. Tomelleri.

Plate 20

Adult Black Bullhead (*Ameiurus melas*).

Adult Yellow Bullhead (*Ameiurus natalis*).

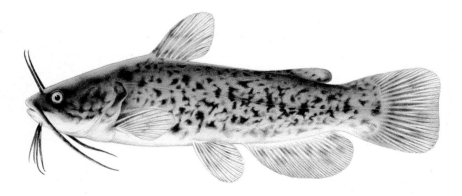

Adult Brown Bullhead (*Ameiurus nebulosus*).

Plate 21

Adult Blue Catfish (*Ictalurus furcatus*).

Juvenile Channel Catfish (*Ictalurus punctatus*).

Young adult Channel Catfish (*Ictalurus punctatus*).

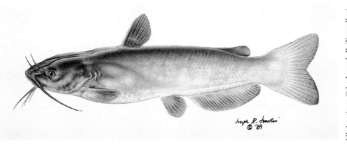

Breeding male Channel Catfish (*Ictalurus punctatus*).

Plate 22

Adult Slender Madtom (*Noturus exilis*).

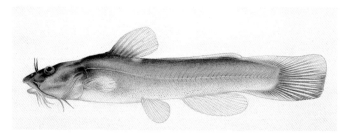

Adult Stonecat (*Noturus flavus*).

Adult Tadpole Madtom (*Noturus gyrinus*).

Adult Brindled Madtom (*Noturus miurus*).

All drawings © by Joseph R. Tomelleri.

Plate 23

Adult Freckled Madtom (*Noturus nocturnus*).

Adult Neosho Madtom (*Noturus placidus*).

Adult Flathead Catfish (*Pylodictis olivaris*).

Plate 24

Adult Northern Pike (*Esox lucius*).

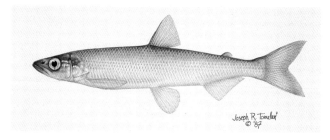

Adult Rainbow Smelt (*Osmerus mordax*).

Adult male Rainbow Trout (*Oncorhynchus mykiss*).

Adult male Brown Trout (*Salmo trutta*).

Adult Burbot (*Lota lota*).

All drawings © by
Joseph R. Tomelleri.

Plate 25

Adult Northern Studfish (*Fundulus catenatus*).

Adult Blackstripe Topminnow (*Fundulus notatus*).

Adult male (top) and female (bottom) Plains Killifish (*Fundulus zebrinus*).

Plate 26

Adult female (top) and male (bottom) Mosquitofish (*Gambusia affinis*).

Adult Brook Silverside (*Labidesthes sicculus*).

Adult Banded Sculpin (*Cottus carolinae*).

Plate 27

From top to bottom: Adult White Bass (*Morone chrysops*); adult Striped Bass (*Morone saxatilis*); hybrid between White Bass and Striped Bass (*Morone chrysops* x *M. saxatilis*).

Plate 28

Adult Rock Bass (*Ambloplites rupestris*).

Breeding male Green Sunfish (*Lepomis cyanellus*).

Juvenile Green Sunfish (*Lepomis cyanellus*).

Adult Warmouth (*Lepomis gulosus*).

Plate 29

Adult female (top) and breeding male Orangespotted Sunfish (*Lepomis humilis*).

Adult female Bluegill (*Lepomis macrochirus*).

Breeding male Bluegill (*Lepomis macrochirus*).

Plate 30

Breeding male (top) and adult female (bottom) Longear Sunfish (*Lepomis megalotis*).

Adult female (top) and breeding male (bottom) Redear Sunfish (*Lepomis microlophus*).

All drawings © by Joseph R. Tomelleri.

Plate 31

Adult Smallmouth Bass (*Micropterus dolomieu*).

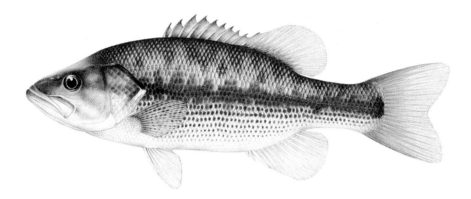

Adult Spotted Bass (*Micropterus punctulatus*).

Adult Largemouth Bass (*Micropterus salmoides*).

Plate 32

Adult White Crappie (*Pomoxis annularis*).

Adult female (top) and breeding male (bottom) Black Crappie (*Pomoxis nigromaculatus*).

Plate 33

Adult Greenside Darter (*Etheostoma blennioides*).

Adult Bluntnose Darter (*Etheostoma chlorosomum*).

Adult female (top) and male (bottom) Arkansas Darter (*Etheostoma cragini*).

Adult Fantail Darter (*Etheostoma flabellare*).

Adult Johnny Darter (*Etheostoma nigrum*).

All drawings © by
Joseph R. Tomelleri.

Plate 34

Adult male Stippled Darter (*Etheostoma punctulatum*).

Breeding male (top) and adult female (bottom) Orangethroat Darter (*Etheostoma spectabile*).

Adult male (top) and female (bottom) Speckled Darter (*Etheostoma stigmaeum*).

Adult Redfin Darter (*Etheostoma whipplii*).

Adult Banded Darter (*Etheostoma zonale*).

All drawings © by Joseph R. Tomelleri.

Plate 35

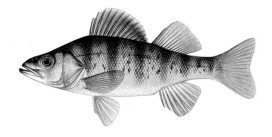

Adult Yellow Perch (*Perca flavescens*).

Adult Logperch (*Percina caprodes*).

Adult Blackside Darter (*Percina maculata*).

Breeding male Slenderhead Darter (*Percina phoxocephala*).

Adult River Darter (*Percina shumardi*).

All drawings © by
Joseph R. Tomelleri.

Plate 36

Adult Sauger (*Stizostedion canadense*).

Adult Walleye (*Stizostedion vitreum*).

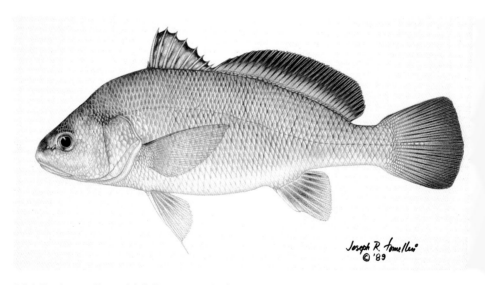

Adult Freshwater Drum (*Aplodinotus grunniens*).

An adult Black Bullhead *(Ameiurus melas)*. Drawing by F. A. Carmichael.

Black Bullhead
Ameiurus melas (Rafinesque) (Plate 20)

Description: Color of back and sides plain yellowish brown to gray or black, without spots or mottling. Belly yellow to white. Barbels on underside of head darker than skin in the area immediately around them. Anal fin with 17–21 rays (supporting rods). Spine at front of pectoral fin short, slender, and nearly smooth rather than saw-edged. Fins dusky, with dark edges and membranes.

Size: Adult Black Bullheads are usually less than 30.5 cm (12 inches) long. The largest black bullhead from Kansas weighed 3.3 kg (7.33 pounds) and was 62.4 cm (24½ inches) long. This fish was caught in a Montgomery County farm pond on rod and reel by David A. Tremain of Havana on 13 May 1985. Apparently, this is the maximum length record for the species throughout its range, although heavier examples have been found outside of Kansas.

Habitat: This common fish lives in calm waters, usually over mud, and it tolerates high turbidity. It frequents quiet backwaters, oxbows, mouths of creeks, headwaters and pools of small intermittent streams, farm ponds, and small lakes. The Black Bullhead is not common in clear, rocky streams, probably due to competition from and predation by sunfish.

Reproduction: The Black Bullhead nests from May to August, beneath protective cover if any is available. The female clears a hole or depression, and one or both adults hover over the yellow egg-mass. After hatching, the young form conspicuous black swarms that are accompanied by one or both adults. Adults remain with the school for a couple of weeks, until the young are 2.5–5 cm (1–2 inches) long. The young grow to maturity in their second year if food supplies permit.

Food: Aquatic insects, some vegetation, and other fishes are the food of the omnivorous Black Bullhead.

Remarks: This is the common bullhead most frequently caught on hook and line in Kansas. Black Bullheads rapidly invade gently sloping spillways after rains, allowing these fishes access to ponds during overflow.

An adult Yellow Bullhead *(Ameiurus natalis)*. Drawing by F. A. Carmichael.

Yellow Bullhead
Ameiurus natalis (LeSueur) (Plate 20)

Description: A plain dark yellowish brown to dark green catfish with a yellow or white belly, rounded tail fin, and long narrow anal fin (about 24–27 supporting rays). Barbels on chin pure white or creamy, no darker than skin on underside of head. Spine at front of pectoral fin saw-edged along its hind margin.

Size: The Yellow Bullhead usually weighs less than 0.4 kg (1 pound), but its maximum size is about 2.3 kg (5 pounds). Adults are usually 25 cm (10 inches) or less, although this fish reaches a maximum length of 47 cm (18¼ inches).

Habitat: The habitat of the Yellow Bullhead complements that of the Black Bullhead. Generally, the Yellow Bullhead inhabits clear, permanently flowing streams with rocky bottoms, not the muddier waters tolerated by the Black Bullhead, but both species may be found at some localities. Yellow Bullheads can live in lakes as well as streams, and they reproduce in either habitat. The species' range seems to have expanded westward as lakes have increased and stream flows have diminished in Kansas.

Reproduction: The Yellow Bullhead nests from May to August. The female clears a hole, and one or both adults hover over the egg-mass. After hatching, the young form schools that are accompanied (and protected) by one or both adults until they are about 5 cm

(2 inches) long. Hollows in submerged fallen trees are sometimes used as nest sites by the Yellow Bullhead.

Food: The Yellow Bullhead eats aquatic insects, crustaceans, snails, some vegetation, and other fish; it is also a scavenger.

Remarks: In Kansas, the Yellow Bullhead is less abundant than the Black Bullhead, is usually smaller than that species, and is less often caught by anglers. Yellow Bullheads can be raised in ponds but their potential in commercial pondfish production has not been investigated.

An adult Brown Bullhead *(Ameiurus nebulosus).* Drawing by F. A. Carmichael.

Brown Bullhead
Ameiurus nebulosus (Le Sueur) (Plate 20)

Description: Similar to Black Bullhead, but body with brown or black mottling or spots. Rays and membranes not contrasting in color on caudal and anal fins; usually 21–24 anal fin rays; 5–8 sawlike teeth on rear of pectoral spine.

Size: Maximum length for an adult of this species is 50 cm (21 inches), with a maximum weight of 2.5 kg (5½ pounds).

Habitat: Prefers the soft bottoms of pools and sluggish channels in creeks and rivers, as well as lakes and ponds with moderate to large amounts of aquatic vegetation.

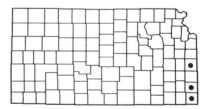

Reproduction: This species spawns from April to July, commonly selecting nest sites adjacent to stones, logs, or other shelter. The nest consists of a shallow excavation cleared of silt and is constantly attended by at least one parent.

Food: The Brown Bullhead has a varied diet, but insects and their larvae are a major part of its food supply. It is also known to eat plants, crustaceans, mollusks, worms, and small fishes.

Remarks: INTRODUCED SPECIES. The Brown Bullhead was introduced into a U.S. Fish and Wildlife Service Fish Hatchery at Farlington in

Crawford County during the 1950s. Also during that decade, it was stocked in many farm ponds and some lakes in eastern Kansas. To our knowledge, it has not become established in any streams in our state, but may reproduce and survive in some ponds or lakes.

An adult Blue Catfish *(Ictalurus furcatus)*. Drawing by Gene Pacheco.

Blue Catfish
Ictalurus furcatus (Le Sueur) (Plate 21)

Description: A very pale (often white) or bluish gray catfish with a deeply forked tail, and usually without spots on its silvery sides. Head short and heavy, back humped in front of dorsal fin. Differs from the Channel Catfish in having a longer anal fin, with about 30–35 supporting rays.

Size: Although Blue Catfish attained weights of 68 kg (150 pounds) or more in Kansas many years ago, the largest caught on hook and line in recent years measured 135 cm (53 inches) in total length and weighed 37.2 kg (82 pounds). It was caught in the Kansas River on rod and reel by Preston Stubbs, Jr., of DeSoto on 18 August 1988. Most Blue Catfish are 38–76 cm (15–30 inches) long. Elsewhere in its range, this species reaches a maximum length of 165 cm (65 inches).

Habitat: This species lives in the main channels of large rivers, particularly in stretches with bedrock, gravel, or sandy bottoms and with swift current, but it frequents reservoirs as well. When not feeding during winter, the 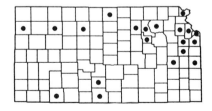 Blue Catfish apparently retreats to deep pools. All of the occurrences mapped from Pottawatomie County westward resulted from introductions in impoundments.

Reproduction: Blue Catfish spawn in late spring or early summer at water temperatures of 21°–24° C (70–75°F) in a nest cavity prepared by the male. Some of them migrate many miles upriver and into tributary streams before spawning, but construction of impoundments can limit their movements. Both parents construct a nest, similar to that of the Channel Catfish.

Food: The Blue Catfish eats crayfishes, aquatic insects and their larvae, freshwater clams, worms, other fishes, and frogs.

Remarks: Many anglers use the names "white cat," "fulton," or "Mississippi cat" for this species.

An adult Channel Catfish *(Ictalurus punctatus)*. Drawing by F. A. Carmichael.

Channel Catfish
Ictalurus punctatus (Rafinesque) (Plate 21)

Description: Channel Catfish are generally slender and blue-gray, blending into white on the belly, and with a few dark spots scattered over their sides. The tail is deeply forked. The anal fin has a rounded edge, and 24–29 supporting rays. Channel Catfish vary in color and shape depending on their size, sex, and habitat, and on the time of year. Young fish less than 10 cm (4 inches) long, and large, old fish often lack spots. Channel Catfish are darker in clear water than in muddy water. Breeding males are often unspotted, dark blue or gray; they also have two fleshy humps on top of the head, and wide fleshy lips. Channel Catfish in rivers are usually more slender than those in lakes and ponds.

Size: The largest Channel Catfish caught on hook and line in Kansas was 98 cm long (38½ inches) and weighed 15.8 kg (34.72 pounds). It was caught in the Kansas River on rod and reel by Larry L. Wright of Kansas City on 22 May 1980. Several Channel Catfish that weigh between 9 and 14 kg (20 and 30 pounds) are caught in Kansas lakes each year—particularly in the smaller, clearer state and county lakes. Farm ponds have produced Channel Catfish that weighed nearly 9 kg (20 pounds). River fish are smaller, seldom exceeding 2.3 kg (5 pounds). Elsewhere in its range, this species reaches a maximum length of 127 cm (50 inches).

Habitat: Channel Catfish inhabit all large streams in Kansas and have been stocked in many lakes and ponds. The rivers where Channel Catfish are most abundant have sandy or rocky bottoms and strong flow, but their waters are often muddy and fluctuate widely with runoff. Young Channel Catfish occupy shallow places strewn with rocks or other cover, usually in the current. The adults occupy

deeper water in pools, near
steep cut-banks, logjams, or
other debris. The adults often
move onto riffles at night for
feeding. However, Channel Catfish do not require flowing water
at any time in their lives.

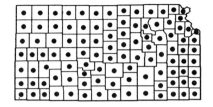

Reproduction: Where Channel Catfish grow rapidly, they mature at an
age of three years, a length of 38–40.5 cm (15–16 inches), and a
weight of about 0.7 kg (1½ pounds). Where they grow slowly, they
mature at an age of four or five years and lengths as small as 28–30.5
cm (11–12 inches). They spawn only once each year, from late May
to early July, when the water temperature is about 21°–26°C
(70°–80°F). Spawning always takes place in cavities of some sort—
holes or crevices along stream banks, beneath rock ledges in the
channel, or in or under logs lodged against the stream bottom. The
male chooses the nest site, enlarges it by cleaning out soft sediment,
and stays with the nest throughout the spawning period. The female
enters only to deposit her eggs. The eggs hatch in about seven days.
The young remain schooled in or near the nest for a few days
longer, then disperse to shallow riffles where they spend their first
summer and fall, retreating to deeper water in winter. They return
to the rocky or sandy shallows for a month or two in spring but
move gradually to deep water as they grow larger.

In ponds, Channel Catfish can be induced to spawn in wooden
boxes, sewer tiles, metal drums, or milk cans. Methods for their
propagation were first developed in Kansas in the 1930s. Most of the
young may be lost to predators in clear ponds, because they seek
shelter in places that are occupied by Largemouth Bass or Green
Sunfish.

Food: Channel Catfish feed mainly on insects, crayfish, mollusks, and
other fishes. They are scavengers in part, eating dead as well as living animals and parts of plants, which they locate by taste and odor
more often than by sight. This fish feeds most actively from sun-
down to midnight.

Remarks: Because Channel Catfish do not require clear water and living food, they do better than most game fish in turbid lakes and
ponds. Yields of 2,000 pounds per acre or more can be had by daily
feeding of pelleted rations available from stores that sell farm supplies
and livestock feed. We advise daily feeding only if all the fishes will

be harvested each year by nets or draining of the pond. If the plan is to catch them on hook and line, for sport and table use, feeding twice a week—using no more than 0.9–.13 kg (2–3 pounds) of pellets for each 100 pounds of fish in the pond at each feeding—is adequate. That amount of supplemental food will more than double the normal production of the pond, from about 68 kg (150 pounds) per acre to 136–227 kg (300–500 pounds) per acre. Few anglers want more catfish than that, and the smaller crop of fish reduces the chance that all will be lost to oxygen depletion on a hot summer day.

Several hundred ponds in Kansas are used for commercial catfish production, which originated in this state. The Kansas Commercial Fish Growers Association, as well as the Kansas Department of Wildlife and Parks, can provide fish for stocking private ponds, as well as information on methods and equipment needed for spawning, feeding, and processing catfish.

An adult Slender Madtom *(Noturus exilis)*. Drawing by F. A. Carmichael.

Slender Madtom
Noturus exilis Nelson (Plates 2, 22)

Description: A thin, plain gray or yellowish brown madtom with small, flattened head and median fins often dark-outlined. Anal fin long and narrow, with about nineteen rays. Lower jaw closing against upper jaw at front of head (tip of snout), but not projecting beyond lower jaw.

Size: Maximum length for an adult of this species in Kansas is 11.5 cm (4½ inches). Elsewhere in its range, this fish reaches a maximum length of 15.2 cm (6 inches).

Habitat: The Slender Madtom inhabits small, permanent streams in the Kansas, Osage, and Spring river basins. It occurs also, but less commonly, in the upper Neosho River drainage in Morris and Wabaunsee counties. Clear water,

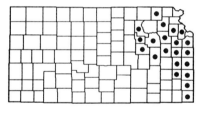

cool temperatures, and rocky bottoms seem necessary for this species. It lives mainly in shallow riffles where it hides in the crevices between stones in daytime, emerging to feed at night. In winter and when flow ceases over riffles, Slender Madtoms sometimes conceal themselves in leaf-litter in deep pools.

Reproduction: During the spring or early summer, the Slender Madtom nests in a cavity constructed by the male in a riffle or pool beneath a large rock and guarded by the male or by both parents.

Food: The Slender Madtom eats insects and their larvae, crustaceans, and snails.

Remarks: The Slender Madtom is an interesting, adaptable aquarium fish that will readily take commercially prepared food such as frozen brine shrimp or dry flakes.

An adult Stonecat *(Noturus flavus)*. Drawing by F. A. Carmichael.

Stonecat
Noturus flavus Rafinesque (Plate 22)

Description: A rather large yellowish brown madtom with a dusky streak through the center of the tail fin (upper and lower edges pale yellowish). Anal fin short, with about sixteen supporting rays. Lower jaw short, closing against upper jaw behind the front edge of the head.

Size: Maximum length for an adult of this species is 20 cm (8 inches) in Kansas. Elsewhere in its range, this fish reaches a maximum length of 31 cm (12¼ inches).

Habitat: The Stonecat is common on shallow riffles and rocky bottoms in currents of large clear, perennial streams, where it hides during the day beneath slabs of shale or limestone. Stones are not a requirement, as this creature has also been taken along sandbars. It sometimes hides in woody debris lodged in the stream bottom, but always in the current.

Reproduction: The Stonecat spawns in spring or early summer at water temperatures near 24°C (75°F). It nests beneath very large rocks in pools or riffles with moderate current. The nest is guarded by the male parent.

Food: The Stonecat eats insects, insect larvae, crustaceans, and other aquatic invertebrates, plus occasional darters and other small fishes.

Remarks: This is the largest of the madtoms and is sometimes caught by anglers. Like all species of *Noturus,* the Stonecat has sharp spines that deliver a mild poison, and it can inflict a painful wound when carelessly handled. Although Stonecats have been recorded throughout the Kansas River basin, they are now rare in the western half of the state.

An adult Tadpole Madtom *(Noturus gyrinus)*. Drawing by F. A. Carmichael.

Tadpole Madtom
Noturus gyrinus (Mitchill) (Plate 22)

Description: A chubby, plain tan or brownish to gray or black madtom with a white belly and a large, rounded tail fin. Skin appears translucent. Anal fin short, with about fifteen rays. Head rounded, not flat-topped. Lower jaw closing against upper jaw exactly at front of head.

Size: Maximum length for an adult of this species is 7 cm (2¾ inches) in Kansas. Elsewhere in its range, this fish reaches a maximum length of 13 cm (5 inches).

Habitat: The Tadpole Madtom lives in the calm water of oxbows and sluggish, lowland streams. It is most common in the Osage River system in eastern Kansas, but has been found also in the Wakarusa River and in small, di-

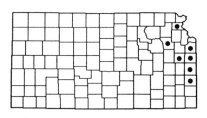

rect tributaries of the Missouri River. During the day this madtom hides beneath woody debris or vegetation. Although found in both clear and muddy water, this species usually lives on a mud bottom rather than the shallow riffles or rocky bottoms preferred by most madtoms in Kansas.

Reproduction: The Tadpole Madtom spawns in June or July. Young are guarded by a single parent.

Food: Algae, larval insects, snails, crustaceans, and small fishes make up the diet of the Tadpole Madtom.

Remarks: SINC SPECIES. Platt et al. (1974) recommended preservation of springs, oxbows, and weedy backwaters where this species occurs. Although it is not thought to be endangered, the Tadpole Madtom is known from so few places in Kansas that efforts for its protection are encouraged.

An adult Brindled Madtom *(Noturus miurus)*. Drawing by F. A. Carmichael.

Brindled Madtom
Noturus miurus Jordan (Plate 22)

Description: A yellowish brown madtom with dark saddles (and bands) on body (and fins). Dorsal fin and tail black-tipped. Adipose fin with a dark blotch that extends to its edge. Anal fin rounded, with about fourteen rays. Upper jaw projecting beyond the lower jaw.

Size: Maximum length for an adult of this species is 8 cm (3¾ inches) in Kansas. Elsewhere in its range, this fish reaches a maximum length of 13 cm (5 inches).

Habitat: The Brindled Madtom prefers the leaf-littered floor of pools in clear streams, usually with mud, sand, or fine gravel bottoms. It avoids riffles in the Kansas portion of its range, and is sometimes found in slow cur-

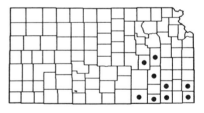

rents in the deeper parts of channels with low to moderate gradients. Brindled Madtoms occur at several localities in the Spring River basin (Cherokee and Crawford counties), and isolated populations have been found in headwaters of the Cottonwood, Verdigris, and Caney drainages.

Reproduction: The Brindled Madtom spawns in late spring or early summer, and the nest is guarded by the male parent.

Food: Insects, insect larvae, and small crustaceans are the preferred diet of the Brindled Madtom.

Remarks: Platt et al. (1974) considered the Brindled Madtom rare in Kansas. They recommended protection of watersheds, and minimizing pollution and physical alteration of streams where this species occurs.

An adult Freckled Madtom *(Noturus nocturnus)*. Drawing by F. A. Carmichael.

Freckled Madtom
Noturus nocturnus Jordan and Gilbert (Plate 23)

Description: A plain brown or gray madtom with tail fin uniformly dark except for a fine clear line along its edge. Underparts finely speckled. Anal fin with about seventeen rays. Lower jaw closing against upper jaw behind the front edge of the head.

Size: Maximum length for an adult of this species is 11 cm (4½ inches) in Kansas. Elsewhere in its range, this fish reaches a maximum length of 15 cm (5¾ inches).

Habitat: The Freckled Madtom prefers streams with moderate or low gradient, but occasionally is found in riffles. It lives in debris piled against streambanks, under rocks in shallow backwaters along a channel, or where roots of trees have been exposed along a shoreline.

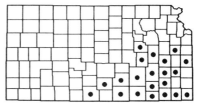

Reproduction: The Freckled Madtom spawns in late spring or early summer, and the nest is guarded by the male parent.

Food: Freckled Madtoms dine on insects, insect larvae, and small crustaceans.

Remarks: Although it is widely distributed in southeastern Kansas, the Freckled Madtom seldom occurs with other madtoms, such as the Slender Madtom. It has been found with the Stonecat and the Neosho Madtom, but those two species usually are in rocky parts of the main channel, swept by currents; the Freckled Madtom stays in calmer water.

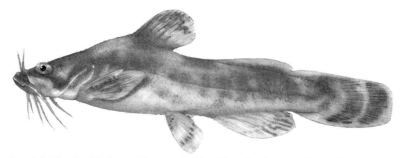

An adult Neosho Madtom *(Noturus placidus)*. Drawing by F. A. Carmichael.

Neosho Madtom
Noturus placidus Taylor (Plate 23)

Description: A small, mottled dark- and light-brown madtom with dark bars on the tail fin. Dorsal and anal fins with dusky streaks but not black-tipped. Dark blotch on adipose fin does not extend to its margin. Lower jaw closes against upper jaw behind front edge of head.

Size: The largest Neosho Madtom on record was found in Kansas, and measured 8.7 cm (3½ inches) in total length.

Habitat: The Neosho Madtom lives only in the mainstream of the Cottonwood, Spring, and Neosho rivers. It occurs in riffles and along sloping gravel bars in moderate to strong currents. Deep deposits of loose, rounded chert gravel seem to be preferred by this fish.

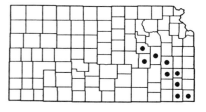

Reproduction: Spawning by the Neosho Madtom probably takes place in June or July during peak stream flow.

Food: The Neosho Madtom eats larval insects that live in crevices between stones on the riverbed. It feeds at night, with the greatest foraging activity occurring during the three hours after sunset.

Remarks: FEDERALLY THREATENED SPECIES IN KANSAS. Platt et al. (1974) considered the Neosho Madtom the most endangered fish in Kansas. They recommended control of pollution by nutrient influx,

avoidance of gravel removal in mainstreams, and careful considera-
tion of any further impoundments where this species occurs. This
fish has disappeared from most of its original range outside Kansas.
In 1990 it was designated for protection by the U.S. Fish and Wildlife Service.

An adult Flathead Catfish *(Pylodictis olivaris)*. Drawing by F. A. Carmichael.

Flathead Catfish
Pylodictis olivaris (Rafinesque) (Plate 23)

Description: A large catfish with very broad head, jutting lower jaw, and shallowly notched (but not forked) tail fin. About fifteen supporting rays in anal fin. Young jet-black with white patch on upper tip of tail fin. Body becomes mottled black and olive-brown as fish grows; large adults plain yellowish brown.

Size: Most adult Flathead Catfish are 46–92 cm (18–36 inches) in total length. The largest specimen taken in Kansas weighed 40.8 kg (90 pounds) and measured 136.2 cm (53½ inches) in total length. It was taken in Pomona Reservoir on rod and reel by Wayne Medlen of Pomona on 15 June 1993. Elsewhere in its range, this fish reaches a maximum length of 155 cm (61 inches).

Habitat: The Flathead Catfish is common in pools of the larger streams in Kansas. It avoids rivers with high gradients or intermittent flows. During the day, it often lies on the bottom, near cover such as fallen trees that have lodged in the stream, below the concrete aprons of dams, or against bridge-supports where pockets of deep water are formed by currents. At night, it actively moves about in search of food. Flathead Catfish are rare in western Kansas except where their numbers have increased locally in the more favorable habitat of reservoirs.

Reproduction: The Flathead Catfish spawns in June or early July, pairing off in cavities similar to those used by the Channel Catfish. Both parents construct the nest.

Food: The Flathead Catfish is carnivorous. Young Flatheads eat aquatic insects; but as they grow, their diet shifts to crayfishes and other fishes. They are not scavengers like Channel Catfish and bullheads.

Remarks: The Flathead Catfish is a good sport fish for those with the patience to seek it. It is not easily caught, especially in the convenient hours of daylight, but it offers greater possibilities for hooking a really big fish than any other species in Kansas.

ORDER SALMONIFORMES

PIKES (Family Esocidae)

An adult Northern Pike *(Esox lucius)*. Drawing by F. A. Carmichael.

Northern Pike
Esox lucius Linnaeus (Plate 24)

Description: Body slender with short dorsal and anal fins located just in front of the forked tail fin. No bony spines in any fin. Broad, flat snout with strong teeth on jaws. Color gray-green with mottled sides, usually with oval or capsule-shaped pale spots on a dark background.

Size: Maximum weight for an adult of this species is about 23 kg (50 pounds). The current Kansas rod-and-reel record weighed 11.2 kg (24.75 pounds) and measured 112 cm (44 inches) in total length. It was taken from Council Grove Reservoir in Morris County by Mr. and Mrs. H. A. Bowman of Manhattan on 28 August 1971. Elsewhere in its range, this fish reaches a maximum length of 133 cm (53 inches).

Habitat: Northern Pike prefer shallow, weedy, clear water. The species is found in both lakes and streams, but its abundance in streams diminishes southward, so that it is mainly a lake fish in the southern part of its range. There is some evidence that Northern Pike occurred naturally in Kansas, perhaps as individual strays, but their presence today is mainly due to introductions into various impoundments beginning in 1962. During the 1960s, Northern Pike were stocked in all major public reservoirs and many of the smaller "state lakes." The stocking program continues but is now very limited because a general lack of suitable spawning habitat deters their permanent establishment through natural reproduction and high water temperature in summer prevents many stocks from surviving.

Reproduction: Northern Pike spawn in late winter or early spring. Prior to spawning, the adults move upstream or inshore into creeks, marshes, or flooded grasslands. The eggs are deposited on debris left over from the previous year's plant growth. The adults then return to their lakes, while the eggs and young develop in the shallow, weedy flats for several weeks. Nutrients released by plant decay, as the water warms, support growth of the abundant food required by young pikes. Kansas impoundments fluctuate too much for nursery areas like these to be available at the times and in the amounts needed to sustain a Northern Pike population. Usually, reservoirs are held at a low level during the critical time, February to April, in anticipation of later runoff for which flood storage will be needed. Fluctuating water levels in summer also prevent establishment of the large weedbeds where pike do best.

Food: Northern Pike are voracious carnivores that grow rapidly to large size. The newly hatched fry feed initially on small crustaceans (animal plankton). Very soon, however, they begin feeding on the young of other fishes that spawn later and grow more slowly than the pike. Adult Northern Pike feed almost solely on fish.

Remarks: INTRODUCED SPECIES. Northern Pike were brought into Kansas for two purposes: first, to provide an additional game fish to meet the increasing recreational demand; and second, to provide an additional large predator to help stabilize reservoir fish populations. Reservoirs are artificial habitats that have no natural counterpart in the southern plains, where no large lakes existed prior to damming. The fish communities of shallow plains rivers do not include many large predatory species like the Northern Pike, Muskellunge, Walleye, and various basses, compared to the number of forage fishes such as suckers, minnows, small catfish, and sunfish. Large predators were not needed to "balance" the river communities, because natural calamities did that. Losses due to drought or to scouring by floods eliminated the excess annual production and balanced the river populations at favorable levels. Reservoirs reduced these natural losses; native fishes quickly occupied the warm, shallow reservoirs, where some of the previous checks on their abundance were removed.

"Balanced" communities in reservoirs are unlikely unless high rates of mortality in some new form replace the old causes of mortality. Increasing the "top carnivores" in the system is the most effective solution to that problem. If the predators added are also gamefish, they can serve a dual purpose—unless so many are cropped by anglers that they cannot accomplish their second, essential function of thinning the ranks of nongame fish to desirable levels.

The Northern Pike was one of several species introduced in the attempt to advance sport fishing in newly created lake habitats of Kansas. They were catchable only for brief periods each year, probably because temperatures here are outside the optimal range for them during much of the summer fishing season. Also, Northern Pike tended to leave reservoirs and disappear, through outlet gates, over spillways, or upstream into habitats less suitable for them than the lakes into which they were stocked.

SMELTS (Family Osmeridae)

Rainbow Smelt
Osmerus mordax (Mitchill) (Plate 24)

Description: A slender, silvery, minnowlike fish with an adipose fin and teeth on its jaws and tongue.

Size: Maximum length for an adult Rainbow Smelt is 33 cm (13 inches).

Habitat: The Rainbow Smelt occurs naturally along the northeastern Atlantic coast, with some
populations in the lower St.
Lawrence River system and landlocked in lakes. It was introduced
successfully into the upper Great

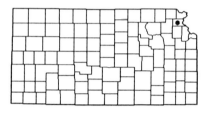

Lakes (above Niagara Falls) in the early 1900s, and into Garrison Reservoir on the upper Missouri River in North Dakota in 1971. Its specific habitat needs are for cold, clear waters along oceanic coast-lines or the open waters of large rivers and lakes, with access to smaller streams for spawning.

Reproduction: In its native range, this species is anadromous, mean-ing that it migrates inland from the ocean to spawn in streams (or, if landlocked, from lakes to tributary streams). Very large schools of Rainbow Smelt migrate upstream together in early spring. Some of these smelt reportedly spawn on offshore rocks of large lakes. Many adults die after the egg-laying occurs. Rainbow Smelts have a life span of about eight years.

Food: Rainbow Smelts eat aquatic invertebrates and small fishes.

Subspecies in Kansas: The race of this introduced fish in Kansas has not yet been determined because too few specimens are available for examination.

Remarks: INTRODUCED SPECIES. Unlike the shallow reservoirs on rivers in Kansas, the large Dakota reservoirs are deep and cold, re-ceiving most of their water from snowmelt. Few of the fishes that were native to the shallow, turbid water of the Missouri River prior to its impoundment can exist in the chain of reservoirs constructed there in the mid-twentieth century. The habitat is now more suitable for cold-water, pelagic fishes, including trout and salmon, and smelt as an open-water forage fish, comparable to Gizzard Shad in impoundments farther south. Rainbow Smelt prospered after their establishment in Garrison Reservoir (Lake Sakakawea) in the early 1970s, spread downstream through the other lakes, and into the lower Missouri River as drifting "outwash." Rainbow Smelt were first captured in the Kansas reach of the Missouri River in 1978. They are not reproductively self-sustaining in this part of the Missouri River, and are not to be expected elsewhere in this area.

Trouts (Family Salmonidae)

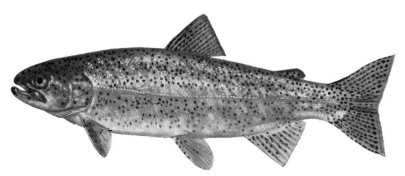

An adult Rainbow Trout *(Oncorhynchus mykiss)*. Drawing by F. A. Carmichael.

Rainbow Trout
Oncorhynchus mykiss (Walbaum) (Plate 24)

Description: Distinguishable from other fishes in Kansas by the combination of an adipose fin and finely scaled body. Differs from the Brown Trout in having many small black spots on head, body, and tail fin, and a pink lateral stripe.

Size: The current Kansas rod-and-reel record weighed 4.2 kg (9.31 pounds) and measured 71.9 cm (28¼ inches) in total length. It was taken from Lake Shawnee in Shawnee County by Raymond Deghand of Topeka on 14 November 1982. Elsewhere, this fish reaches a maximum length of 114 cm (45 inches).

Habitat: Rainbow Trout prefer clear-water streams and lakes that remain saturated with oxygen and are never warmer than 24°C (75°F).

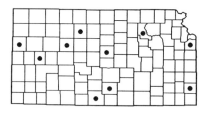

Reproduction: Reproductive populations of the Rainbow Trout do not exist in Kansas.

Food: The Rainbow Trout eats aquatic and terrestrial insects, as well as snails and small fishes.

Remarks: INTRODUCED SPECIES. Kansas has so little water suitable for the Rainbow Trout that no self-sustaining populations exist in the state. Nevertheless, at least six species of trout and salmon have been introduced here in the past, and some trout probably are present in private waters at all times.

A few springs in the state have enough flow to maintain limited numbers of the Rainbow Trout year-round (for example, Rock Springs 4-H camp in Dickinson County). Elsewhere wells have been used to provide cool water for small, permanent trout-ponds. Seasonal trout-fishing can be had practically anywhere in the state by releasing catchable-size trout, bought from private hatcheries, into farm ponds when their water cools in October or November; the pond conditions generally remain acceptable to the Rainbow Trout until the following May or June.

A few very local, highly artificial public trout fisheries have been established in the state, but that effort seems less worthwhile to us than equal effort toward the conservation of species that are better adapted to the natural environment of our state.

Brown Trout
Salmo trutta Linnaeus (Plate 24)

Description: Distinguishable from other fishes in Kansas by the combination of an adipose fin and finely scaled body. Differs from the Rainbow Trout in having comparatively large red and black spots on the head and body, and no distinctive lateral stripe. Spots absent from tail fin or, if they are present, confined along upper margin.

Size: The Brown Trout attains a maximum length of 103 cm (40½ inches).

Habitat: Brown Trout inhabit cool streams and lakes, but tolerate slightly warmer water than other trouts. They frequent pools below riffles and areas beneath undercut banks or submerged logs.

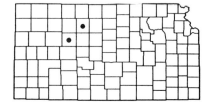

Reproduction: Reproductive populations of the Brown Trout do not exist in Kansas.

Food: The diet of Brown Trout is similar to that of the Rainbow Trout, but it consumes a greater number of small fishes and feeds more frequently on crayfishes.

Remarks: INTRODUCED SPECIES. See the Remarks section for the Rainbow Trout.

ORDER GADIFORMES

Codfishes (Family Gadidae)

An adult Burbot *(Lota lota).* Drawing by F. A. Carmichael.

Burbot
Lota lota (Linnaeus) (Plate 24)

Description: Slender body, mottled greenish brown. Long dorsal and anal fins, without bony spines, and small rounded tail fin. One barbel on lower jaw. Scales so small that body appears naked.

Size: Maximum known weight 27.8–34.8 kg (60–75 pounds). Kansas specimens are juveniles, mostly less than 51 cm (20 inches) long and 1.4 kg (3 pounds) in weight. Elsewhere in its range, this fish reaches a maximum length of 84 cm (33 inches).

Habitat: The Burbot occurred in the mainstream of the Missouri River, and formerly entered the lower Kansas River during floods.

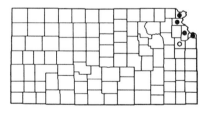

Reproduction: Burbots gather to spawn in groups in winter. The eggs are scattered over firm bottoms and abandoned.

Food: Fishes and aquatic insect larvae make up the diet of the Burbot.

Remarks: The Burbot is the only codfish that occurs widely in freshwater. Kansas is at the southern limit of its range, which extends northward throughout Canada to Alaska and Siberia. Before the

Missouri River was impounded in Montana and the Dakotas, some Burbots moved down the channel as far as Missouri and Kansas. They were caught occasionally by anglers, and by commercial fishing operations in hoopnets. Platt et al. (1974) placed the Burbot on their peripheral list of endangered species in Kansas. To our knowledge, none has been caught in Kansas for several years.

ORDER ATHERINIFORMES

KILLIFISHES (Family Fundulidae)

The topminnows are a small group of species that resemble true minnows in size and habits but differ from them in four respects: (1) they have peculiar jaws adapted for feeding at the water surface; (2) their head is covered by scales or plates; (3) they have rounded tail fins; (4) there is no line of pored scales along their sides. Four kinds of topminnows have been found in Kansas, but only two are common enough to be caught regularly.

Topminnows and killifish are slender fishes with a strongly arched mouth that opens nearly level with the top of the head. The back is long and straight, and the rounded dorsal fin arises near the tail fin. These are adaptations to swimming at or near the water surface. Much of the food of topminnows consists of tiny animals, such as mosquito larvae, that are associated with the surface film. By living at the surface, topminnows are partly safeguarded against one of the major hazards of aquatic life—loss of oxygen, which is as necessary to fishes as to land animals. Oxygen is rarely absent from the very surface of the water, where it dissolves from the air, even in cases of serious pollution. Therefore, topminnows and killifish (and Mosquitofish) sometimes survive "fish-kills" in streams, or appear in large numbers soon after these kills. Some species also occur in places where the water seems foul due to natural accumulations of organic material on soft mud bottoms. Apart from this advantage over most other kinds of fishes, topminnows are poor competitors. They are not abundant where many other kinds of fishes live, and (unlike minnows), no two kinds of topminnows are likely to be found in the same place.

Most topminnows and killifish prefer clear, quiet water, in pools or near shore. Such places often have aquatic vegetation. The Plains Killifish is exceptional, living mainly in shallow, barren, sandy streams.

Topminnows and killifish are most active in daytime. Their food is varied, including most organisms in the plankton as well as organisms associated with the surface film.

Most topminnows and killifish have bright colors or sharply contrasting patterns of dark and light pigment, especially in males. The sexes usually differ in color, most obviously during the breeding season but also at other times of the year. In some instances the sexes differ in size also, so that the males and females may at first appear to be different species. All four species are egg-layers.

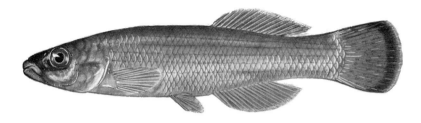

An adult Northern Studfish *(Fundulus catenatus)*. Drawing by Gene Pacheco.

Northern Studfish
Fundulus catenatus (Storer) (Plate 25)

Description: Color plain greenish, with 8–10 thin brownish lines along sides. Breeding males with shiny blue sides and yellow-orange lengthwise lines; tail orange-tipped and with black band just inside its margin. Dorsal fin with 13–16 rays; anal fin with 15–18 rays (both fins longer than in other Kansas topminnows).

Size: Maximum length for an adult of this species is 18 cm (7 inches).

Habitat: This fish inhabits clear streams having permanent flow and rocky bottoms. The Northern Studfish is extremely rare in Kansas, having been collected only in Drywood Creek, Crawford County.

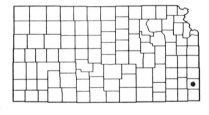

Reproduction: The Northern Studfish spawns in late spring and summer over gravel in calm, shallow water.

Food: Small insects found in riffle areas are the preferred food of the Northern Studfish. See the family account for killifish.

Remarks: The Northern Studfish is abundant in Ozark streams of southwestern Missouri, but it barely enters Kansas. Thus, it was listed by Platt et al. (1974) as a peripheral species, one that is rare in Kansas because this is the extreme edge of its range. It might be found in the Spring and Osage river systems in Cherokee, Crawford, Bourbon, and Linn counties, but records elsewhere are very unlikely.

An adult Blackstripe Topminnow *(Fundulus notatus).* Drawing by Victor Hogg.

Blackstripe Topminnow
Fundulus notatus (Rafinesque) (Plates 2, 25)

Description: Black stripe full length of sides (straight-edged in females, broken by crossbars in males). Fins plain or sometimes yellow. Dorsal fin with about nine rays; anal fin with twelve rays.

Size: Maximum length for an adult of this species is 7.4 cm (3 inches).

Habitat: This fish inhabits clear, small streams in southeastern Kansas that have rocky or muddy bottoms. It avoids strong currents, living in pools and along the shoreline, especially where leaf litter and other organic sediments accumulate. Our only record from the Kansas River basin came from Lyon Creek, Dickinson County, in 1975; it may have been introduced. The Blackstripe Topminnow is easily observed due to its surface-dwelling habit.

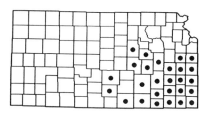

Reproduction: The Blackstripe Topminnow spawns from May to mid-August. Adults tend to pair off and remain together. Eggs are deposited singly in vegetation, to which the eggs adhere during development. There is no parental attention to the eggs.

Food: The Blackstripe Topminnow feeds on surface-dwelling insects, crustaceans, and their larvae.

Remarks: This is the most common topminnow in eastern Kansas. It makes a striking and handsome addition to any home aquarium.

An adult Plains Topminnow *(Fundulus sciadicus)*. Drawing by Thomas H. Swearingen.

Plains Topminnow
Fundulus sciadicus Cope

Description: Color plain greenish, sides without stripes or bars. Fins red-tipped, sides with bluish reflections in summer. Body shorter and thicker (chubbier) than that of other topminnows in Kansas. Dorsal fin with 9–11 rays; anal fin with 12–15 rays.

Size: Maximum length for an adult Plains Topminnow is 7 cm (2¾ inches).

Habitat: The single record for the Plains Topminnow from Kansas was taken from a small, weedy pool alongside the channel of Shoal Creek in Cherokee County.

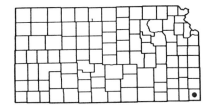

Reproduction: The Plains Topminnow spawns in late spring on algal strands or other aquatic vegetation.

Food: The Plains Topminnow eats mainly insects, and some algae. See the family account for killifish.

Remarks: Outside Kansas, the Plains Topminnow inhabits sandy spring runs in the Platte River system (Nebraska), and small streams in the western Ozark Region of Missouri. It has been found also in the westernmost part of the Republican River drainage in Nebraska. Therefore, Kansas records are most likely from two extreme places: the southeastern corner (Cherokee County) and the northwestern corner (Cheyenne County). It might also be looked for in northeastern Kansas, along the Missouri River. Platt et al. (1974) considered this fish a peripheral species on their endangered list for Kansas.

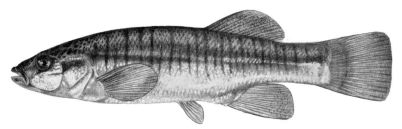

An adult Plains Killifish *(Fundulus zebrinus)*. Drawing by F. A. Carmichael.

Plains Killifish
Fundulus zebrinus (Garman) (Plate 25)

Description: Straw-colored with many narrow vertical (transverse) bars on sides. Bars fewer, wider, and more prominent in males than in females (female shown above). Fins, except dorsal, become bright orange in breeding males. Dorsal fin with about fifteen rays; anal fin with 13–14 rays.

Size: Maximum length for an adult of this species is 10 cm (4 inches).

Habitat: This species is common in many western Kansas streams. It prefers shallow streams that have sandy bottoms and are highly alkaline or saline. Plains Killifish can be abundant either in rapid current or in backwaters, but rarely in water more than 15 cm (6 inches) deep.

Reproduction: This fish spawns from May through July at water temperatures of 26°C (80°F) or higher. Because the water temperature varies greatly during a 24-hour interval in shallow, exposed streams, the reproductive activity of the Plains Killifish may be restricted to a short period each day. The eggs are deposited in coarse sand where the current is not rapid, and are left unattended. Plains Killifish mature as yearlings, and seldom live more than two years.

Food: This fish eats insects, mainly midge larvae and mayflies, both at the surface and the bottom.

Subspecies in Kansas: A Mississippi River basin race, *Fundulus zebrinus kansae.*

Remarks: Often called "zebra minnow" or "penitentiary minnow" in Kansas. The Plains Killifish tolerates salinities and temperatures that are too extreme for many other Kansas fishes, so it is often the dominant species where it occurs. It has declined or disappeared from western Kansas streams where flow became highly intermittent due to irrigation withdrawals in recent years. In the eastern part of our state, this fish has been found only as a rare vagrant in the Missouri River and Kansas River mainsteams, and in the Walnut River (Butler County) when that stream was polluted by saline oilfield and refinery wastes many years ago. Other fishes replaced the Plains Killifish after those pollution sources were curtailed.

LIVEBEARERS (Family Poeciliidae)

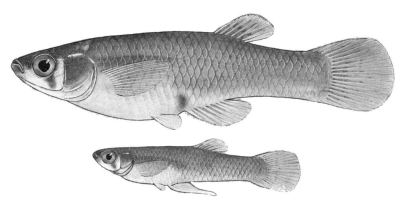

An adult female (top) and adult male (bottom) Mosquitofish *(Gambusia affinis)*. Drawings by Victor Hogg.

Mosquitofish
Gambusia affinis (Baird and Girard) (Plate 26)

Description: Small size, plain greenish gray color. Females stout, often with a dark spot on each side in front of anal fin. Males much smaller and more slender than females, with rodlike anal fin. Anal fin farther forward than dorsal fin, both with seven rays.

Size: Maximum length for an adult of this species is 6.5 cm (2½ inches).

Habitat: The Mosquitofish prefers calm, shallow pools and backwaters of streams. It has a limited tolerance of cold, so only a few individuals survive over winter.

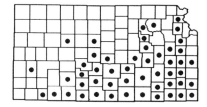

Reproduction: The Mosquitofish is the only Kansas fish that gives birth to young rather than depositing eggs. Litters of as many as 140 fully developed, active, independent young are produced repeatedly during the summer.

Food: This fish feeds on many kinds of aquatic insect larvae and on small crustaceans, mostly at the surface. Because it eats mosquito larvae, and thrives in small, shallow, weedy pools where mosquitoes often breed, the Mosquitofish is widely introduced for mosquito control.

Remarks: INTRODUCED SPECIES. The Mosquitofish was introduced into Kansas in the Ninnescah River, probably during the 1930s. Due to this and later introductions, it spread gradually throughout much of Kansas. Its range has now expanded northward into Nebraska.

SILVERSIDES (Family Atherinidae)

An adult Brook Silverside *(Labidesthes sicculus)*. Drawing by Victor Hogg.

Brook Silverside
Labidesthes sicculus (Cope) (Plate 26)

Description: Tiny first dorsal fin (often folded against back). Slender body, transparent with narrow, bright silvery lateral stripe. Upper jaw long, beaklike. Forked tail.

Size: Maximum length for an adult of this species is 13 cm (5 inches).

Habitat: This species prefers calm, clear water, but inhabits many small streams that have considerable current. The Brook Silverside is numerous in pools having rocky bottoms. It is attracted to light, and collections at night yield many more specimens than daylight collecting.

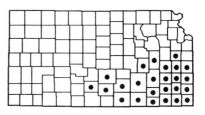

Reproduction: The Brook Silverside spawns from May to July. Male fish in streams congregate over gravel bottoms where they are joined by females that enter the breeding area when ready to spawn. The eggs are extruded singly, and each has a sticky thread that anchors it on contact with a stone, vegetation, or debris. This species matures quickly; its life span rarely exceeds a year.

Food: Brook Silversides feed mainly on small crustaceans and insects on or near the water surface.

Subspecies in Kansas: The nominate race, *Labidesthes s. sicculus.*

Remarks: Normally scarce, the Brook Silverside sometimes becomes abundant in new impoundments. It increased in the Cottonwood and Neosho rivers after most fishes there were killed by pollution in 1967. Predation probably keeps its numbers low in well-established, mixed fish populations. The Brook Silverside is not hardy enough for use as a bait minnow or aquarium fish. It is the most widespread freshwater species in a family that is mainly marine.

ORDER SCORPAENIFORMES

Sculpins (Family Cottidae)

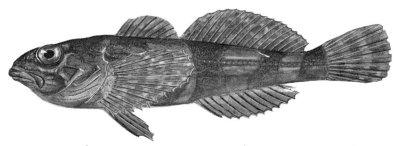

An adult Banded Sculpin *(Cottus carolinae)*. Drawing by Gene Pacheco.

Banded Sculpin
Cottus carolinae (Gill) (Plate 26)

Description: Naked skin. When viewed from above, entire body outline is wedge-shaped due to large head and mouth. Small soft first dorsal and very long second dorsal fin. Color brown with broad darker brown "saddles."

Size: Maximum length for an adult of this species is 18 cm (7¼ inches).

Habitat: The Banded Sculpin lives in swift riffles over rubble bottom in clear, permanent streams.

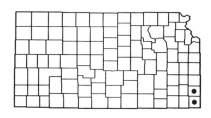

Reproduction: Little is known of the reproductive habits of the Banded Sculpin. Spawning probably occurs in March. In other species of sculpins outside Kansas, males establish territories in crevices beneath stones. Females enter the nests only to deposit eggs, which are attached to the underside of the stone. The male guards the eggs.

Food: The Banded Sculpin eats the larvae of stoneflies, mayflies, and caddisflies, as well as amphipods, small mollusks, crayfishes, and small fish.

Subspecies in Kansas: The nominate race, *Cottus c. carolinae.*

Remarks: SINC SPECIES. Abundant in Ozark streams, the Banded Sculpin enters Kansas only where reliable springs maintain a stream flow cool and clear enough to sustain the species through the summer. It is now known only from Shoal Creek, Cherokee County. If that stream should fail or be impounded, the Banded Sculpin and several other species would be lost from the state's fish fauna. Platt et al. (1974) included the Banded Sculpin on their list of endangered fishes as a peripheral species.

ORDER PERCIFORMES

Temperate Basses (Family Moronidae)

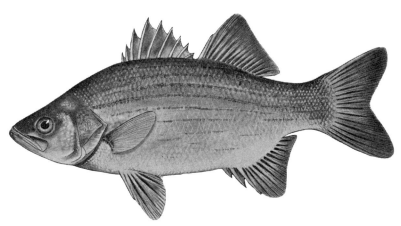

An adult White Bass *(Morone chrysops)*. Drawing by Victor Hogg.

White Bass
Morone chrysops (Rafinesque) (Plate 27)

Description: Dorsal fins separate, both high, the second dorsal nearly straight along its edge. Body slab-sided, silver with faint lengthwise lines. Gill cover with a sharp spine. Differs from Striped Bass as follows: teeth on tongue usually in a single patch; less than 56 scales in the lateral-line row on sides; second dorsal and anal fins with one more flexible ray (usually 12–13).

Size: The largest Kansas White Bass weighed 2.5 kg (5.52 pounds), and measured 56.3 cm (22⅛ inches) in total length. It was caught on rod and reel by Jeffery L. Clark of Clay Center from a sand pit in Clay County on 7 March 1992. Apparently, this is the maximum length for the species throughout its range. The usual size of adults is 0.4–1.4 kg (1–3 pounds).

Habitat: The White Bass lives in reservoirs and large rivers. It probably occurred naturally in eastern Kansas, but its present abundance results from introductions into reservoirs throughout the state. An

abundance of Gizzard Shad as
prey appears to be necessary for
the White Bass to become established.

Reproduction: White Bass spawn
in spring, along shoals in lakes
and in the shallow water of rivers where currents expose a firm,
clean streambed. Groups of fishes spawn together without preparing nest sites. The eggs receive no parental attention. This species is
short-lived, reaching full adult weight in two to four years.

Food: This fish feeds on schools of small fishes such as Gizzard Shad.

Remarks: The White Bass is a good game fish and an unusually effective predator on schooling fishes such as Gizzard Shad because the
White Bass themselves rove about in schools, hunting prey in open
water.

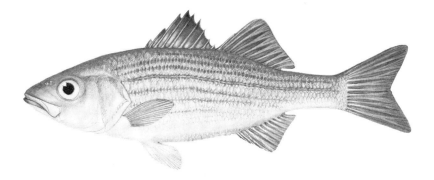

An adult Striped Bass *(Morone saxatilis)*. Drawing by Thomas H. Swearingen.

Striped Bass
Morone saxatilis (Walbaum) (Plate 27)

Description: Resembles the White Bass, but more slender, with sides more prominently lined, and growing to much larger size. Two parallel patches of teeth on the tongue. Second dorsal fin with one spine and 11–12 soft rays; anal fin with three spines and 10–11 rays. More than 56 scales in the lateral-line row on midsides.

Size: The largest Striped Bass caught since the introduction of this species into Kansas weighed 19.7 kg (43½ pounds) and measured 108.8 cm (42¾ inches) in total length. It was taken with rod and reel by Chester Nily of Sylvan Grove in Wilson Reservoir on 18 May 1988. Elsewhere in its range, this species reaches a maximum length of 200 cm (79 inches).

Habitat: The natural habitat of the Striped Bass is along the Atlantic coast, where it occurs in saltwater and enters the lower parts of rivers to spawn. The localities shown on the map are those where Striped Bass have 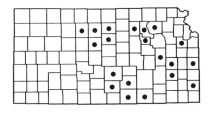 been stocked in reservoirs by the Kansas Department of Wildlife and Parks. The most succeful of these stockings is that in Wilson Reservoir, on the Saline River.

Reproduction: This fish spawns during April and early May at water temperatures of 14°C (58°F) or above. Where spawning by stocked populations occurs, the sites generally are in flowing water 90–180 cm

(3–6 feet) deep in rivers above lakes or below lake outlets. A single female Striped Bass can produce over 30,000 eggs. Little, if any, natural reproduction occurs in Kansas.

Food: The Striped Bass feeds on schools of smaller fishes such as the Gizzard Shad.

Remarks: INTRODUCED SPECIES. See the accounts of the Gizzard Shad and Northern Pike for information on the ecological role of this fish in Kansas. At the time of this writing, the Kansas Department of Wildlife and Parks continues to stock this species, but now also produces hybrids (called "wipers"—see Plate 27) between Striped Bass and White Bass for release in Kansas reservoirs.

SUNFISHES (Family Centrarchidae)

Sunfishes are known to almost everybody, because they are bold, active fishes that are readily seen in clear water along the edges of streams and ponds. Sunfishes are also the "first catch" of many young anglers dabbling worms or other bait from short poles near shore. One or more kinds of sunfish occur in every part of the state. Nearly all live in stream pools, and lakes provide even better habitat for most species. Sunfishes, especially the Largemouth Bass and Bluegill, are the fishes used most for stocking new lakes and ponds. Whether or not sunfish are stocked, they normally get into new lakes by moving downstream into them or swimming upstream over spillways during overflow. Because of the additional habitat provided by tens of thousands of ponds built for water supply, sunfish now occur much more widely in Kansas than they did when the state was first settled by Europeans.

Twelve kinds of sunfish live in Kansas. These are conveniently divided into three groups. The Black Basses (Largemouth Bass, Smallmouth Bass, and Spotted Bass, genus *Micropterus*) grow larger than other sunfishes, are more slender than the other members of the family, and are the most prized as game fish. Second, the Black Crappie and White Crappie (genus *Pomoxis*) are white or silvery, slab-sided fishes that are easily recognized by their having about as many bony spines in the anal fin as in the dorsal fin; crappies abound in most lakes but are caught less often in streams of Kansas. The third group consists of several small, compact, often colorful fishes variously called "panfish," "perch," and "goggleye" as well as sunfish; six of the seven species in Kansas are in the genus *Lepomis*. Each kind differs from all others in details of shape and color, as described in accounts on later pages.

Sunfishes are most active in daytime. They feed on various living animals that they locate mainly by sight, so sunfishes do best in clear water. All of them have highly movable jaws that enable them to inhale their food whole. As they approach their prey, they thrust the jaws forward and outward, automatically sucking the prey into the greatly enlarged mouth cavity. The prey is then forced backward into the stomach as the mouth is closed. Underwater, this feeding method is surer and tidier than biting and chewing. It is the method of attack used by the most advanced, most successful groups of modern fishes. The size of the mouth limits the size of the prey that can be consumed, of course, and differs among sunfishes. Some, like the Largemouth Bass and the Green Sunfish, are able to swallow items up to half their own size—other fishes, frogs, large insects, or fishing plugs. Motion of the prey, as much as its appearance, attracts sunfishes. That is why they are such fine sport fishes, subject to capture on a nearly unlimited assortment of artificial lures and live baits.

All sunfishes in Kansas have similar reproductive habits in that they prepare and guard nests, mainly in spring, for the development of their eggs. Winters are spent quietly in deep water, but as the water warms in March and April, sunfishes disperse into shallow places along shore. Males precede females, and select the nest sites. Each male clears a small area of the bottom, sweeping away silt to expose a solid surface underneath—gravel or firm clay—that forms the floor of the circular nest. Sunfishes sometimes make their nests next to a large stone or log, but they almost never conceal the nest beneath overhead cover. Thus the nest is often visible from above, looking like a light-colored patch of clean bottom with the male fish hovering in the open water nearby. Males of some species (Bluegill, for example) sometimes place their nests so close together that the bottom appears pockmarked by colonies of nests, separated only by ridges of fine silt. Other species (Largemouth Bass, for example) nest in isolation from males of their own kind, but they may not avoid the nests of other species. We have seen Green Sunfish on nests that were surrounded by the nests of Bluegills. Maybe this accounts for some of the hybrids of those two species, found rather commonly in Kansas ponds and streams.

When a female sunfish is ready to deposit her eggs, she approaches the nest area and is urged into a nest by its guardian male. Once she has given up her eggs, however, she is no longer welcome near the nest. The eggs stick to the hard floor of the nest. They are so small as to be barely visible, and are transparent. But they can be seen on pebbles lifted from an active nest, looking like small glass beads or dewdrops. The male remains to protect them as the embryos develop, and to receive additional females seeking a place to spawn. Within a week or two, the young have hatched, risen as a school from the nest bottom, and begun to wander as they seek the microscopic animals that are their first food.

The small sunfishes (*Lepomis* species) spawn repeatedly through the late spring and summer, but the larger kinds (basses and crappies) normally reproduce only during a few weeks in spring. The larger species also make their nests in deeper water, where they are less likely to be seen than those of Bluegill, Green Sunfish, Longear Sunfish, or Orangespotted Sunfish.

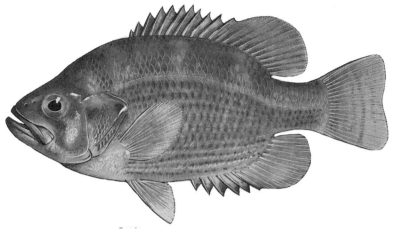

An adult Rock Bass *(Ambloplites rupestris)*. Drawing by Victor Hogg.

Rock Bass
Ambloplites rupestris (Rafinesque) (Plate 28)

Description: Color black or dark brown with a spot on each scale. Anal fin with 5–6 sharp, bony spines; dorsal fin with eleven spines. Mouth large. Gill cover stiff to its bony edge, without a strong "ear spot."

Size: The Rock Bass grows to a length of 43 cm (17 inches) and a maximum weight of 1 kg (2 pounds).

Habitat: The Rock Bass prefers large, clear streams and lakes that have a rocky bottom. Rock Bass usually occupy pools, where they stay near shore or adjacent to boulders, ledges, fallen timber or other cover.

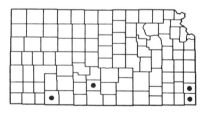

Reproduction: See the family account for sunfish.

Food: Rock Bass eat insects, crustaceans, mollusks, and small fish.

Remarks: INTRODUCED SPECIES. This species is a fair sport fish, most easily caught on live bait (worms, crayfishes, or minnows). At present, self-sustaining populations exist only in Shoal Creek, Cherokee County. At various times in the past, Rock Bass have been kept by the Kansas Department of Wildlife and Parks in hatchery ponds in Pratt and Meade counties; some have been stocked in lakes elsewhere.

An adult Green Sunfish *(Lepomis cyanellus)*. Drawing by Victor Hogg.

Green Sunfish
Lepomis cyanellus Rafinesque (Plates 2, 28)

Description: Color greenish with dull orange breast and pale blue streaks on head. Fins usually yellow-edged; dorsal and anal fins with dark blotch. Mouth large. Tongue usually toothless. Gill cover stiff to the edge of the black "ear-spot." Anal fin with three spines.

Size: The largest Kansas Green Sunfish weighed 1.1 kg (2⅖ pounds), and measured 29.4 cm (11½ inches) in total length. It was taken on rod and reel by Fae Vaupel of Russell from a farm pond on 26 September 1982. Most Green Sunfish weigh less than 200 g (6 ounces). Elsewhere in its range, this species reaches a maximum length of 31 cm (12 inches).

Habitat: This species occurs throughout Kansas in many types of habitats. It commonly occupies small, muddy creeks that have temporary flow. Few other fishes penetrate so far up drainageways during wet periods as do Green Sunfish, and few are so successful in surviving drought in residual pools. Green Sunfish usually occur singly, very near shore, alongside bits of cover such as rocks, stems of vegetation, and woody debris at the water's edge.

Reproduction: See the family account for sunfish.

Food: Green Sunfish feed on both terrestrial and aquatic insects, and on small fishes.

Remarks: The Green Sunfish is the most abundant sunfish in Kansas, readily catchable on worms or artificial flies. When no other fish will bite in lakes, try this one by bouncing popping bugs off the rock riprap along the dam. Keep the bait within a foot of the shore.

An adult Warmouth *(Lepomis gulosus)*. Drawing by Victor Hogg.

Warmouth
Lepomis gulosus (Cuvier) (Plate 28)

Description: Color brown and yellow, with red eye and brown streaks on side of head. Mouth large, with patch of teeth on tongue. Anal fin with three spines. Resembles the Rock Bass and Green Sunfish.

Size: The largest Warmouth from Kansas weighed 0.5 kg (1⅛ pounds), and measured 26.8 cm (10½ inches) in total length. It was taken on rod and reel by Vivian A. Bradley of Pittsburg from a pond within Mined Land Wildlife Area No. 7, Crawford County, on 30 April 1988. Elsewhere in its range, this species reaches a maximum length of 31 cm (12 inches).

Habitat: This fish occurs mainly in impoundments in Kansas, but it can also be found in sluggish streams of the southeastern part of the state. The Warmouth prefers pools and backwaters with soft mud bottoms and 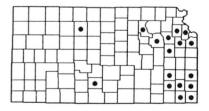 dense weed beds. Adult Warmouths do not school. Instead, they are scattered sparsely in the shallows near shore, usually adjacent to emergent vegetation.

Reproduction: See the family account for sunfish.

Food: Warmouths eat aquatic insects, crayfishes, and smaller fish.

Remarks: The Warmouth is a fair sport fish. To catch it, move along the shoreline, using worms as bait, or a fly rod with popping bugs, beetles, or small spinners.

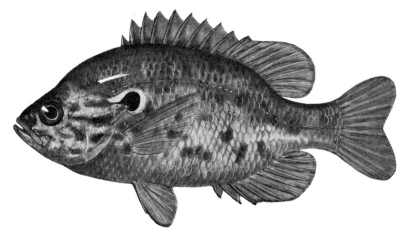

An adult Orangespotted Sunfish *(Lepomis humilis)*. Drawing by Victor Hogg.

Orangespotted Sunfish
Lepomis humilis (Girard) (Plate 29)

Description: Color silvery with scattered brown or reddish spots. In breeding male, sides of head blue streaked with orange, breast and fins orange. "Ear" flap long and flexible with rounded black spot and broad white margin. Mouth moderately large. Gill rakers slender. Most resembles Longear Sunfish.

Size: Maximum length for an adult of this species is 15 cm (6 inches).

Habitat: The Orangespotted Sunfish occurs throughout Kansas, rivaling the Green Sunfish in abundance. It appears to prefer sandy streams, but it tolerates muddy water and extensive water level fluctuation and seems indifferent to bottom type—rocky, sandy, or muddy.

Reproduction: See the family account for sunfish.

Food: The Orangespotted Sunfish eats mainly insects, and some smaller fishes.

Remarks: The Orangespotted Sunfish does not grow large enough to qualify as a game fish. It is, however, an important food item in the diet of larger fishes. Breeding males are the most strikingly colorful of all the sunfish.

An adult Bluegill *(Lepomis macrochirus).* Drawing by Victor Hogg.

Bluegill
Lepomis macrochirus Rafinesque (Plate 29)

Description: Pale blue-green to rust-colored, often barred. "Ear-spot" dark to its edge, short but flexible. Mouth small—smallest of any sunfish. Pectorals pointed but shorter than in Redear Sunfish. Dark blotch near back of dorsal fin (but not anal fin).

Size: The largest Kansas Bluegill weighed 1 kg (2.31 pounds), and measured 28 cm (11 inches) in total length. It was caught on rod and reel by Robert Jeffries of Modoc in a Scott County farm pond on 26 May 1962. The average size in Kansas is about 15 cm (6 inches) and 113 g (4 ounces). Elsewhere in its range, this species reaches a maximum length of 41 cm (16¼ inches).

Habitat: The Bluegill is native to streams in eastern Kansas and has been introduced into farm ponds and lakes throughout the state. This species does best in clear ponds with steep shore-lines and some aquatic vegetation.

Reproduction: See the family account for sunfish.

Food: This fish primarily feeds on small crustaceans and insects.

Subspecies in Kansas: The nominate race, *Lepomis m. macrochirus.*

Remarks: The Bluegill is a fine game fish, abundant and very easily caught on worms, grasshoppers, mayflies, larvae of paper wasps, and almost all artificial lures used with a fly rod. It commonly fails to grow large unless bass or other predators thin the ranks of young Bluegills. The only realistic way to obtain large Bluegills is to leave some large bass in the pond. See also the accounts of the Largemouth Bass and Northern Pike.

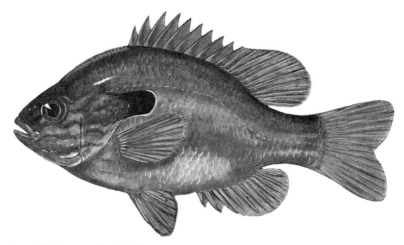

An adult Longear Sunfish *(Lepomis megalotis)*. Drawing by Gene Pacheco.

Longear Sunfish
Lepomis megalotis (Rafinesque) (Plate 30)

Description: Color blue-green with amber fins and belly. Crest of back with amber stripe. "Ear" flap very long in adults, with thin white edge. Mouth small. Pectoral fins short and rounded. Gill rakers short and knobby.

Size: Maximum length for an adult Longear Sunfish is 24 cm (9½ inches).

Habitat: This species is abundant in the eastern part of the Arkansas River drainage. It inhabits upland streams having numerous pools, a permanent or semipermanent flow of clear water, and unsilted bottoms of stone or firm

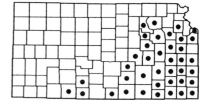

clay. The Longear Sunfish is less abundant in the Marais des Cygnes and Osage river drainages, and in some tributaries of the Kansas River (notably Mill Creek in Wabaunsee County, and the Wakarusa River).

Reproduction: See the family account for sunfish.

Food: Insects are the primary food of the Longear Sunfish.

Remarks: This species is often caught by fly-rod anglers, especially in streams of the Flint Hills, but it never grows large enough to qualify as an important sport fish. The Longear Sunfish is a handsome fish suitable for a home aquarium.

An adult Redear Sunfish *(Lepomis microlophus).* Drawing by Thomas H. Swearingen.

Redear Sunfish
Lepomis microlophus (Günther) (Plate 30)

Description: Color pale, silvery or with faint brownish mottling; red crescent at edge of dark "ear-spot." Body deep and slab-sided. Mouth small. Pectoral fin long and sharply pointed. Most resembles Bluegill.

Size: The largest Redear Sunfish from Kansas weighed 0.7 kg (1½ pounds) and measured 29.4 cm (11½ inches) in total length. It was taken on rod and reel by Shane Hill of Redfield from a Crawford County pond on 27 May 1992. Apparently, this is the maximum length for the species throughout its range.

Habitat: In Kansas, the Redear Sunfish inhabits lakes and ponds, where it has been introduced. This species occupies deeper water than other small sunfish, usually remaining near the bottom away from the shore-line.

Reproduction: See the family account for sunfish.

Food: Aquatic insects (burrowing mayflies, bloodworms) and mollusks (snails, fingernail clams) make up the diet of the Redear Sunfish.

Remarks: INTRODUCED SPECIES. The Redear Sunfish is not native to Kansas, but has been introduced into many farm ponds and small reservoirs. The Redear Sunfish is a good sport fish but is difficult to catch. Try a generous gob of worms on a small hook, attached to monofilament line with no sinker and no bobber. Cast well offshore and allow bait to settle to bottom. Redears often bite gently, lifting the bait and moving away with it; if resistance is felt, they may drop the bait.

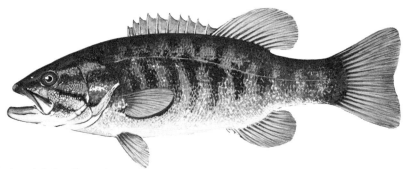

An adult Smallmouth Bass *(Micropterus dolomieu)*. Drawing by Victor Hogg.

Smallmouth Bass
Micropterus dolomieu Lacépède (Plate 31)

Description: Color plain brown or with vague vertical (transverse) bars, never a lengthwise stripe. First dorsal fin low, its last (shortest) spine more than one-half as long as the tallest spine. Scales on cheek and gill cover very small and granular, scarcely visible.

Size: The Smallmouth Bass can attain weights of 2.8–3.7 kg (6–8 pounds), but rarely weighs more than 0.9–1.4 kg (2–3 pounds). The fish now holding the Kansas angling record weighed 1.2 kg (5½ pounds) and was 55.7 cm (21⅞ inches) in total length. It was taken on rod and reel by Rick O'Bannon of Westfall at Wilson Reservoir on 9 October 1988. Elsewhere in its range, this species reaches a maximum length of 69 cm (27¼ inches).

Habitat: Smallmouth Bass inhabit clear, cool, rocky streams in the southeastern corner of the state, and have been introduced into reservoirs elsewhere. Most introductions have failed, probably due to competition from 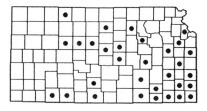 Largemouth Bass that were already established. In streams, Smallmouth Bass usually occupy pools, especially those having undercut banks, boulders, or fallen trees as cover.

Reproduction: See the family account for sunfish.

Food: The Smallmouth Bass feeds on crayfishes, aquatic insects, and other fish.

Subspecies in Kansas: An Arkansas River basin race, *Micropterus dolomieu velox,* is found naturally in the streams of southeastern Kansas, but the nominate race, *M. d. dolomieu* has been introduced into impoundments elsewhere in the state.

Remarks: The Smallmouth Bass is native to streams of southeastern Kansas, but the extent of its original range is uncertain. Probably its range included Spring River (Cherokee County) and nearby parts of the Osage system. Smallmouth Bass were present in the Neosho basin in Chase County in 1886, but the species had also been introduced by that year.

An adult Spotted Bass *(Micropterus punctulatus)*. Drawing by Victor Hogg.

Spotted Bass
Micropterus punctulatus (Rafinesque) (Plate 31)

Description: Color greenish with a blotchy lengthwise stripe on sides, and parallel rows of dark dots below the main lateral band. First dorsal fin low, its shortest spine (in notch) more than one-half as long as the tallest spine. Upper jaw ending below eye. Scales on cheek granular, smaller than scales on gill cover.

Size: The largest Spotted Bass from Kansas weighed 2.0 kg (4½ pounds) and measured 47 cm (18½ inches) in total length. It was taken on fly rod by Clarence E. McCarter of Wichita in Marion County Lake on 16 April 1977. Elsewhere in its range, this species reaches a maximum length of 61 cm (24 inches).

Habitat: The Spotted Bass is common in streams of the Arkansas River system that drain limestone uplands. The streams inhabited are small, clear, and spring-fed, but some of them dry back to pools in late summer 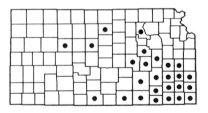 and fall. Spotted Bass also occur in the Marmaton River drainage in Bourbon and Crawford counties, but are not native farther north in the Kansas and Osage river basins. This species has been introduced in a few state lakes and reservoirs.

Reproduction: See the family account for sunfish.

Food: Crayfishes and insects are the principal food of the Spotted Bass.

Subspecies in Kansas: The nominate race, *Micropterus p. punctulatus.*

Remarks: Spotted Bass in Flint Hills streams of the Cottonwood and Verdigris basins afford some of the finest angling to be found in Kansas. These streams are fished easily by walking along their banks and riffles, stopping to make a few casts into each of the frequent small, clear pools. The bass are not large, rarely weighing much more than a pound, but they eagerly attack small spinners, flies, or minnows.

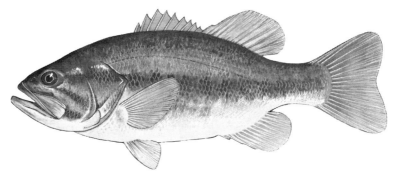

An adult Largemouth Bass *(Micropterus salmoides).* Drawing by Victor Hogg.

Largemouth Bass
Micropterus salmoides (Lacépède) (Plate 31)

Description: Green-backed with white sides and a dusky lengthwise stripe. Lateral stripe nearly the same width throughout its length (even-edged), rather than blotchy as in the Spotted Bass. Lower sides sometimes spotted, but scales not lined with dark dots. First dorsal fin arched, shortest spine in notch less than one-half as long as tallest spine. Mouth large, upper jaw extending backward beyond eye in adults. Scales on cheek and gill cover equally large.

Size: The record Largemouth Bass from Kansas was caught on a spinning rod; it weighed 5.3 kg (11¾ pounds) and was 63.5 cm (25 inches) long. Kenneth M. Bingham of Topeka caught it from a farm pond in Jefferson County on 20 March 1977. Elsewhere in its range, this species reaches a maximum length of 97 cm (38 inches). Large-mouth Bass rarely become even half as large as the one Mr. Bing-ham caught, let alone approach the national length record. The size to which any fish grows depends on at least three factors: (1) the length of its life, because fish normally grow larger as long as they live; (2) the amount of food (of the kinds and sizes it prefers at each stage in life) available to it throughout its life; (3) the number of other fishes with which it must compete for that same food.

Ordinarily, Largemouth Bass are 10–12.5 cm (4–5 inches) long at the end of their first year of life. Few survive even that long, perhaps no more than a hundredth of those hatched. Losses are less in later years, about half the remaining population each year. The survivors commonly are 23 cm (9 inches) long and weigh 170 g (6 ounces) at the end of their second year, and 31 cm (12 inches) long and weigh 340 g (12 ounces) at the end of the third growing season. At this time, about 0.25 percent (one-quarter of 1 percent) of those hatched might still be alive. Beyond the second or third year, Largemouth Bass and other fishes usually add less to their length, but more to their weight, during each season as their age advances.

There is much individual variation in growth rate among Largemouth Bass, even among those that hatch from the same group of eggs. Even greater variation arises from differences in the food production and fish populations in the places where these basses occur. In exceptionally productive lakes with low Largemouth Bass populations, some four-year-old bass weigh 2.3 kg (5 pounds) or more. At the other extreme, all the four-year-old bass in one pond we know weighed less than 226 g (8 ounces).

Habitat: The Largemouth Bass occurs throughout Kansas, partly as a result of construction of thousands of impoundments, most of which have been stocked with this species. Lakes and ponds are its principal habitat.

The Largemouth Bass is native to rivers in eastern Kansas, and fishable populations exist in streams from the Walnut River (Butler County) eastward and northward to the Marais des Cygnes. A few of these bass now occur in nearly all other streams of the state, perhaps due to their escape from lakes. Largemouth Bass are more tolerant of warm, slightly muddy water than are Smallmouth Bass and Spotted Bass. Largemouth Bass grow best at a temperature of about 26°C (80°F). They prefer streams with low gradient and large, deep pools, often mud-bottomed rather than rocky. Nevertheless, the water must be clear during most of the growing season for this fish to do well, either in streams or in lakes, because Largemouth Bass locate their food by sight. Large individuals usually occur alone, near shore, and near brushy or weedy cover. The young often occur in small groups.

Reproduction: See the family account for sunfish. The Largemouth Bass spawns for a brief period in spring, when the water temperature is a little below 21°C (70°F). Its nests are built where the water is about 76 cm (30 inches) deep and the bottom is firm.

Food: Largemouth Bass will eat almost anything that moves and that they can swallow. The main food of adults consists of minnows, Gizzard Shad, small suckers, catfish, other sunfish, insects, and crayfishes.

In their first year of life, Largemouth Bass eat microcrustaceans and small insects—the same food as Bluegills and all other carnivorous fishes that live with them.

Subspecies in Kansas: The nominate race, *M. s. salmoides.*

Remarks: In most lakes and ponds, the Largemouth Bass is both the most sought-after game fish and the main "top carnivore" required for balancing populations of other fishes at favorable levels. Stunting of Bluegills, crappies, and other species may result from excessive harvest of this bass. See also the account of Northern Pike.

An adult White Crappie *(Pomoxis annularis).* Drawing by Victor Hogg.

White Crappie
Pomoxis annularis Rafinesque (Plate 32)

Description: Anal fin about as large as dorsal fin; both of these fins with 5–6 stiff spines. Color plain white or silvery, usually with faint vertical bars. Males dark, head and breast nearly black, in spring and early summer. Resembles Black Crappie, but body less rounded, never irregularly spotted with black, and rarely with more than six dorsal spines.

Size: The largest Kansas White Crappie weighed 1.8 kg (4 pounds), and measured 44.6 cm (17½ inches). It was taken by Frank Miller of Eureka from a farm pond in Greenwood County on 30 March 1964. Elsewhere in its range, this species reaches a maximum length of 53 cm (21 inches).

Habitat: The White Crappie is one of the commonest fishes in Kansas. Its abundance in the state has undoubtedly increased due to construction and stocking of lakes and ponds, but pre-impoundment records indicate that this species was present in most rivers of eastern Kansas. In lakes, White Crappie usually occur in schools in moderately deep water offshore. They enter shallow, brushy areas before spawning in spring, and again as the water cools in autumn.

Reproduction: See the family account for sunfish.

Food: Young White Crappie feed on small crustaceans and other zoo-plankton. Adults 15 cm (6 inches) or longer prefer small fishes, especially minnows and young Gizzard Shad.

Remarks: The White Crappie may be the most important sport fish in Kansas, in terms of numbers caught.

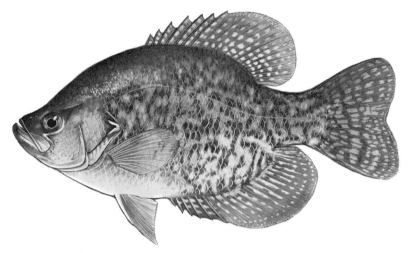

An adult Black Crappie *(Pomoxis nigromaculatus)*. Drawing by Victor Hogg.

Black Crappie
Pomoxis nigromaculatus (Le Sueur) (Plate 32)

Description: Anal fin with six spines and nearly as large as dorsal fin. Dorsal fin with 7–8 spines. Body irregularly flecked by dark spots, never banded. Breeding males with head and breast black. Resembles White Crappie.

Size: The largest Kansas Black Crappie weighed 2.1 kg (4½ pounds) and measured 56 cm (22 inches) in total length. It was taken on rod and reel by Hazel Fey of Toronto from Woodson County State Lake on 21 October 1957. This is apparently the maximum length for the species throughout its range.

Habitat: This species is rare in Kansas streams. It occurs in lakes and ponds throughout the state, where it has been stocked.

Reproduction: See the family account for sunfish.

Food: The Black Crappie eats insects and small crustaceans. Adults also eat other fishes.

Remarks: INTRODUCED SPECIES. The Black Crappie was introduced in Kansas prior to 1895, and the Kansas Department of Wildlife and Parks has increasingly focused its hatchery and lake-stocking program on this species in preference to White Crappie. Black Crappie seem less prone to overpopulation and stunting in lakes.

PERCHES (Family Percidae)

The name "perch" is confusing as applied to these fishes, because it is used commonly for only one species in the family—the Yellow Perch or "ring" perch. "Perch" is used more often as a general name for some of the small sunfish, family Centrarchidae. Nevertheless, the name "perch" should be limited to the species in the family Percidae, because that scientific name, from the type genus *Perca*, literally means "perch." Maybe the problem can be blamed on our European ancestors. True perch (family Percidae) are common in Europe, where there are no sunfish (family Centrarchidae). Europeans arriving in America found few perch; instead, they found a number of unfamiliar but comparable fishes for which a name was needed. "Perch" was convenient, and probably came into general use before anyone suggested "sunfish" as a more appropriate name for the American centrarchid fishes.

The difficulty with names goes further. After the Yellow Perch, the best known fish in this group is the Walleye, or "walleyed pike." Obviously that species is a perch, not a pike (family Esocidae). Few anglers would go along with the name walleyed perch, although some of them call it a "pikeperch." We should simply call it a "Walleye." Besides the Yellow Perch and the Walleye, one other member of the family grows large enough to be a good game fish and food fish. That is the Sauger, which resembles the Walleye. Probably, it is the only one of the three species that occurred in Kansas at the time of settlement. The same fish is commonly known as "jack salmon," but it is clearly not a salmon (family Salmonidae).

The Yellow Perch, the Walleye, the Sauger, and seventeen smaller kinds of perch in Kansas are true perch because they share the following structural characteristics. They have two dorsal fins, completely separated near the middle of the back. The first (anterior) dorsal fin is supported entirely by stiff spines (bone), whereas the second (posterior) fin is supported by flexible branched rays (cartilage). Sunfish also have bony spines and cartilaginous rays in the dorsal fin, but the spines and rays are joined by membranes into a single dorsal fin. Pikes—and salmon or trout—have a short dorsal fin without any spines. The anal fin of perches has one or two thin, weak spines, in contrast to the three or more obvious spines at the front of the anal fin in sunfish; pikes and salmon have no spines in the anal fin. The scales of perches are rather small, and rough to the touch (smooth in other groups, or only a little rough in sunfish). No perches have a dark "ear" spot on the gill cover, and none of them is strongly flattened from side to side.

The many species of small perch native to Kansas are commonly called *darters*. Typically, they perch on stones on the bottom of streams, with head high, using their fins as props. Then they dart forward a few inches and settle onto a new perch. Most of the species live in swift water in small, clear streams. As a group, they are riffle fishes, although a few species have adapted to calm water having dense plant growth. All of them feed mainly on small insects. All are most active in daylight.

Most darters are colorful, having shades of yellow, orange, or red in combination with blue or green. One of these colors may cover much of the body and fins (background color) while the other color is restricted to bands or spots. Darters that lack bright (chromatic) colors have brown or black blotches in a definite pattern on a pale background. Each of the species differs from every other species in color, or in the pattern formed by various colors. These specific differences would make identification of darters an easy matter if all the members of each species were colored alike, but they are not. In most species, the adult males differ in color from the females, and both may differ from their young. Males are nearly always more strikingly colored than females, but the males are much more colorful in spring, when they are spawning, than at other times of year. As a result of these complex differences, color is useful for identifying darters only if you know all the variations to expect in each species. So, we urge that you use the key to species in this book when identifying these fascinating little fishes.

The fishes themselves know all about their differences, of course. The differences help them to recognize one another and to know how to act when they meet. If one highly colored male is approached by another brightly colored male of the same species, he is likely to threaten the intruder or to fight. If he is approached by a mature female, he behaves differently. Juveniles may avoid the adults, especially the breeding males. Therefore, in seining a stream in spring, you may find mostly males in one place—the best breeding sites—but not schooling together. Most females stay elsewhere until each is ready to enter the spawning area and accept the attentions of a male; she does not want them constantly. Juveniles may be in a third place or in company with the females.

The colors developed by breeding darters tend to match the nest sites used by each species. Orangethroat Darters spawn on open, gravel riffles. From above, their orange and blue colors blend surprisingly with the rust-colored and gray gravels of the stream bottom. Greenside Darters spawn in strands of algae attached to large stones in riffles. Johnny Darters, which nest in dark cavities beneath stones, are nearly black. Some kinds of darters remain with the eggs throughout their development. Others, as well as the Walleye, the Sauger, and the Yellow Perch, soon abandon the sites where the eggs are placed.

An adult Greenside Darter *(Etheostoma blennioides).* Drawing by Victor Hogg.

Greenside Darter
Etheostoma blennioides Rafinesque (Plate 33)

Description: Snout blunt, rounded, overhanging the small, crescentic mouth. Gill membranes broadly joined across throat; 6–8 large W-shaped, brownish olive markings on sides. Breeding males solidly green or with 5–6 broad green bands around body. Upper sides and bases of dorsal fins with dark red dots. Dorsal fins with 12–14 spines and 12–14 soft rays. Large size.

Size: Maximum length for an adult of this species is 17 cm (6½ inches).

Habitat: The Greenside Darter inhabits deep, swift riffles over rubble bottom (stones egg-size or larger). It requires permanent flow and is most abundant in streams having a large, stable volume of flow, allowing the growth

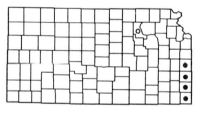

of filamentous algae on riffles. The water must remain clear and cool.

Reproduction: The Greenside Darter spawns in April in Kansas. Eggs are deposited near the bases of dense strands of algae attached to stones in fast water.

Food: Greenside Darters eat small animals, including insects, that live on the surfaces of stones or attached vegetation, along the stream bottom.

Subspecies in Kansas: Two subspecies of the Greenside Darter are found in Kansas. They are *Etheostoma blennioides newmani* in the Spring

River system in Cherokee and Crawford counties, and *E. b. pholido-tum* in the Osage River drainage in Bourbon County.

Remarks: SINC SPECIES. The Greenside Darter originally occupied streams in the Kansas River basin as far west as Manhattan, and probably occurred more widely in the Osage and Arkansas river systems than it does now. It has been taken recently only in the Little Osage, Marmaton, and Spring rivers or their tributaries.

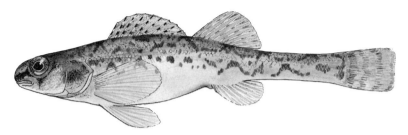

An adult Bluntnose Darter *(Etheostoma chlorosomum)*. Drawing by Victor Hogg.

Bluntnose Darter
Etheostoma chlorosomum (Hay) (Plate 33)

Description: Slender, transparent body with a few wavy dark lines. Head very small, densely scaled. Snout short and rounded. Mouth small and horizontal, not quite terminal. A continuous black "bridle" crosses tip of snout, from eye to eye, above upper lip. Dorsal fins with 8–9 spines and 9–11 soft rays.

Size: Maximum length for an adult of this species is 6 cm (2½ inches).

Habitat: The Bluntnose Darter inhabits small, slowly flowing creeks with bottoms of mud or clay in the eastern part of the Arkansas River system. The creeks may be intermittent during severe drought. This species

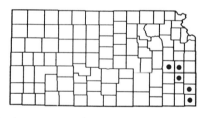

is also found in oxbows and overflow pools, especially if they remain clear and have aquatic vegetation.

Reproduction: The Bluntnose Darter probably spawns in April or May in Kansas. Little is known of its reproductive habits in the state.

Food: Bluntnose Darters eat larval insects (especially midges) and microcrustaceans.

Remarks: SINC SPECIES. The Bluntnose Darter occurs in only a few places in the Spring and Neosho river basins, always in small numbers. It resembles the Johnny Darter but is never found with that species in Kansas.

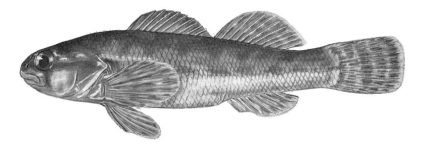

An adult Arkansas Darter *(Etheostoma cragini)*. Drawing by Gene Pacheco.

Arkansas Darter
Etheostoma cragini Gilbert (Plate 33)

Description: Mottled brown. Body stout. Head short and blunt, snout shorter than eye. Gill membranes separate, forming deep V-notch on throat. Head usually scaleless. About fifty scales in lateral-line row on sides, but fewer than twenty-five pored. Dorsal fins with nine spines and 11–13 soft rays. Breeding males orange along entire ventral surface; dorsal fin with diffuse orange band, otherwise plain brown. No blue or green pigment.

Size: Maximum length for an adult of this species is 6 cm (2¼ inches).

Habitat: The Arkansas Darter prefers small springs or seeps that are partly overgrown by watercress or other aquatic plants. It occurs only in the Arkansas River basin, in small prairie streams as well as in streams

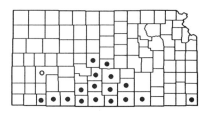

along the western Ozark border. It seems to require shallow, clear water where there is not much current and where cover is provided by aquatic vegetation or by willow roots and grasses along the stream bank.

Reproduction: The Arkansas Darter spawns from March to May. Eggs are deposited in sandy substrate and abandoned. For more information about the reproductive habits of this fish (based on captive specimens), refer to Distler (1972).

Food: Arkansas Darters eat insects.

Remarks: THREATENED SPECIES IN KANSAS. Platt et al. (1974) recommended that special attention be given to the Arkansas Darter to ensure its survival in Kansas. This species is endemic (restricted in its range) to the Arkansas River system. Most of its surviving populations in Kansas are in small streams south of the "big bend" of the Arkansas River in south-central Kansas, where small, sandy streams are fed continuously by seepage from a high water table. Irrigation and drought have dried much of its habitat farther west, including the site where it was discovered and named, near Garden City, in 1885. This remarkable little darter has somehow managed to sustain itself by finding new habitats at other sites in streams overlying the Ogallala and Great Bend aquifers as flows decline due to receding water tables. This process of water depletion in our state and elsewhere may not continue indefinitely, as its biological and economic consequences become more apparent.

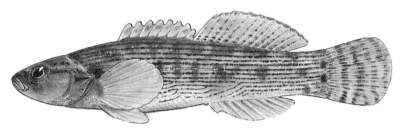

An adult Fantail Darter *(Etheostoma flabellare)*. Drawing by Victor Hogg.

Fantail Darter
Etheostoma flabellare Rafinesque (Plate 33)

Description: Body lined with thin black or brown stripes. Tail broad, fin strongly barred. First dorsal fin low, nearly flat-topped, with 8–9 spines. Head small, scaleless. Gill membranes broadly joined across throat. Snout sharp, mouth small and nearly vertical. Breeding males with black head, body dark brown.

Size: Maximum length for an adult of this species is 8.4 cm (3¼ inches).

Habitat: The Fantail Darter lives in many small, clear tributaries of the Spring, Osage, and Cottonwood rivers, and in a few tributaries of the lower Neosho River. It is locally abundant over bottoms of small gravel or of bedrock strewn with small stones. It prefers riffles having slowly flowing water less than 40 cm (8 inches) deep.

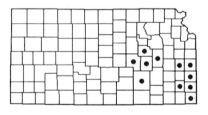

Reproduction: Male Fantail Darters establish nests in spaces beneath stones during April or May. The undersurface of the stone is rubbed clean by the dorsal fins and the thickened skin atop the head and nape of the nuptial male. A female enters the nest, turns upside down, and deposits about 35 eggs in a single layer on the underside of the stone. They are fertilized by the male who then chases the female from the nest. The male remains to guard the nest and to clean and aerate the eggs.

Food: The Fantail Darter eats small insects.

Subspecies in Kansas: The nominate race, *Etheostoma f. flabellare.*

An adult Slough Darter *(Etheostoma gracile).* Drawing by Victor Hogg.

Slough Darter
Etheostoma gracile (Girard)

Description: Mottled olive-brown, three spots at base of tail. Tail slender. Snout short, head scaly. Fins small, first dorsal with 8–9 spines, second with 10–11 soft rays. Lateral line arched, parallel to back below dorsal fin. Breeding males with a row of green spots on sides, first dorsal fin black with red dots near its margin.

Size: Maximum length for an adult of this species is 6 cm (2¼ inches).

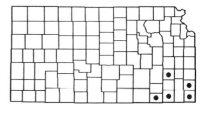

Habitat: Unlike most darters, this species inhabits quiet lowland pools having muddy bottoms. It prefers small, shaded streams and overflow ponds where there is leaf litter or aquatic vegetation. The Slough Darter tolerates occasional muddy water but always avoids strong currents. It is known in Kansas from six sites in Chautauqua, Cherokee, Crawford, Montgomery, and Woodson counties.

Reproduction: The Slough Darter spawns in April or May in Kansas. The female attaches eggs in a single row on a thin plant stem or twig, and the male follows to fertilize each egg as it is laid.

Food: Larval midges, mayflies, and microcrustaceans are the preferred diet of the Slough Darter.

Remarks: SINC SPECIES. Agricultural developments that eliminate permanent, weedy overflow pools alongside stream channels reduce the habitat for the Slough Darter and several other species of fishes.

An adult Least Darter *(Etheostoma microperca).* Drawing by Thomas H. Swearingen.

Least Darter
Etheostoma microperca Jordan and Gilbert

Description: Small size. Body densely speckled, brownish black. Fins short, first dorsal with 6–7 spines, second with 9–10 soft rays. Head not scaled. No line of pored scales on sides. Males without bright breeding colors, except for orange spots through center of first dorsal fin.

Size: Maximum length for an adult of this species is 4.4 cm (1¾ inches).

Habitat: This species is known in Kansas only from a backwater pool alongside Shoal Creek in Cherokee County. The Least Darter normally occurs near the headwaters of streams or in springs, where the water is calm 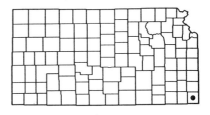 and densely vegetated, and the bottom is covered by organic sediment or detritus.

Reproduction: Least Darters deposit eggs singly on stems or leaves of plants above the stream bottom, while maintaining a vertical posture. The large pelvic fins of the male are adapted for holding to the back of the female as she releases eggs. Spawning occurs during April and May.

Food: Small insects and microcrustaceans make up the diet of the Least Darter.

Remarks: The Least Darter barely enters Kansas, along the Ozark border, and thus is extremely rare in the state. Platt et al. (1974) included the Least Darter as a peripheral species on their list of rare and endangered fishes in Kansas.

An adult Johnny Darter *(Etheostoma nigrum).* Drawing by Gene Pacheco.

Johnny Darter
Etheostoma nigrum Rafinesque (Plate 33)

Description: Slender, translucent body with fine brownish W-marks on sides. Head small, snout blunt, mouth small and nearly horizontal. First dorsal fin short but very high with 8–10 spines; second dorsal fin with 11–13 soft rays. Breeding color dark brown or black.

Size: Maximum length for an adult of this species is 7.2 cm (2¾ inches).

Habitat: The Johnny Darter is likely to be found only in small, spring-fed tributaries of the Kansas River, especially in the Flint Hills, although it formerly occurred as far west as Trego and Decatur counties. It usually occu-

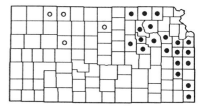

pies shallow pools where there is not much current, but it may invade nearby riffles. The species is rare in the Marais des Cygnes, Little Osage, and Spring river basins and is absent elsewhere in Kansas.

Reproduction: The Johnny Darter spawns in April or May. Males establish individual nesting territories beneath sloping stones, and clean the undersurface of the stone by brushing it with their fins. A female enters the nest and flips over to attach her eggs to the stone's lower surface while they are being fertilized by the male. The male stays in the nest to protect the eggs and young.

Food: The Johnny Darter feeds mainly on bloodworms and other immature insects.

Subspecies in Kansas: The nominate race, *Etheostoma n. nigrum.*

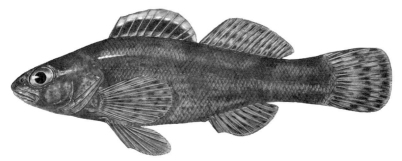

An adult Stippled Darter *(Etheostoma punctulatum)*. Drawing by Gene Pacheco.

Stippled Darter
Etheostoma punctulatum (Agassiz) (Plate 34)

Description: Mottled brown, head densely flecked with black. Body stout; head large, mouth large and terminal. Gill membranes separate, V-notched on throat. No scales on head. Scales on body small, about sixty in lateral line, more than thirty pored. Dorsal fins with 10–11 spines, 13–15 soft rays. Breeding males dark brown with orange belly, and first dorsal fin black with orange band near its margin.

Size: Maximum length for an adult of this species is 10 cm (4 inches).

Habitat: This species lives in brooks near sources of springs. It prefers small, clear pools or recesses beneath cut-banks, where it conceals itself near large stones, in hanging roots, or among fallen leaves. Stippled Darters also occupy shallow overflow and seepage pools, maintained by groundwater, alongside channels of larger streams.

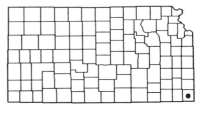

Reproduction: This fish probably spawns in April in Kansas. Its reproductive habits are unknown.

Food: The Stippled Darter eats various aquatic insects and small crustaceans.

Remarks: SINC Species. This is an Ozarkian species that barely enters Kansas, where it occurs rarely in the Spring River drainage, Cherokee County. Platt et al. (1974) placed the Stippled Darter on their peripheral list due to its small range in the state. This is the "Sunburst Darter" listed as *Etheostoma* sp. (a new undescribed species) by Page and Burr (1991).

An adult Orangethroat Darter *(Etheostoma spectabile).* Drawing by Victor Hogg.

Orangethroat Darter
Etheostoma spectabile (Agassiz) (Plate 34)

Description: Body banded or lined, nearly always with blue and dull orange pigment. Head short, rather blunt, mouth terminal. Gill membranes separate, V-notched on throat. Lateral line with 45–55 scales, more than twenty with pores; dorsal fins with 9–10 spines, 12–14 soft rays. Breeding males with blue bands around body; dorsal fins orange with blue border; tail orange without blue border, anal fin solidly blue.

Size: Maximum length for an adult of this species is 7.2 cm (2¾ inches).

Habitat: This species lives mainly in small streams, on shallow riffles having bottoms of fine gravel or mixed gravel and sand. Orangethroat Darters also inhabit rocky shorelines of some lakes, and pools of streams that are briefly intermittent. This adaptability, together with the species' tolerance of warm water, allows the Orangethroat Darter to be the most widespread of Kansas darters. It occurs in all the main river systems, but diminishes in abundance westward.

Reproduction: The Orangethroat Darter spawns from March through May at water temperatures between 15° and 21°C (60° and 70°F). Brilliantly colored males gather on shallow riffles, while the less colorful females occupy adjacent shallow pools. When ready to breed, a female enters the riffle and buries her eggs in gravel by vibrating against the substrate until she penetrates it, while an attendant male fertilizes them. No fixed territory or nest is established, and no parental attention is shown the eggs or young.

Food: The Orangethroat Darter feeds on blackfly larvae, bloodworms, and caddisfly larvae, as well as other insects and fish eggs.

Subspecies in Kansas: The Orangethroat Darter has three subspecies in Kansas. They are *Etheostoma s. spectabile* in the Osage River system, *E. s. squamosum* in tributaries of the Spring River in Cherokee County, and *E. s. pulchellum* elsewhere in the state.

Remarks: This attractive fish makes an excellent addition to the home aquarium. However, the Orangethroat Darter will remain brightly colored only if the water remains cool—21°C (70°F) or less. It can be fed frozen brine shrimp, although it prefers living food (brine shrimp or small worms).

An adult Speckled Darter *(Etheostoma stigmaeum)*. Drawing by Victor Hogg.

Speckled Darter
Etheostoma stigmaeum (Jordan) (Plate 34)

Description: Brownish with six dorsal blotches and a line of 9–11 small dark blotches along sides. Mouth terminal. Gill membranes joined across throat. Dorsal fins with 11–12 spines and 10–11 soft rays. Breeding males with brassy sheen and pale blue spots on sides. First dorsal fin black with orange band near margin.

Size: Maximum length for an adult of this species is 6 cm (2½ inches).

Habitat: This fish lives in rather large streams having moderate or steep gradients. The Speckled Darter prefers pools below riffles, often at depths of 60 cm (2 feet) or more, except when spawning. In Kansas, it is found only in the Spring River basin in Cherokee and Crawford counties.

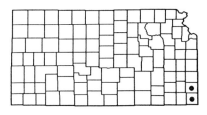

Reproduction: The Speckled Darter spawns in April. Males gather on broad, shallow riffles over clean, rounded gravel of uniformly small size. The spawning activity of this species is similar to that of the Orangethroat Darter.

Food: The diet of the Speckled Darter is not known.

Remarks: SINC Species. The Speckled Darter is listed by Platt et al. (1974) as a peripheral species, of interest because of its very localized occurrence in Kansas.

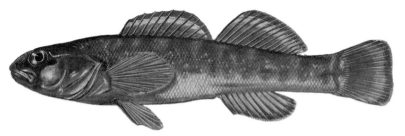

An adult Redfin Darter *(Etheostoma whipplii).* Drawing by Gene Pacheco.

Redfin Darter
Etheostoma whipplii (Girard) (Plate 34)

Description: A slender, plain brownish darter with large, terminal mouth. Gill membranes narrowly joined but forming V-notch on throat. Scales small, sixty or more in lateral line along middle of side, forty or more with pores. Dorsal fins with 10–12 spines and 13–15 soft rays. Fins in breeding males with red, white, and blue bands, sides with red dots. Anal fin red with blue border.

Size: Maximum length for an adult of this species is 9 cm (3½ inches).

Habitat: The Redfin Darter inhabits streams having moderate
or low gradient, where the bottom consists of small gravel,
mixed sand and gravel, broken
shale, and bedrock. It is not
abundant but has been found in

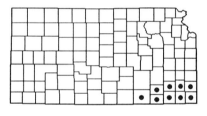

many streams from Caney River eastward to the Spring River, in slowly flowing water and on gentle riffles.

Reproduction: The Redfin Darter spawns in April. Little is known of its reproductive habits.

Food: The diet of the Redfin Darter is not known; but like other darters, this species must feed mainly on insects.

Subspecies in Kansas: The nominate race, *Etheostoma w. whipplii.*

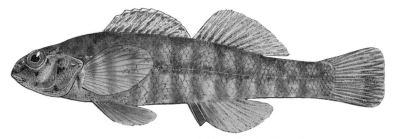

An adult Banded Darter *(Etheostoma zonale)*. Drawing by Victor Hogg.

Banded Darter
Etheostoma zonale (Cope) (Plate 34)

Description: Head short, snout very blunt; mouth small, horizontal, below level of eye. Gill membranes broadly connected across throat, rather than forming deep V-notch. Lateral line with 51–58 scales, all with pores. Dorsal fins with 10–11 spines and 11–12 soft rays. Sides of breeding males with 9–12 bright green vertical bars; fins with red-dish spots near base, otherwise green or yellow.

Size: Maximum length for an adult of this species is 7.8 cm (3 inches).

Habitat: This species is common in Shoal Creek, Cherokee County, and the neighboring Spring River. It has also been found in Cow Creek, Crawford County. This fish inhabits clear, perma-nently flowing streams of moder- 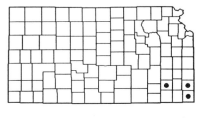 ate size. The Banded Darter prefers deep riffles over a rocky bottom, but also uses clumps of algae-covered debris where water flows slowly over smooth bottoms.

Reproduction: The Banded Darter spawns in April or May in Kansas, probably attaching its eggs to strands of algae or other fibrous mate-rial on stones in flowing water.

Food: Larval insects are the primary food of the Banded Darter.

Remarks: SINC SPECIES. Because of its localized occurrence, the Banded Darter was listed by Platt et al. (1974) as a peripheral species in Kansas. One record from the Verdigris River in Wilson County in-dicates that this darter formerly occupied a larger area in southeast-ern Kansas. All recent records are from the Spring River drainage.

An adult Yellow Perch *(Perca flavescens)*. Drawing by F. A. Carmichael.

Yellow Perch
Perca flavescens (Mitchill) (Plate 35)

Description: Sides yellowish, flattened, with 6–7 distinct dark bars. Two dorsal fins, the first with about thirteen spines, second with 1–2 spines and thirteen rays. Anal fin with two spines plus eight soft rays. Head scaly, mouth large and terminal. Large size.

Size: The largest Kansas Yellow Perch weighed 0.3 kg (¾ pound) and measured 29.4 cm (11½ inches) in total length. It was taken on rod and reel by Merlin Sprecher of Manhattan from Lake Elbo in Pottawatomie County on 12 July 1970. Elsewhere in its range, this species attains a maximum length of 40 cm (16 inches).

Habitat: The Yellow Perch has been stocked in impoundments throughout Kansas. Self-sustaining populations are known from lakes in Clark, Douglas, Leavenworth, Pottawatomie, Shawnee, and Wabaunsee counties, among 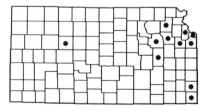 others. This species is not found in Kansas creeks and rivers. It prefers clear lakes having aquatic vegetation, and rocky or sandy bottoms near shore. The adults prefer deep water.

Reproduction: The Yellow Perch spawns in winter and early spring at water temperatures of 4° to 10°C (40° to 50°F). Eggs are deposited in gelatinous strands several feet long. The strands are sometimes entwined in aquatic vegetation or submerged branches of fallen trees, but egg deposition on rocky shoals is known also.

Food: Yellow Perches feed mainly on larval insects and crustaceans, and to a lesser extent on small fishes. Most anglers catch them with earthworms or minnows.

Remarks: INTRODUCED SPECIES. The Yellow Perch was introduced in Kansas prior to 1885, and later in many of the lakes built in the 1930s by the Civilian Conservation Corps.

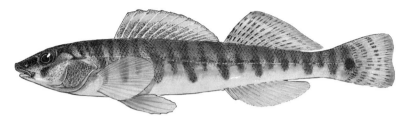

An adult Logperch *(Percina caprodes)*. Drawing by Victor Hogg.

Logperch
Percina caprodes (Rafinesque) (Plate 35)

Description: Yellowish green with many dark vertical bars on sides, and round black spot at base of tail fin. Snout cone-shaped, mouth not quite terminal. Orange band in dorsal fin of males. Lateral line with more than 80 scales.

Size: Maximum length for an adult of this species is 18 cm (7¼ inches).

Habitat: This species lives in the large tributaries of all major rivers in eastern Kansas, except those north of the Kansas River. It is common in clear, permanent streams that cross surface exposures of limestone. It is found

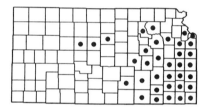

most often in deep riffles or in pools at the base of riffles, over bottoms of gravel and rubble. Logperch occupy clear lakes also.

Reproduction: The Logperch spawns in swift riffles over gravel bottoms. In early April, males congregate on the riffles; females are in pools and eddies nearby. When ready to deposit eggs, a female joins the males in the riffle. The eggs are extruded, fertilized, and then buried in the gravel by means of vigorous vibratory movements of both parents against the substrate. The parents pay no further attention to the eggs.

Food: This fish eats immature insects, crustaceans, and some algae.

Remarks: This is the largest of the darters found in Kansas. Anglers sometimes catch Logperch on worms in lakes and in the pools of streams.

Subspecies in Kansas: A central U.S. race, *Percina caprodes fulvitaenia,* occurs in Kansas.

An adult Channel Darter *(Percina copelandi)*. Drawing by Gene Pacheco.

Channel Darter
Percina copelandi (Jordan)

Description: Greenish gray with several small dark spots connected by a thin line along sides. X-marks on scales on upper part of sides. No orange band in dorsal fin. Snout short and blunt, mouth small. Lateral line with 55–60 scales.

Size: Maximum length for an adult of this species is 7.2 cm (2¾ inches).

Habitat: The Channel Darter inhabits most tributaries of the Arkansas River system east of its mainstream but is seldom abundant in Kansas. Its principal habitat is in shallow pools having a rocky bottom and just enough current to sweep the bottom free of sediment.

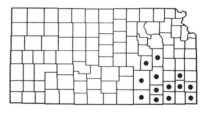

Reproduction: In Kansas, the Channel Darter probably spawns in late April and May. Males establish territories behind stones in strong currents near shore. Males become dark, nearly black, in the breeding season, but they lack bright colors except for a bluish sheen on the throat.

Food: The Channel Darter feeds on bloodworms, larval caddisflies, and microcrustaceans.

Remarks: This species is most common in the Verdigris and Caney river drainages. It is often found with Orangethroat Darters and Slenderhead Darters, but never with Johnny Darters, which it resembles most.

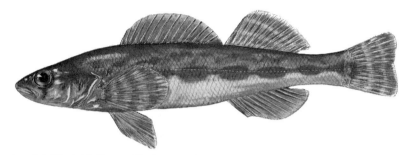

An adult Blackside Darter *(Percina maculata).* Drawing by Gene Pacheco.

Blackside Darter
Percina maculata (Girard) (Plate 35)

Description: Green and gray (or black), sides with 6–8 large, oblong dark blotches. No orange band in dorsal fin. Snout short, mouth terminal, Gill membranes separate, forming a narrow V-notch on throat. Lateral line with about 63–65 scales.

Size: Maximum length for an adult of this species is 11 cm (4¼ inches).

Habitat: The Blackside Darter inhabits cool, clear, medium-size streams, where it occupies shallow pools having moderate current and bottoms of gravel or mixcd gravcl and sand. This fish does not cling to the stream bottom, as do most darters, but is often found in midwater and sometimes rises to the surface for food.

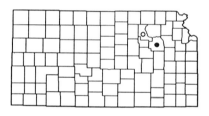

Reproduction: The Blackside Darter spawns during April and early May at water temperatures of 15°C (60°F) or slightly warmer. Spawning takes place in pools or runs, rather than riffles, at a depth of 30 cm (1 foot) or more. The eggs are buried in fine gravel or sand as they are extruded and fertilized by the paired fish. No parental concern is shown for the eggs.

Food: The Blackside Darter eats insects.

Remarks: THREATENED SPECIES IN KANSAS. The Blackside Darter is found only in Mill Creek, Wabaunsee County. Platt et al. (1974) recommended that this creek be protected.

An adult Slenderhead Darter *(Percina phoxocephala)*. Drawing by Victor Hogg.

Slenderhead Darter
Percina phoxocephala (Nelson) (Plate 35)

Description: Mottled brownish or greenish, with more than eight small dark blotches in a line on sides. Orange band in dorsal fin of males. Snout sharply pointed, mouth terminal. Gill membranes joined by a membrane across throat. Lateral line with about seventy scales.

Size: Maximum length for an adult of this species is 9.6 cm (3¾ inches).

Habitat: This fish inhabits the larger, permanent streams of the Arkansas and Osage river systems in Kansas. It prefers swift-flowing, shallow water over a bottom of loose gravel or of bedrock littered with stones. In

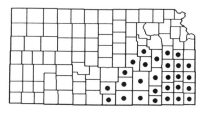

streams where it occurs, the Slenderhead Darter is often the dominant darter.

Reproduction: The Slenderhead Darter spawns between late March and early May at water temperatures of about 21°C (70°F). The spawning sites are in swift riffles, over bottoms of rubble and gravel, at depths of 45 cm (18 inches) or more.

Food: The Slenderhead Darter eats bloodworms and immature blackflies, dragonflies, and mayflies, as well as other aquatic invertebrates.

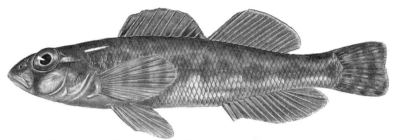

An adult River Darter *(Percina shumardi)*. Drawing by Gene Pacheco.

River Darter
Percina shumardi (Girard) (Plate 35)

Description: Greenish or gray, with 6–10 faded gray or brownish blotches on sides. Blotches higher than long. Dorsal fin with dark spot at front and back, without an orange band. Head large, blunt. Dark streak extending downward below eye. Lateral line with about 55 scales.

Size: Maximum length for an adult of this species is 7.8 cm (3 inches).

Habitat: The River Darter is known in Kansas from the lower Neosho River (Labette County) and the Spring River (Cherokee County). Its habitat is shallow, rocky areas with moderate current in large rivers.

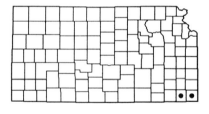

Reproduction: River Darters spawn in April at a water depth of 60 cm (2 feet) or less, on rocks in currents near shore.

Food: The River Darter preys on insects.

Remarks: SINC SPECIES. This species barely enters Kansas. Our only records for the River Darter are from the broad, shallow channels of the Neosho and Spring rivers. The only other darters likely to occur with it are the Logperch and the Slenderhead Darter.

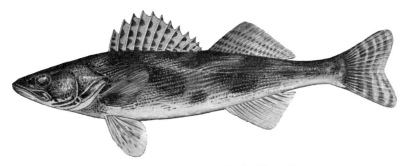

An adult Sauger *(Stizostedion canadense).* Drawing by Victor Hogg.

Sauger
Stizostedion canadense (Smith) (Plate 36)

Description: Resembles Walleye, but with 2–4 large, dark brown "saddles" angling downward onto sides. First dorsal fin colorless except for small scattered black spots. Cheeks scaled.

Size: The largest Sauger from Kansas weighed 1.5 kg (3.27 pounds) and measured 54.3 cm (21⅜ inches) in total length. It was taken on rod and reel by Dennis Barnhart of Topeka from Melvern Reservoir on 16 May 1993. Elsewhere in its range, this species attains a maximum length of 76 cm (30 inches).

Habitat: The Sauger occurs naturally in the Missouri River and in the Kansas River basin westward to the Blue River. It is mostly confined to large, rather turbid rivers, seldom entering their tributaries. Based on a single nineteenth-century record, Saugers may have occurred in the Neosho River drainage at the time of European settlement. Recently, this species and hybrids between it and the Walleye (called "saugeye") have been propagated in hatcheries and stocked in several state lakes and reservoirs.

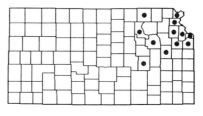

Reproduction: Early spring reproductive migrations of Saugers are known below the Kansas River dam at Lawrence. We have found young of the year in pools along sandbars in the Missouri River and the lower Kansas River.

Food: The Sauger feeds on small fish.

Remarks: The Sauger is a good game fish that can be caught on live bait or artificial lures.

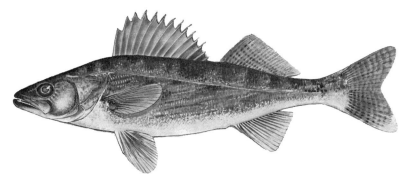

An adult Walleye *(Stizostedion vitreum)*. Drawing by Victor Hogg.

Walleye
Stizostedion vitreum (Mitchill) (Plate 36)

Description: Back with 6–8 dark blotches, not angling downward onto sides. First dorsal fin plain dusky, unspotted except for a large dark blotch where the fin joins the body. Lower tip of tail fin white. Cheeks usually scaleless.

Size: The largest Walleye from Kansas weighed 6 kg (13.06 pounds) and measured 80 cm (31½ inches) in total length. It was caught on rod and reel by David Watson of Manhattan at Rocky Ford Dam on the Blue River below Tuttle Creek Reservoir (Riley County) on 29 March 1972. Elsewhere in its range, this species attains a maximum length of 91 cm (36 inches).

Habitat: The Walleye occurs mainly in large lakes. It has been common in Kansas since its introduction into several reservoirs about 1960. Most Walleyes occupy fairly deep water near steeply sloping banks or bars without much cover. They often move to shallower parts of lakes at night. Many Walleyes leave reservoirs to move long distances upstream and downstream, so the species may now be caught in rivers nearly anywhere in Kansas. Fishing for them is often best in "tailwaters" below dams, during the cool months.

Reproduction: Walleyes spawn in March and April, when the water is 7° to 10°C (45° to 50°F). Males gather in shallow areas with clean, rocky bottoms—along the riprap of dams and on riffles of some large streams in Kansas. Females remain in other, deeper areas until ready to spawn, then move singly onto the breeding grounds occupied by males. The eggs are fertilized as they are released, and adhere to stones on the bottom during their development, which requires about two weeks to hatching.

Food: Newly hatched Walleyes eat small crustaceans, but soon begin feeding on small fishes, and are chiefly piscivorous thereafter.

Remarks: INTRODUCED SPECIES. The Walleye was recorded from Kansas as early as 1865; thus it may have occurred naturally in rivers of eastern Kansas at the time of settlement. If so, it soon disappeared. Efforts were made to establish the species by introduction at least as early as the 1880s, but all attempts were unsuccessful until the 1960s.

DRUMS (Family Sciaenidae)

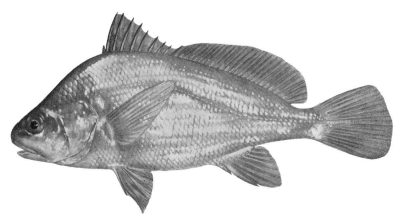

An adult Freshwater Drum *(Aplodinotus grunniens).* Drawing by F. A. Carmichael.

Freshwater Drum
Aplodinotus grunniens Rafinesque (Plate 36)

Description: Arched back, straight belly line. Tail rounded at tip. Long dorsal fin, with about ten spines and thirty or more soft rays. Mouth horizontal, lips thin. Gray-backed with silvery sides.

Size: The largest Freshwater Drum caught in Kansas weighed 14.2 kg (31.25 pounds) and was 95.4 cm (37½ inches) in length, apparently the longest example on record. It was caught on a trotline in the Verdigris River on 17 July 1982 by Arthur C. Hyatt of Coffeyville.

Habitat: The Freshwater Drum occurs in rivers throughout Kansas. It became more common westward after construction of impoundments in the central and western parts of the state.

Reproduction: Freshwater Drums spawn between May and July in lakes or deep pools. The "booming" sounds made by this species relate to its reproductive activity, which occurs in open water. The buoyant eggs drift freely near the surface.

Food: The Freshwater Drum feeds on larval insects (especially burrowing mayflies), small clams, snails, and rarely fish.

Remarks: This is the only common freshwater species of a large marine family that feeds mainly on hard-shelled animals such as mollusks. Knobby tooth plates in the throat are adapted for crushing these shells. Freshwater Drums get their name from the ability to make booming sounds by muscular action against the air bladder. The large otoliths ("lucky stones") in the head, the large sensory canals on the sides of the head, and the long lateral line extending to the tip of the tail fin are all adaptations for receiving these (and other) sounds.

The Freshwater Drum is readily caught on hook and line, usually on worms or other live bait. It is also an important commercial food fish. Many anglers call this species the "white perch."

TECHNICAL KEYS TO THE FISHES OF KANSAS

HOW TO USE THE KEYS

A key offers a more precise way to identify a fish (particularly when examining preserved specimens in a classroom setting). It consists of a sequence of numbered couplets (paired, contrasting statements). Both parts of each couplet should be read carefully before deciding which of the two statements better describes the fish at hand. Use of these keys starts with couplet number 1 under the Key to the Families of Fishes in Kansas.

Before you begin, read the next three numbered paragraphs, which explain how a key is used:

1. If your fish lacks jaws, has a mouth that resembles a suction cup, and has a line of seven gill-pits rather than a single slotlike gill-opening (Fig. 1), you are fortunate to have found a Chestnut Lamprey (Family Petromyzontidae), and you may turn to the species account for further information about it. If, on the other hand, your specimen does have jaws and a single gill-opening, continue your use of the key by proceeding to couplet number 2.

2. Read both alternatives in couplet 2. If you conclude that the caudal fin of your fish is symmetrical and has a vertical base (homocercal; Fig. 2), go to couplet number 6 (otherwise, go to couplet 3).

3. In couplet 6, if the first statement accurately describes your specimen, it is an American Eel (Fig. 1). If the second statement better fits the fish at hand, proceed to couplet number 7, and continue as before until a specific (or family) identification can be obtained. Often, identification requires use of a second set of keys, to the kinds of fishes within families that are represented by more than one species in Kansas.

It is essential, when using these keys, to have a minimum number of instruments and tools available. Most important is the need for a dissecting (binocular) microscope. Also have at hand a pair of small dissecting scissors, a fine probe, a pair of forceps, a ruler, and a pair of calipers or engineer's dividers. In addition, be sure to consult the figures and glossary to ensure that you understand the language used in the keys.

As a precautionary measure, you should check the characteristics of several individual fish that you believe to be alike, while utilizing these keys (and specifically Figures 1 to 45) to identify them. Most kinds of fish have a wide range of individual variation, as is implied by the range in scale count or fin ray count that is cited in each half of many couplets. The range of variation given is inclusive of most (but not necessarily all) individuals of a species; therefore, failure of a specimen to "fit the key," or misidentification of the specimen, may result from unusual features of that specimen relative to others of its kind. Examination of several specimens (if available) will minimize this problem. Users of this key may encounter particular difficulty in identifying minnows (Family Cyprinidae), suckers (Family Catostomidae), and darters (Family Percidae).

Some difficulties encountered in identifying particular fish reflect unusual but still "normal" characteristics of the species. Nevertheless, users of this book should remember that knowledge of our fish fauna is incomplete. Additional species are likely to be found within the state, and extensions of the known distributions of other species are certain. Therefore, "unidentifiable" specimens command real interest, as do specimens caught outside the areas of known occurrence as given in the species accounts. Such specimens should be taken to the nearest college, university, or regional office of the Kansas Department of Wildlife and Parks for verification.

KEY TO THE FAMILIES OF FISHES IN KANSAS

1. Jaws absent, mouth an oval suction cup; seven small gill-openings in a line behind head (Fig. 1) .... Lampreys, Family Petromyzontidae

   Jaws present, mouth not cuplike; gill-opening single, slotlike, at back of head 2

2. Caudal fin at least slightly asymmetrical, its base slanting downward and forward (heterocercal, Fig. 2) 3

   Caudal fin symmetrical, its base vertical (usually homocercal, Fig. 2) 6

3. Body naked or with five rows of bony plates; caudal fin forked, strongly heterocercal (Fig. 2) 4

   Body completely scaled; caudal fin rounded, abbreviate-heterocercal (Fig. 2) 5

4. Body naked (except for a small patch of scales on tail); mouth opening forward, beneath paddlelike snout; gill cover long, flexible, pointed posteriorly (Fig. 1) .... Paddlefishes, Family Polyodontidae

   Body with five rows of bony plates; mouth protrusible downward; gill cover short, rounded posteriorly (Fig. 1)
   .... Sturgeons, Family Acipenseridae

5. Jaws prolonged into a toothed beak; scales diamond-shaped, hard; dorsal fin far back on body, with fewer than twelve rays; gular plate absent (Fig. 1) .... Gars, Family Lepisosteidae

   Jaws short, snout blunt; scales rounded, flexible; dorsal fin extending most of length of back, with more than 45 rays; gular plate present (Fig. 1) .... Bowfins, Family Amiidae

6. Body form snakelike; dorsal, caudal, and anal fins united; pelvic fins absent (Fig. 1) .... Freshwater Eels, Family Anguillidae

   Body form not snakelike; dorsal, caudal, and anal fins separate; pelvic fins present 7

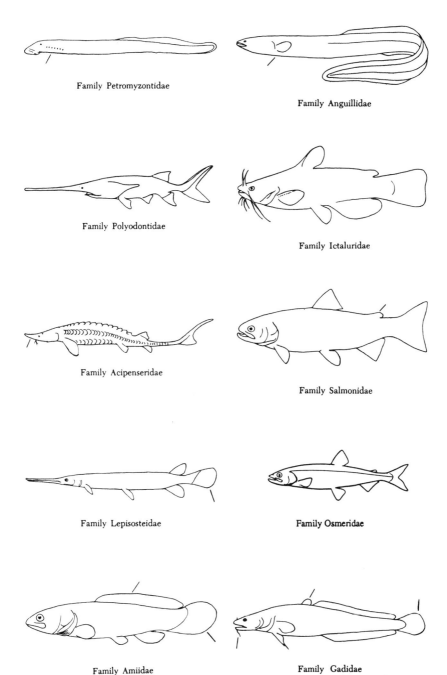

Figure 1. General body shape, fin shape, and fin placement (diagrammatic) of ten families of fishes in Kansas. The family Osmeridae was redrawn from Nelson (1994). If your fish does not resemble any of the above outlines, turn the page and continue. Once you have established the identity of the family to which your fish belongs, turn to the appropriate following key for that family. Drawings by Thomas H. Swearingen.

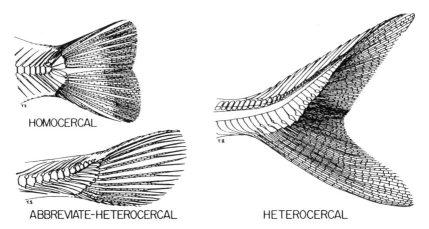

HOMOCERCAL

ABBREVIATE-HETEROCERCAL   HETEROCERCAL

Figure 2. Kinds of caudal fins in fishes. Homocercal fin shown is that of a Black Crappie; abbreviate-heterocercal, Shortnose Gar; heterocercal, Paddlefish. Drawings by Thomas H. Swearingen.

7. Adipose fin present (sometimes as a low fleshy ridge joined to caudal fin) (Figs. 3A, 35) 8

   Adipose fin absent 10

8. Body naked; each pectoral fin with a strong spinous ray; eight barbels on front of head (Fig. 1) .... Catfishes, Family Ictaluridae

   Body scaled; pectoral fins entirely soft-rayed; no barbels 9

9. Scales tiny, a hundred or more along lateral line; anal fin rays fewer than sixteen .... Trouts, Family Salmonidae

   Scales larger, about sixty along lateral line (fewer than twenty pored); anal fin rays sixteen or more .... Smelts, Family Osmeridae

10. A single barbel on middle of chin; base of pelvic fins anterior to base of pectoral fins; two dorsal fins, both entirely soft-rayed; more than fifty rays in second dorsal fin and anal fin (Fig. 1)
    .... Codfishes, Family Gadidae

    No barbel on chin; base of pelvic fins not anterior to base of pectoral fins; one or two dorsal fins, the first spinous if present; fewer than 35 rays in anal and second dorsal fins 11

11. Pelvic fins abdominal (their base nearer tip of pectoral fin than base of pectoral fin when pectoral fin is laid straight back along body; Fig. 3A); dorsal fin never with more than one spine, except in Family Atherinidae (one species, see 12) 12

    Pelvic fins thoracic (their base nearer base of pectoral fin than tip of pectoral fin when pectoral fin is laid back along body; Fig. 3B); dorsal fin with several spines 19

12. A small dorsal finlet, containing 4–5 spines, in front of and well separated from the large soft dorsal fin (Fig. 4)
    .... Silversides, Family Atherinidae

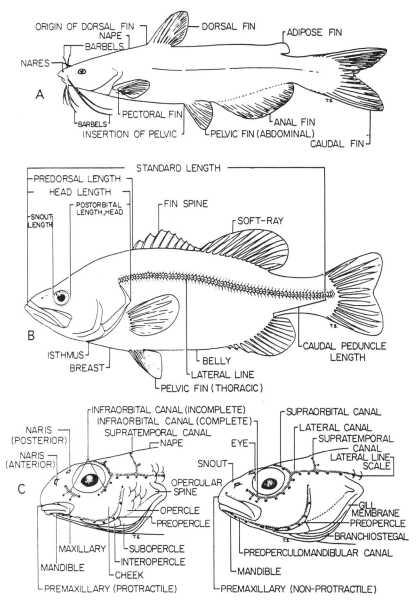

Figure 3. Structural features of fishes that are often used for identification of fishes and that appear in the various keys that follow. Species shown are (A) Channel Catfish, (B) Largemouth Bass, and (C) Johnny Darter [left] and Stippled Darter [right]. Drawings by Thomas H. Swearingen.

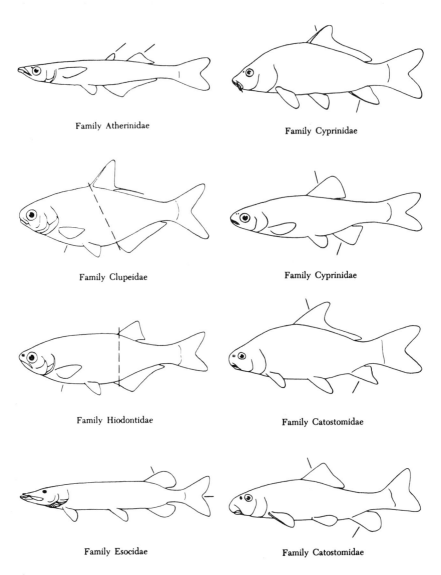

Figure 4. General body shape, fin shape, and fin placement (diagrammatic) of eight families of fishes in Kansas. If your fish does not resemble any of the above outlines, turn the page and continue. Once you have established the identity of the family to which your fish belongs, turn to the appropriate following key for that family. Drawings by Thomas H. Swearingen.

Dorsal fin single, without true spines (first ray sometimes hardened and spinelike) 13

13. Anal fin with eighteen or more rays; longest ray in anal fin only about half, or less than half, length of fin base 14

Anal fin with fewer than eighteen rays; longest ray in anal fin more than half length of fin base 15

14. Lateral line absent; belly with modified, sharp-edged scales that catch or tear when rubbed forward; gill rakers numerous and slender (Figs. 4, 5A) .... Herrings, Family Clupeidae

Lateral line well-developed; belly smooth, with ordinary scales; gill rakers few and knoblike (Figs. 4, 5B) .... Mooneyes, Family Hiodontidae

15. Jaws produced into a flattened, ducklike bill (Fig. 4); teeth large .... Pikes, Family Esocidae

Jaws not produced into a ducklike bill; teeth inconspicuous or absent ... 16

16. Head scaleless; gill membranes joined to isthmus (opercular clefts terminating ventrally at a point behind level of eye, the membranes not overlapping each other anteriorly; Fig. 6A); caudal fin forked 17

Head partly scaled, or with scaly plates; gill membranes free from isthmus (opercular clefts extending forward below eye, the membranes usually overlapping anteriorly; Fig. 6C); caudal fin not forked 18

17. Dorsal fin short with 8–10 principal rays and lacking a spine at origin, or, if longer, with up to 21 fin rays and containing a single spinelike, saw-edged ray at origin (Fig. 4); pharyngeal arch with 1–3 rows of teeth, never more than six teeth in primary row (Fig. 7C); lips thin (Figs. 17, 18) .... Minnows, Family Cyprinidae

Dorsal fin with ten or more principal rays; first dorsal ray flexible at tip, never saw-edged posteriorly (Fig. 4); pharyngeal arch with single row of more than twenty teeth (Fig. 7A); lips usually thick and fleshy (Figs. 15, 16) .... Suckers, Family Catostomidae

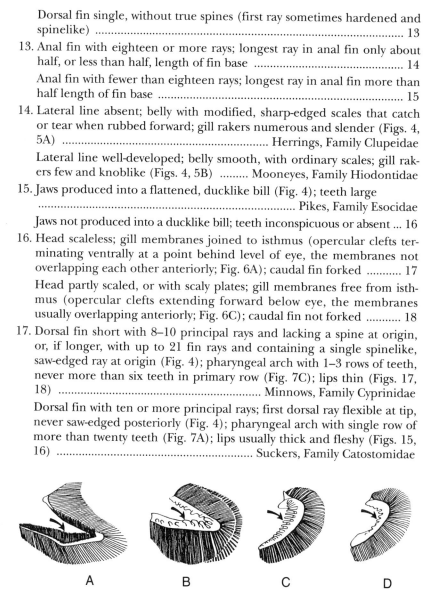

A   B   C   D

Figure 5. First gill arches of four fishes, showing differences in number and shape of gill rakers (on left or concave side of each arch, see arrows). A. Rakers numerous and slender, as in Clupeidae (Gizzard Shad illustrated). B. Rakers short and knoblike, as in Hiodontidae (Goldeye illustrated). C. Rakers slender, as in species of *Lepomis* other than the Longear Sunfish and the Redear Sunfish (Green Sunfish illustrated). D. Rakers short and knoblike, as in the Longear Sunfish (illustrated) and the Redear Sunfish. Drawings by Thomas H. Swearingen.

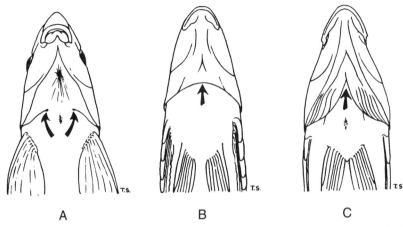

Figure 6. Gill membranes of fishes in relation to ventral body wall (note arrows). A. Right and left membranes bound down to isthmus, as in minnows and suckers (carpsucker illustrated): a needle-tip slipped into the gill cleft on one side cannot be moved freely across to the opposite side; gill membranes free from isthmus (as in B and C). B. Gill membranes broadly joined across isthmus, as in Banded Darter. C. Gill membranes separate (right and left sides not conjoined), as in Stippled Darter. Drawings by Thomas H. Swearingen.

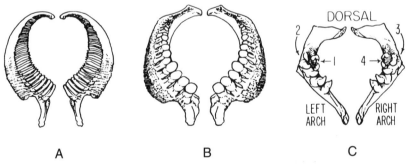

Figure 7. Pharyngeal arches of suckers (A and B) and a minnow (C). As shown, arches have been laid on a horizontal surface with teeth projecting upward. (Redrawn from Bailey 1956, Fig. 5.) A. Golden Redhorse: teeth numerous and slender, in a single row (comblike). B. River Redhorse: lower teeth stumplike or molariform, but numerous and uniserial. C. Creek Chub: teeth few, confined to central part of arch, often hooked (two-rowed in this species); the sequence in which rows are counted is indicated by numerals 1, 2, 3, 4; the count of number of teeth therefore is 2,5–4,2. Drawings by Thomas H. Swearingen.

18. Dorsal fin with nine or more rays; anal rays twelve or more (Fig. 8A); anal fin of males large, not rodlike; egg-laying (Fig. 9)
.... Topminnows and Killifishes, Family Fundulidae
Dorsal fin with 7–8 rays; anal rays fewer than ten; anal fin of males a slender, rodlike organ (gonopodium); livebearing (Fig. 9)
.... Livebearers, Family Poeciliidae

19. Body nearly naked; head width more than ⅔ predorsal length; pelvic fin with fewer than five soft rays (Fig. 9) .... Sculpins, Family Cottidae
Body scaled; head width less than ⅔ predorsal length; pelvic fin with five soft rays 20

20. Anal fin with three or more spines 21
Anal fin with one or two spines.. 22

21. Spinous and soft-rayed parts of dorsal fin separate or scarcely joined (Fig. 9; shortest spine in notch between dorsal fins not more than ⅕ length of longest dorsal spine); sides with several narrow, longitudinal stripes; pseudobranchia well developed
.... Temperate Basses, Family Moronidae
Spinous and soft-rayed parts of dorsal fin continuous (Fig. 9; if fin is notched, next-to-last dorsal spine more than ⅕ length of longest dorsal spine); sides not marked by several distinct longitudinal stripes; pseudo-branchia absent or inconspicuous .... Sunfishes, Family Centrarchidae

22. Lateral line not extending onto caudal fin; dorsal fin divided into two parts, the second with fewer than 25 soft rays; second anal spine weak if present; species mostly small and mottled or barred with color (Fig. 9)
.... Perches, Family Percidae
Lateral line extending onto caudal fin; dorsal fin single, with 25 or more soft rays; second anal spine long and stout; plain silvery, deep-bodied species of large size (Fig. 9) .... Drums, Family Sciaenidae

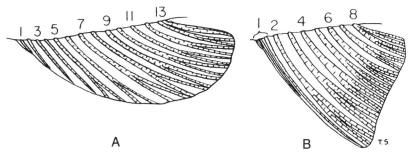

Figure 8. Hypothetical anal fins (or, in effect, inverted dorsal fins) showing how fin rays are counted. (Redrawn from Bailey 1956, Fig. 7.) A. Total ray count, as taken in fins that slope gradually away from the body contour. B. Principal ray count, as taken in fins that have a straight leading edge (rudimentary [procurrent] rays contiguous anteriorly). Drawings by Thomas H. Swearingen.

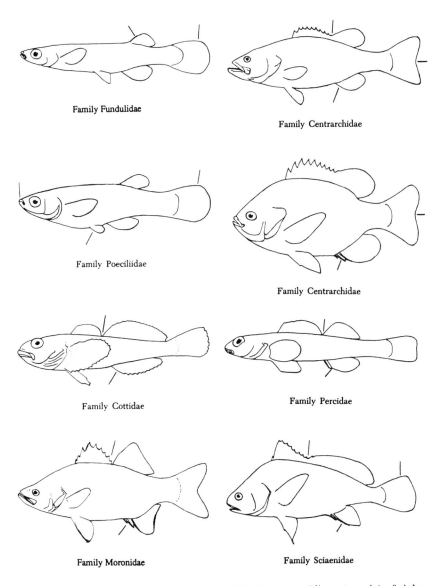

Figure 9. General body shape, fin shape, and fin placement (diagrammatic) of eight families of fishes in Kansas. Once you have established the identity of the family to which your fish belongs, turn to the appropriate following key for that family. Drawings by Thomas H. Swearingen.

KEY TO THE STURGEONS (FAMILY ACIPENSERIDAE)

1. Caudal peduncle partly naked, its length much less than distance from origin of anal fin to insertion of pelvics; spiracle present (Fig. 10) .... Lake Sturgeon, *Acipenser fulvescens*
   Caudal peduncle covered by scaly plates, its length greater than distance from origin of anal fin to insertion of pelvics; spiracle absent 2

2. Barbels arising near middle of snout length; distance from base of inner barbel to front of mouth contained 1.3–2.2 times in distance from base of outer barbel to tip of snout; length of inner barbels contained 1.2–1.5 times in length of outer barbels; breast (in front of pelvic fins) scaled except in young (Fig. 11A) .... Shovelnose Sturgeon, *Scaphirhynchus platorynchus*
   Barbels arising much nearer front of mouth than tip of snout; distance from base of inner barbel to front of mouth contained 2.3–3.3 times in distance from base of outer barbel to tip of snout; length of inner barbels contained 1.6–2.4 times in length of outer barbels; breast naked in front of pelvic fins (Fig. 11B) .... Pallid Sturgeon, *Scaphirhynchus albus*

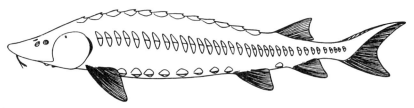

Figure 10. Lateral view of a Lake Sturgeon, showing the short, partially naked caudal peduncle. Drawing by Anne Musser and Joseph T. Collins.

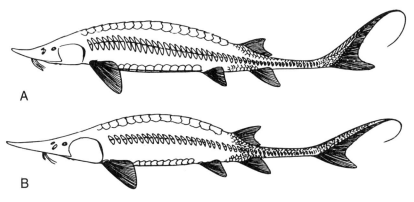

Figure 11. Lateral views of sturgeons. A. Shovelnose Sturgeon, showing placement of barbels and scaled caudal peduncle; note narrow space between lateral row of scales and those on belly. B. Pallid Sturgeon, showing placement of barbels and scaled caudal peduncle; note wider space between lateral row of scales and those on belly. Drawings by Anne Musser and Joseph T. Collins.

KEY TO THE GARS (FAMILY LEPISOSTEIDAE)

1. Distance from front of eye to back of operculum less than half the distance from front of eye to tip of snout; least width of snout less than diameter of eye .... Longnose Gar, *Lepisosteus osseus*
Distance from front of eye to back of operculum more than half the distance from front of eye to tip of snout; least width of snout greater than diameter of eye 2
2. Scales on midline of back, from occiput to dorsal fin, fifty or more; top of head and back plain greenish, unblotched
.... Shortnose Gar, *Lepisosteus platostomus*
Fewer than fifty scales on midline of back, from occiput to dorsal fin; top of head and back with dark blotches
.... Spotted Gar, *Lepisosteus oculatus*

KEY TO THE HERRINGS (FAMILY CLUPEIDAE)

1. Dorsal fin with 15–16 rays (Fig. 8B), the last one not prolonged as a flexible filament; anal fin low, with about eighteen rays; twenty or more sharp-edged scutes (scales) along ventral midline before base of pelvic fins; mouth large, lower jaw projecting
.... Skipjack Herring, *Alosa chrysochloris*
Dorsal fin with about twelve rays, the last one long and filamentous; anal fin with twenty or more rays; fewer than twenty scutes along ventral midline before pelvic fins; mouth variable... 2
2. Mouth subterminal, snout bluntly rounded; anal fin rays 25–33; ventral scutes before pelvic fins 17–19 .... Gizzard Shad, *Dorosoma cepedianum*
Mouth terminal; anal fin rays 20–25; ventral scutes before pelvic fins 14–17... Threadfin Shad, *Dorosoma petenense*

KEY TO THE MINNOWS (FAMILY CYPRINIDAE)

1. Dorsal fin with more than fifteen soft rays and an anterior spine (Fig. 12A) 2
Dorsal fin with fewer than twelve soft rays and lacking saw-edged spine (Fig. 12B) 3
2. Two barbels on each side of mouth (Fig. 13A)
.... Common Carp, *Cyprinus carpio*
Barbels absent (Fig. 13B)................................ Goldfish, *Carassius auratus*
3. Caudal peduncle stout, its depth at least ⅔ its length and half the distance from origin of anal fin to caudal base (Fig. 14A); head broad, interorbital width greater than head depth at orbit; pharyngeal teeth 2,5–5,2 and strongly grooved .... Grass Carp, *Ctenopharyngodon idella*

Figure 12. Lateral view of dorsal fins of fishes. A. Fin with an anterior spine and more than fifteen soft fin rays. B. Fin without anterior spine and fewer than twelve soft fin rays. Drawings by Anne Musser.

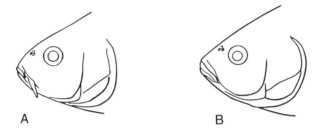

Figure 13. Lateral view of heads of fishes. A. Common Carp, showing location of barbel on side of mouth. B. Goldfish, showing lack of barbel on side of mouth. Drawings by Anne Musser.

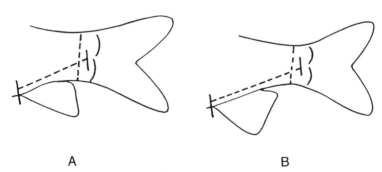

Figure 14. Lateral view of rear portion of bodies of fishes. A. Caudal peduncle stout. B. Caudal peduncle more slender. Drawings by Anne Musser and Joseph T. Collins.

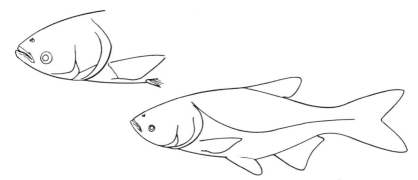

Figure 15. Lateral views of Bighead Carp, showing placement of eye and aspect of pectoral fins. Drawings by Anne Musser.

Caudal peduncle more slender, its least depth less than ⅔ its length and less than half the distance from origin of anal fin to caudal base (Fig. 14B); interorbital width usually much less than head depth at orbit; pharyngeal teeth not as above 4

4. Eye entirely below axis of body; pectoral fins long, extending well beyond base of pelvic fins; scales small, 85 or more in lateral-line series (Fig. 15) .... Bighead Carp, *Hypophthalmichthys nobilis*

Eye not entirely below axis of body; pectoral fins rarely extending beyond base of pelvic fins; lateral-line scales usually fewer than 85 5

5. Groove above upper lip not extending across tip of snout (premaxillae nonprotractile; Fig. 16A) .... Blacknose Dace, *Rhinichthys atratulus*

Groove above upper lip extending completely across snout (premaxillae protractile; Fig. 16B) 6

6. Principal dorsal fin rays usually ten, sometimes nine; pharyngeal teeth usually 3,5–5,3; dorsal, anal, and caudal fins red in life
.... Rudd, *Scardinius erythrophthalmus*

Principal dorsal fin rays usually eight; pharyngeal arch never with more than two teeth in secondary row; fin color may or may not be red 7

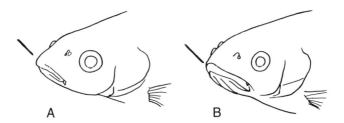

Figure 16. Lateral view of heads of fishes. A. Groove above upper lip not extending across snout. B. Groove above upper lip extending across snout. Drawings by Anne Musser.

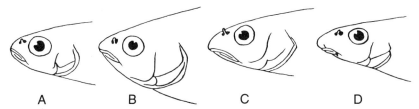

Figure 17. Characteristics of mouths of minnows (lateral view). A. Mouth terminal and oblique, upper and lower jaws equal (Bigeye Shiner illustrated). B. Mouth nearly terminal, oblique, but lower jaw shorter than upper jaw, closing within it (Bluntface Shiner illustrated). C. Mouth subterminal, scarcely oblique, lower jaw shorter than upper jaw, closing within it (Bigmouth Shiner illustrated). D. Mouth ventral and nearly horizontal; note also barbel projecting from groove at corner of mouth, absent in A, B, and C (Gravel Chub illustrated). Drawings by Thomas H. Swearingen.

7. Barbels present (one or two at each corner of mouth; Figs. 17D, 18A) 8
   Barbels absent 18
8. A false barbel (in breeding males) consisting of a fleshy outgrowth on lips near their juncture (Fig. 19A); nuptial tubercles or their pits usually present, and confined to snout, where they are arranged in transverse rows .... Bluntnose Minnow, *Pimephales notatus*
   Barbels genuine, persistent in both sexes, usually projecting from groove above or behind lips (Fig. 19B); nuptial tubercles, if present, not arranged in definite rows across snout 9
9. Two barbels on each side of mouth ... Speckled Chub, *Extrarius aestivalis*
   One barbel on each side of mouth 10

Figure 18. Characteristics of mouths in four kinds of minnows (ventral view). A. Flathead Chub: Deeply U-shaped mouth, as in most minnows (note also terminal barbels, projecting from groove behind lips at each corner of mouth). B. Plains Minnow: Shallowly crescentic mouth, as in genus *Hybognathus* (barbels absent). C. Suckermouth Minnow: note uniquely lobed lips. D. Central Stoneroller: cartilaginous edge exposed along front of lower jaw, not covered by thickened epidermis of lower lip. Drawings by Gene Pacheco.

Figure 19. Lateral view of heads of fishes. A. False barbel and tubercles. B. Genuine barbel. Drawings by Anne Musser.

10. Barbel minute and flat, in groove above maxillary (Fig. 16B); mouth terminal and oblique, upper lip expanded at center; dorsal fin with dark spot anteriorly near base; pharyngeal teeth usually 2,5–4,2
.... Creek Chub, *Semotilus atromaculatus*

Barbel minute to large, conical, at angle of jaws (Fig. 19B); mouth terminal or ventral, upper lip not expanded at center; dorsal fin without dark spot anteriorly; pharyngeal teeth never 2,5–4,2 11

11. Pectoral fins falcate (Fig. 20A); lateral-line scales 44 or more; eye small, its diameter usually less than ⅙ of the head length 12

Pectoral fins rounded at tip (Fig. 20B); lateral-line scales fewer than 44; eye diameter usually greater than ⅙ of the head length 13

12. Head wider than deep at occiput; snout acute; breast scaled; pharyngeal teeth 2,4–4,2 .... Flathead Chub, *Platygobio gracilis*

Head width at occiput less than head depth; snout bluntly rounded; breast mostly scaleless; pharyngeal teeth 0,4–4,0
.... Sicklefin Chub, *Macrhybopsis meeki*

13. Anal fin rays eight (Fig. 8B); body pallid; lower lobe of caudal fin darker than upper lobe, but with lowermost ray white; breast scaleless except in *Macrhybopsis storeriana* 14

Anal fin rays seven; body well-pigmented; caudal fin pigmented uniformly; breast with scales 16

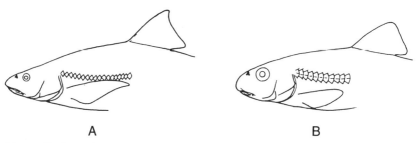

Figure 20. Lateral view of fishes. A. Pectoral fin falcate. B. Pectoral fin rounded. Drawings by Anne Musser.

14. Eye large, its diameter equal to distance from hind margin of eye to upper end of gill cleft; head depth at occiput greater than distance from tip of snout to hind margin of eye; breast with scales .... Silver Chub, *Macrhybopsis storeriana*

Eye diameter less than distance from hind margin of eye to upper end of gill cleft; head depth at occiput less than distance from tip of snout to hind margin of eye; breast mostly naked 15

15. Scales with fleshy ridges or keels; lateral-line scales 39–43; pharyngeal teeth 1,4–4,1; dorsum uniformly dusky, without tiny scattered black spots .... Sturgeon Chub, *Macrhybopsis gelida*

Scales without fleshy ridges or keels; lateral-line scales 35–39; pharyngeal teeth 0,4–4,0; dorsum pallid, with tiny scattered black spots .... Speckled Chub, *Extrarius aestivalis*

16. Mouth ventral (Fig. 21A); eye large, its diameter equal to distance from hind margin of eye to upper end of gill cleft, and equal to or greater than length of upper jaw; sides with scattered X-markings; pharyngeal teeth 0,4–4,0 .... Gravel Chub, *Erimystax x-punctatus*

Mouth terminal or subterminal, not overhung by snout; eye moderate, its diameter much less than distance from hind margin of eye to upper end of gill cleft, and less than length of upper jaw; sides plain or with a dark lateral band; pharyngeal teeth 1,4–4,1 17

17. Breeding males with tubercles only on head and pectoral fins (Fig. 21B); Missouri River basin .... Hornyhead Chub, *Nocomis biguttatus*

Breeding males with tubercles on upper sides of body as well as on head and pectoral fins (Fig. 21C); Neosho River basin .... Redspot Chub, *Nocomis asper*

18. Anal rays usually nine or more; pharyngeal arch with one or more teeth in secondary row (Fig. 7C), except in *Notemigonus crysoleucas* 19

Anal rays usually eight or fewer; pharyngeal arch lacking teeth in secondary row, except in *Cyprinella spiloptera, Hybopsis dorsalis, Notropis blennius, Notropis boops,* and *Semotilus atromaculatus* 29

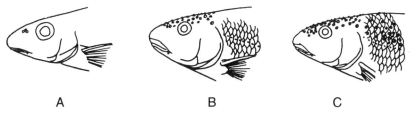

A   **B**   **C**

Figure 21. Lateral view of heads of fishes. A. Mouth ventral. B. Presence of tubercles on head only. C. Presence of tubercles on head and upper side of body. Drawings by Anne Musser.

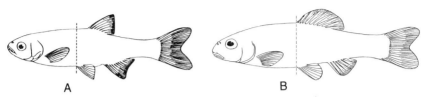

Figure 22. Differences in position and shape of dorsal fins of minnows. A. Origin of dorsal fin posterior to insertion of pelvic fins, as indicated by vertical dashed line. Also, dorsal fin is triangular (pointed at tip), and its anterior rays would extend to or beyond tips of posterior rays if fin were folded downward against body. B. Origin of dorsal fin approximately over insertion of pelvic fins. Also, dorsal fin is rounded, and its anterior rays would not extend to tips of posterior rays if fin were folded downward against body. Drawings by Thomas H. Swearingen.

19. Anal rays usually more than nine; insertion of pelvic fins distinctly anterior to origin of dorsal fin (Fig. 22A) 20

    Anal rays usually nine; insertion of pelvic and origin of dorsal fin approximately equidistant from tip of snout (Fig. 22B) 24

20. Midline of belly (behind base of pelvic fins) with fleshy keel; lateral-line scales more than 45; pharyngeal teeth 5–5
    .... Golden Shiner, *Notemigonus crysoleucas*

    Midline of belly (behind base of pelvic fins) not keeled; lateral-line scales fewer than 45; pharyngeal teeth 4–4 21

21. Body slender, scarcely compressed, greatest width (thickness) equal to distance from crest of back to lateral-line row of scales (at point of greatest decurvature of lateral line); body depth usually contained four or more times in standard length 22

    Body deep, compressed, greatest width (thickness) less than distance from crest of back to lateral-line row of scales (at point of greatest decurvature of lateral line); body depth usually contained less than four times in standard length 23

22. Snout blunt, its length about equal to eye diameter and contained more than 1.5 times in postorbital length of head; least depth of caudal peduncle usually exceeding distance from tip of snout to middle of pupil; tip of dorsal fin pointed; rosy pigment lacking (Fig. 23A)
    .... Emerald Shiner, *Notropis atherinoides*

    Snout acute, its length greater than eye diameter and contained less than 1.5 times in postorbital length of head; least depth of caudal peduncle less than distance from tip of snout to middle of pupil; tip of dorsal fin rounded; usually rosy color on head, breast, and base of dorsal fin (Fig. 23B) .... Rosyface Shiner, *Notropis rubellus*

23. Predorsal scale rows 25 or more (scales minute and crowded); lateral-line scales more than 37; slight dark spot at origin of dorsal fin; fins seldom red or orange (in Kansas specimens)
    .... Redfin Shiner, *Lythrurus umbratilis*

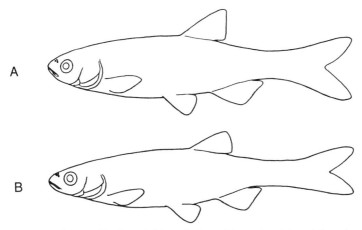

Figure 23. Lateral view of bodies of fishes. A. Snout blunt; tip of dorsal fin pointed. B. Snout acute; tip of dorsal fin rounded. Drawings by Anne Musser.

Predorsal scale rows fewer than twenty (scales not minute and crowded); lateral-line scales fewer than 37; no dark spot at origin of dorsal fin; fins often red or orange .... Red Shiner, *Cyprinella lutrensis*

24. Dorsal fin acutely pointed, first principal ray longer than head length; predorsal stripe indistinct or absent; body almost unpigmented, transparent in life; sides with thin, bright silvery longitudinal stripe .... Silverband Shiner, *Notropis shumardi*

Dorsal fin not acutely pointed, first principal ray shorter than head length; predorsal stripe usually prominent; body well-pigmented, not transparent in life; sides generally silvery, without longitudinal stripe ... 25

25. Predorsal length (Fig. 24A) less than or equal to distance from dorsal origin to base of caudal fin; lining of body cavity black; lateral-line scales 37 or more 26

Predorsal length (Fig. 24B) usually greater than distance from dorsal origin to base of caudal fin; lining of body cavity silvery or dusky; lateral-line scales 37 or fewer 28

26. Scales on anterior part of sides not notably diamond-shaped, about twice as high as long (Fig. 25A); lateral-line scales usually 40–44 .... Cardinal Shiner, *Luxilus cardinalis*

Scales on anterior part of sides narrowly diamond-shaped, about three times as high as long (Fig. 25B); lateral-line scales usually 37–40 27

27. Predorsal scales much smaller than scales on sides, more than eighteen scale rows before dorsal fin; no dark lines between dorsolateral scale rows .... Common Shiner, *Luxilus cornutus*

Predorsal scales not much smaller than scales on sides, fewer than eighteen scale rows before dorsal fin; dark zigzag lines, converging posteri-

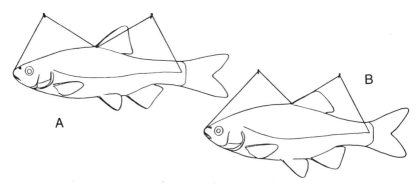

Figure 24. Lateral view of fishes, showing method by which predorsal length is determined as a comparative character. A. Predorsal length less than or equal to distance between dorsal fin origin and caudal fin base. B. Predorsal length greater than distance between dorsal fin origin and caudal fin base. Drawings by Anne Musser.

orly atop caudal peduncle, evident between dorsolateral scale rows
.... Striped Shiner, *Luxilus chrysocephalus*

28. Lower jaw shorter than upper jaw, closing into it (Fig. 17B); posterior membranes of dorsal fin blotched, darker than anterior membranes; caudal fin pale (unpigmented) basally, darker distally
.... Bluntface Shiner, *Cyprinella camura*

Upper and lower jaws equal (Figs. 17A, 22A); posterior part of dorsal fin not blotched, not darker than anterior part; caudal fin uniformly pigmented .... Red Shiner, *Cyprinella lutrensis*

29. Intestine forming single, flattened S-shaped loop longitudinally (Fig. 26A); lining of body cavity silvery, sometimes dusky, black only in *Notropis boops* 30

Intestine looped transversely (Fig. 26B) across body cavity (only one loop crossing midline, anteriorly, in *Pimephales notatus*); lining of body cavity black 46

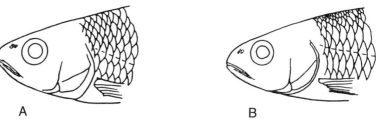

Figure 25. Lateral view of anterior portion of fishes. A. Scales on side of body not diamond-shaped, about twice as high as long. B. Scales on side of body diamond-shaped, about three times as high as long. Drawings by Anne Musser.

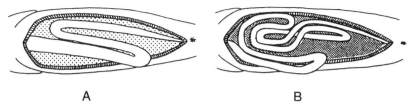

A   B

Figure 26. Ventral views (diagrammatic) of body cavities in minnows, as they would appear if lower body wall were cut away. A. Intestine short, forming a single S-shaped loop; peritoneum silvery. B. Intestine long, looped transversely across body cavity; peritoneum dark (usually black). Drawings by Thomas H. Swearingen.

30. Anal rays usually eight 31

 Anal rays usually seven 40

31. Lateral-line scales more than fifty; dorsal fin with dark spot at origin; pharyngeal teeth 2,5–4,2 .... Creek Chub, *Semotilus atromaculatus*

 Lateral-line scales fewer than 42; dorsal fin without dark spot at origin; pharyngeal teeth never 2,5–4,2 32

32. Body compressed, lateral line decurved; greatest width of body less than distance from crest of back to lateral line; dorsal fin rounded, anterior rays extending approximately to tips of posterior rays when fin is depressed against body 33

 Body terete, lateral line nearly straight; greatest width of body about equal to distance from crest of back to lateral line; dorsal fin pointed, anterior rays extending beyond tips of posterior rays when fin is depressed against body 34

33. Posterior membranes of dorsal fin more densely pigmented than anterior membranes; lateral-line scales usually more than 35; greatest depth of body 3.6–4.3 in standard length; pharyngeal teeth 1,4–4,1 .... Spotfin Shiner, *Cyprinella spiloptera*

 Posterior membranes of dorsal fin not more densely pigmented than anterior membranes; lateral-line scales usually 35 or fewer; greatest depth of body 3.0–3.6 in standard length; pharyngeal teeth usually 0,4–4,0 .... Red Shiner, *Cyprinella lutrensis*

34. Mouth strongly oblique, upper and lower jaws equal or the lower jaw protruding (Fig. 17A); lower lip pigmented 35

 Mouth scarcely oblique, lower jaw shorter than upper jaw, closing within it (Fig. 17C); lower lip unpigmented 36

35. Dorsal rays nine; lateral-line scales 36–40; pharyngeal teeth 0,5–5,0; lining of body cavity silvery .... Pugnose Minnow, *Notropis emiliae*

 Dorsal rays eight; lateral-line scales 34–36; pharyngeal teeth 1,4–4,1; lining of body cavity black .... Bigeye Shiner, *Notropis boops*

36. Eye diameter less than length of upper jaw; anterior lateral-line scales not higher than scales in rows above and below lateral line; circumferential scales 26 or more 37

Eye diameter greater than length of upper jaw (Fig. 27); anterior lateral-line scales higher than scales in rows above and below lateral line; circumferential scales fewer than 26 38

37. Origin of dorsal fin nearer tip of snout than base of caudal fin (Fig. 24A); eye diameter less than ¼ head length; predorsal stripe faint or absent, small caudal spot present; pharyngeal teeth 0,4–4,0 .... Arkansas River Shiner, *Notropis girardi*

Origin of dorsal fin nearer base of caudal fin than tip of snout (Fig. 24B); eye diameter greater than ¼ head length; predorsal dark stripe well-developed, caudal spot absent; pharyngeal teeth 1,4–4,1 .... Bigmouth Shiner, *Hybopsis dorsalis*

38. Dark lateral stripe intense, continuous around snout; anterior lateral-line scales with chevronlike markings with apices directed forward; snout length not less than eye diameter .... Blacknose Shiner, *Notropis heterolepis*

Dark lateral stripe faint or absent; anterior lateral-line scales lacking chevronlike markings; snout length less than eye diameter 39

39. Dorsolateral scales outlined by dark pigment, upper sides about as well-pigmented as dorsal surface; longest ray in dorsal fin usually shorter than head length; infraorbital canal complete (Fig. 3C) .... Mimic Shiner, *Notropis volucellus*

Dorsolateral scales not outlined by dark pigment, upper sides with an unpigmented space; longest ray in dorsal fin longer than head length; infraorbital canal incomplete (Fig. 3C) .... Ghost Shiner, *Notropis buchanani*

40. Lower lip thick, with prominent lobes at corners of mouth (Fig. 18C) .... Suckermouth Minnow, *Phenacobius mirabilis*

Lower lip uniformly thin, without lobes at corners of mouth 41

41. Dorsal fin pointed at tip, unspotted; anterior fin rays of dorsal extending to or beyond tips of posterior rays when fin is depressed against body (Fig. 22A); lateral-line scales 32–37 42

Figure 27. High lateral line scales, eye diameter greater than length of upper jaw. Drawing by Anne Musser.

Dorsal fin rounded, with anterior dark spot; anterior fin rays of dorsal not extending to tips of posterior rays when fin is depressed against body; (Fig. 22B) lateral-line scales 37–41 45

42. Dark lateral band present, terminating in discrete triangular caudal spot; length of caudal peduncle equal to head length; mouth small, distance from front of mandible to end of maxilla about ½ distance from end of maxilla to lower end of gill cleft (union of gill membrane to isthmus) .... Topeka Shiner, *Notropis topeka*

Dark lateral band absent; length of caudal peduncle less than head length; mouth large, distance from front of mandible to end of maxilla at least ⅔ distance from end of maxilla to lower end of gill cleft (union of gill membrane to isthmus) 43

43. Eye diameter less than snout length, 4.0 or more in head length; nape naked anteriorly (scales embedded); pectoral fins falcate, first (unbranched) fin ray the longest, tips of pectoral fin extending to base of pelvic fins in males .... Red River Shiner, *Notropis bairdi*

Eye diameter about equal to snout length, 3.5–4.0 in head length; nape fully scaled (scales not embedded behind occiput); pectoral fins not falcate, second or third fin rays the longest, not reaching base of pelvic fins when depressed (either sex) 44

44. Mid-dorsal stripe divided around base of dorsal fin, not intensified within base (no black dash in base of dorsal); lateral line not accented by melanophores; pharyngeal teeth 1 or 2,4–4,2 or 1
.... River Shiner, *Notropis blennius*

Mid-dorsal stripe not divided around base of dorsal fin, intensified within base (black dash present in base of dorsal); lateral line usually accented by melanophores; pharyngeal teeth 0,4–4,0
.... Sand Shiner, *Notropis ludibundus*

45. Dorsum not cross-hatched (pigment dispersed on scales); spot at base of caudal fin wedge-shaped; dark lateral stripe indistinct or absent; least depth of caudal peduncle usually greater than ½ its length (body stout); nuptial tubercles usually nine, in two rows
.... Bullhead Minnow, *Pimephales vigilax*

Dorsum cross-hatched (pigment concentrated along margins of scales); spot at base of caudal fin vertically elongate; dark lateral stripe well-defined; least depth of caudal peduncle usually less than ½ its length (body slender); nuptial tubercles usually 11–13, in three rows
.... Slim Minnow, *Pimephales tenellus*

46. Intestine wound spirally around air bladder; lower jaw with hardened cartilaginous cutting edge (often concealed, pry mouth open) and submarginal fold of thick skin (Fig. 18D)
.... Central Stoneroller, *Campostoma anomalum*

Intestine with all its loops ventral to air bladder, never completely encircling it; lower jaw not as above, its edge sometimes thin and hard but without submarginal fold of skin 47

47. Lateral line incomplete; scales minute, 65–90 in lateral-line row; origin of dorsal fin behind insertion of pelvics; body with two dark lateral stripes; pharyngeal teeth 0,5–5,0
.... Southern Redbelly Dace, *Phoxinus erythrogaster*

Lateral line usually complete; scales large, fewer than fifty in lateral-line row; origin of dorsal fin not behind insertion of pelvics; body not with two dark lateral stripes; pharyngeal teeth 0,4–4,0................................. 48

48. Dorsal fin rounded, anterior rays not extending to tips of posterior rays when fin is depressed against body (Fig. 22B); lateral-line scales usually more than forty; anal rays usually seven; breast naked (below pectoral fins) 49

Dorsal fin triangular, anterior rays extending to tips of posterior rays when fin is depressed against body (Fig. 22A); lateral-line scales usually fewer than forty; anal rays usually eight; breast scaled (below pectoral fins) 50

49. Scale rows around body 38 or more; caudal fin usually lacking basal spot; intestine with several loops across body cavity
.... Fathead Minnow, *Pimephales promelas*

Scale rows around body 32 or fewer; caudal fin with distinct black basal spot; loops of intestine few and mostly longitudinal
.... Bluntnose Minnow, *Pimephales notatus*

50. Mouth narrowly U-shaped (Fig. 28A); eye diameter more than ¼ head length, equal to snout length; pharyngeal teeth hooked; lateral line outlined by dark dots .... Ozark Minnow, *Notropis nubilus*

Mouth broadly crescentic (Fig. 28B); eye diameter usually less than ¼ head length, less than snout length; pharyngeal teeth not hooked; lateral line not outlined by dark dots 51

51. Dorsal fin rounded at tip; caudal fin uniformly pigmented (lower rudimentary rays pigmented); sides with a brassy sheen in life, dusky lateral band usually evident .... Brassy Minnow, *Hybognathus hankinsoni*

Dorsal fin pointed at tip; caudal fin pale-edged ventrally (lower rudimentary rays unpigmented); sides silvery in life, no dusky lateral band 52

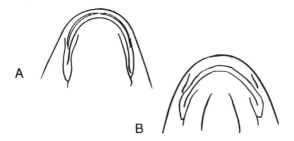

Figure 28. Ventral view of heads of fishes. A. Mouth narrowly U-shaped. B. Mouth broadly crescentic. Drawings by Anne Musser.

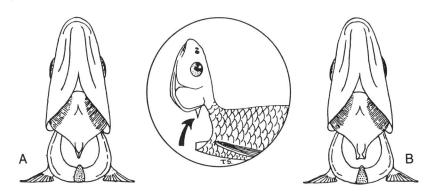

Figure 29. Basioccipital bones in two species of *Hybognathus*. The three figures indicate a method of revealing the structure, by cutting across the isthmus and bending the head backward. A. Plains Minnow: posterior process of basioccipital rodlike. B. Western Silvery Minnow: posterior process of basioccipital expanded. Drawings by Thomas H. Swearingen.

52. Ventral scale rows (below lateral-line series, crossing in front of pelvic fins) usually 15–18; posterior process of basioccipital bone rodlike (Fig. 29A) .... Plains Minnow, *Hybognathus placitus*

Ventral scale rows (below lateral-line series, crossing in front of pelvic fins) usually 12–14; posterior process of basioccipital bone expanded (Fig. 29B)........................... Western Silvery Minnow, *Hybognathus argyritis*

KEY TO THE SUCKERS (FAMILY CATOSTOMIDAE)

1. Dorsal fin rays more than twenty (Fig. 30A) 2

   Dorsal fin rays 10–15 (Fig. 30B) 8

2. Lateral-line scales more than fifty; lips papillose (Fig. 31C); eye closer to back of head than tip of snout .... Blue Sucker, *Cycleptus elongatus*

   Lateral-line scales fewer than fifty; lips plicate or smooth (Fig. 31A or B); eye closer to tip of snout than back of head 3

3. Color usually dull bronze or olivaceous; lower fins dark-pigmented; anterior fontanelle (on midline of top of head, between nostrils and eyes) closed in adults; lower margin of subopercle evenly curved, not angular (widest at midpoint of its length; Fig. 32A); pelvic rays usually 10–11, anal rays 8–9, sum of pelvic and anal rays eighteen or more 4

   Color silvery white; lower fins cream-colored or clear; anterior fontanelle open in adults; marginal curvature of subopercle somewhat angular (widest anterior to midpoint of its length; Fig. 32B); pelvic rays usually 8–10, anal rays 7–9, sum of pelvic and anal rays usually seventeen or fewer except in *C. velifer* 6

Figure 30. Lateral view of dorsal fins of fishes. A. Dorsal fin rays number more than twenty. B. Dorsal fin rays number 10–15. Drawings by Linda Greatorex.

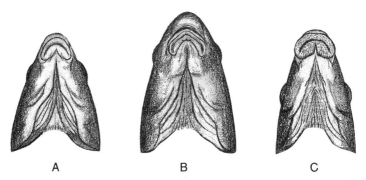

Figure 31. Mouths in three genera of suckers *(Ictiobus, Carpiodes, Catostomus)*. A. Small-mouth Buffalo: note moderately thick lips and rounded mouth. B. River Carpsucker: note relatively thin lips and angular mouth; lower lip with median nipplelike projection. C. White Sucker: note thick, papillose lips. Drawings by Gene Pacheco.

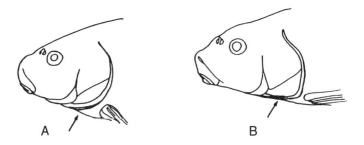

Figure 32. Lateral view of heads of fishes. A. Lower margin of subopercle evenly curved. B. Lower margin of opercle angular. Drawings by Anne Musser, Linda Greatorex, and Joseph T. Collins.

4. Mouth terminal and oblique; anterior tip of upper lip nearly level with lower edge of eye; lips thin; upper jaw about as long as snout .... Bigmouth Buffalo, *Ictiobus cyprinellus*

Mouth ventral and horizontal; tip of upper lip far below level of eye; lips fleshy; upper jaw shorter than snout 5

5. Distance from tip of lower jaw to end of maxilla equal to or greater than eye diameter in young, about twice eye diameter in adults; height of anterior rays in dorsal and anal fins often less than ⅔ head length; greatest depth of body 2.6–3.2 in standard length; not notably ridgebacked .... Black Buffalo, *Ictiobus niger*

Distance from tip of lower jaw to end of maxilla less than eye diameter in young, about equal to eye diameter in adults; height of anterior dorsal and anal fin rays greater than ⅔ head length; greatest depth of body 2.2–2.8 in standard length; back highly arched, ridgelike .... Smallmouth Buffalo, *Ictiobus bubalus*

6. Mouth farther forward than nostrils; front of lower lip rounded; distance from tip of snout to anterior nostril greater than diameter of eye; lateral line scales usually 37 or more .... Quillback, Carpiodes cyprinus

Mouth almost directly below nostrils; front of lower lip with small, median, nipplelike projection (Fig. 31B); distance from tip of snout to anterior nostril less than diameter of eye; lateral-line scales 34–36 7

7. Anterior (longest) rays of dorsal fin exceeding basal length of fin; body depth goes less than 2.7 times in standard length; anal rays 8–9, pelvic rays usually ten .... Highfin Carpsucker, *Carpiodes velifer*

Anterior (longest) rays of dorsal fin shorter than basal length of fin; body depth goes 2.7 or more times in standard length; anal rays 7–8, pelvic rays usually nine .... River Carpsucker, *Carpiodes carpio*

8. Lips papillose (Fig. 31C) 9

Lips plicate (Fig. 33) 10

9. Lateral-line scales 45–54; distance from hind margin of orbit to upper end of gill cleft contained 2.0 or more times in snout length; pelvic rays usually nine .... Northern Hogsucker, *Hypentelium nigricans*

Lateral-line scales more than 55; distance from hind margin of orbit to upper end of gill cleft contained less than 2.0 times in snout length; pelvic rays usually ten .... White Sucker, *Catostomus commersonii*

10. Lower lip thin, not coarsely striated, its width at center contained 2.5 or more times in width of gape (Fig. 33A); sides usually striped by rows of dots; air bladder divided into two chambers .... Spotted Sucker, *Minytrema melanops*

Lower lip thick, coarsely striated, its width at center contained less than 2.5 times in width of gape; sides never conspicuously striped by rows of dots; air bladder divided into three chambers..................................... 11

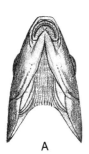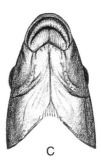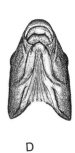

A   B   C   D

Figure 33. Differing forms of mouths in suckers having plicate lips. A. Spotted Sucker. B. Black Redhorse. C. Golden Redhorse. D. Shorthead Redhorse. Drawings by Gene Pacheco.

11. Pharyngeal arch fragile, with slender teeth in comblike series (Fig. 7A); no semicircular line of melanophores on caudal lobes; caudal fin red or not 12

    Pharyngeal arch heavy, with molarlike teeth (Fig. 7B); last caudal scales outlined by melanophores, forming a semicircular line of pigment on each lobe of caudal fin; caudal fin red in life
    .... River Redhorse, *Moxostoma carinatum*

12. Posterior margin of lower lip notched rather than straight across, the right and left halves meeting at an obtuse angle (Fig. 33B or C); plicae of lower lip not broken by transverse grooves; upper lip not thickened at center; caudal fin not red 13

    Posterior margin of lower lip nearly straight or convex (Fig. 33D); plicae of lower lip partly broken by transverse grooves; upper lip thickened medially in most examples; caudal fin red in life
    .... Shorthead Redhorse, *Moxostoma macrolepidotum*

13. Lateral-line scales fewer than 45; pelvic rays nine
    .... Golden Redhorse, *Moxostoma erythrurum*

    Lateral-line scales usually 45 or more; pelvic rays usually ten
    .... Black Redhorse, *Moxostoma duquesnii*

KEY TO THE CATFISHES (FAMILY ICTALURIDAE)

1. Caudal fin deeply forked 2
   Caudal fin not forked 3

2. Anal rays 24–29 (Fig. 8A); margin of anal fin curved
   .... Channel Catfish, *Ictalurus punctatus*

   Anal rays 32–35; margin of anal fin nearly straight
   .... Blue Catfish, *Ictalurus furcatus*

3. Adipose fin completely separated from caudal fin (Fig. 34A) 4

   Adipose fin joined to caudal fin (Fig. 34B) 7

4. Anal rays 14–17 (Fig. 8A); premaxillary band of teeth continuous back-ward along sides of jaw (Fig. 35A) .... Flathead Catfish, *Pylodictis olivaris*

   Anal rays usually more than seventeen; premaxillary band of teeth con-fined to front of jaw (Fig. 35B) 5

5. Anal rays 24–27; chin barbels white, no darker than underside of head; caudal fin usually rounded .... Yellow Bullhead, *Ameiurus natalis*

   Anal rays 17–24; chin barbels pigmented, darker than underside of head; caudal fin slightly notched 6

6. Anal rays 17–21; pectoral spine nearly smooth posteriorly; body and anal fin not mottled, belly yellowish

   .... Black Bullhead, *Ameiurus melas*

   Anal rays 21–24; pectoral spine saw-edged posteriorly; body and anal fin often mottled or barred, belly white

   .... Brown Bullhead, *Ameiurus nebulosus*

7. Body conspicuously mottled; caudal fin vertically banded or with dark basal bar; posterior end of dorsal fin base about equidistant from tip of snout and base of caudal fin (central rays), or nearer the latter 8

   Body color plain or nearly so; caudal fin without vertical dark bars; pos-terior end of dorsal fin base nearer tip of snout than base of central caudal rays 9

8. Dark blotch on adipose fin extending to fin margin; dorsal and caudal fins black-tipped; least depth of caudal peduncle contained about 3.0 times in distance from adipose notch to posterior end of dorsal fin base

   .... Brindled Madtom, *Noturus miurus*

   Dark blotch on adipose fin not extending to fin margin; dorsal and cau-dal fins with dark bands medially, not black-tipped; least depth of cau-dal peduncle contained 3.5 or more times in distance from adipose notch to posterior end of dorsal fin base

   .... Neosho Madtom, *Noturus placidus*

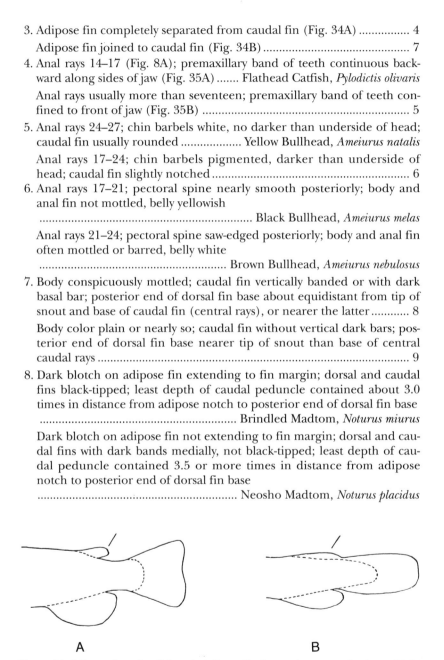

A   B

Figure 34. Adipose fins of catfishes. A. Adipose fin free, as in genera *Ameiurus, Ictalu-rus,* and *Pylodictis.* B. Adipose fin adnate (joined) to caudal fin, as in genus *Noturus.* Drawings by Thomas H. Swearingen.

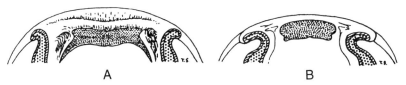

Figure 35. Upper jaws of two kinds of catfish, illustrating differences in form of premaxillary toothpatch (central stippled area, above letter A and letter B). A. With backward extensions of toothpatch along each side of jaw. B. Without backward extensions of toothpatch. Drawings by Thomas H. Swearingen.

9. Upper and lower jaws approximately equal 10

   Lower jaw shorter than upper jaw (snout projecting beyond mouth) ... 11

10. Notch at juncture of adipose and caudal fins much nearer tip of depressed dorsal fin than end of caudal fin; body stout; fins evenly pigmented (not dark-edged) .... Tadpole Madtom, *Noturus gyrinus*

   Notch at juncture of adipose and caudal fins nearer tip of caudal fin than tip of depressed dorsal fin; body slender; dorsal, caudal, and anal fins dark-edged, pale basally .... Slender Madtom, *Noturus exilis*

11. Band of teeth on upper jaw with backward extension on each side of jaw (Fig. 35A); pectoral spine saw-edged anteriorly; caudal fin light-edged dorsally and ventrally, with broad central dark band from base to tip .... Stonecat, *Noturus flavus*

   Teeth on upper jaw confined to narrow band without backward extensions (Fig. 35B); pectoral spine nearly smooth anteriorly; caudal fin uniformly dark or narrowly white-edged .... Freckled Madtom, *Noturus nocturnus*

KEY TO THE TOPMINNOWS AND KILLIFISHES
(FAMILY FUNDULIDAE)

1. Dorsal fin with 9–11 rays (total count; Fig. 8A), originating behind origin of anal fin; scales fewer than forty in lengthwise series 2

   Dorsal fin with 13–16 rays (total count), originating over or in front of origin of anal fin; scales more than forty in lengthwise series 3

2. Sides with broad black lateral band, continuous around snout; caudal peduncle slender, its least depth goes 7.5 or more times in standard length .... Blackstripe Topminnow, *Fundulus notatus*

   Sides plain, without dark lateral band; caudal peduncle deep, its least depth goes 6.5 or less times in standard length
   .... Plains Topminnow, *Fundulus sciadicus*

3. Sides with 12–20 dark vertical bars; lateral scales partly embedded, in more than fifty rows; gill membrane joined to body wall below upper end of opercle, opposite upper end of pectoral fin base
   .... Plains Killifish, *Fundulus zebrinus*

Sides plain or with fine longitudinal streaks; lateral scales exposed, in 40–45 rows; gill membrane joined to body wall at upper end of opercle, above upper end of pectoral fin base
.... Northern Studfish, *Fundulus catenatus*

KEY TO THE TEMPERATE BASSES (FAMILY MORONIDAE)

Body depth in adults greater than head length, more than ⅓ of standard length; lateral stripes weak and often interrupted; anal rays usually 12–13; lateral-line scales 50–58; tongue with one tooth patch, two coalescent patches, or two patches unequal in size .... White Bass, *Morone chrysops*
Body depth less than head length, less than ⅓ of standard length; lateral stripes prominent and usually continuous; anal rays usually 9–11; lateral-line scales 57–67; tongue with two distinct tooth patches of equal size .... Striped Bass, *Morone saxatilis*

KEY TO THE SUNFISHES (FAMILY CENTRARCHIDAE)

1. Anal fin spines 5–7... 2
   Anal fin spines three... 4
2. Dorsal fin spines 11–12 .... Rock Bass, *Ambloplites rupestris*
   Dorsal fin spines 5–8.. 3
3. Dorsal fin spines 5–6; length of dorsal fin base less than distance from origin of dorsal fin to eye .... White Crappie, *Pomoxis annularis*
   Dorsal fin spines 7–8; length of dorsal fin base equal to or greater than distance from origin of dorsal fin to eye
   .... Black Crappie, *Pomoxis nigromaculatus*
4. Greatest depth of body usually less than ⅓ standard length; lateral-line scales more than 55.. 5
   Greatest depth of body more than ⅓ standard length; lateral-line scales fewer than 55 7
5. Dorsal fin deeply notched, shortest posterior spine less than ½ length of longest spine; anal and soft dorsal fins scaleless; scales on cheeks large, in 9–12 rows .... Largemouth Bass, *Micropterus salmoides*
   Dorsal fin slightly notched, shortest posterior spine more than ½ length of longest spine; anal and soft dorsal fins with small scales between rays near fin bases; scales on cheeks minute, in more than twelve rows 6
6. Dorsal soft rays twelve; sides with dark lateral band, sometimes broken into blotches; lower sides usually with rows of dark dots anteriorly
   .... Spotted Bass, *Micropterus punctulatus*
   Dorsal soft rays 13–15; sides plain greenish brown, or with indistinct vertical bars .... Smallmouth Bass, *Micropterus dolomieu*

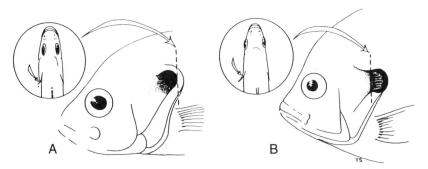

Figure 36. Differences in flexibility of opercles in sunfishes. A. Opercle inflexible posteriorly, its bony edge sharply defined where joined by the marginal gill-membrane (as in the Warmouth, Green Sunfish, and Redear Sunfish). B. Opercle flexible posteriorly, attenuated as a thin, fimbriate, cartilaginous extension into the gill membrane (as in the Bluegill, Longear Sunfish, and Orangespotted Sunfish). Drawings by Thomas H. Swearingen.

7. Opercle bone stiff to the posterior edge of the dark "earspot" (only the narrow, transparent marginal membrane flexible; Fig. 36A) 8

   Opercle attenuated into flexible dark "earspot" (Fig. 36B).................. 10

8. Upper jaw shorter than highest dorsal fin spine; pectoral fins long and pointed; gill rakers short, knoblike (Fig. 37A)
   .... Redear Sunfish, *Lepomis microlophus*

   Upper jaw longer than highest dorsal spine; pectoral fins short and rounded; gill rakers long and slender (Fig. 37B) 9

9. Tongue with central patch of sandpaperlike teeth; lateral-line scales fewer than 45; supramaxilla well-developed
   .... Warmouth, *Lepomis gulosus*

   No teeth on tongue; lateral-line scales usually more than 45; supramaxilla weak, inconspicuous .... Green Sunfish, *Lepomis cyanellus*

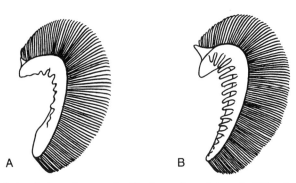

Figure 37. Lateral view of exposed gill rakers of sunfishes. A. Gill rakers short and knoblike. B. Gill rakers long and slender. Drawings by Anne Musser.

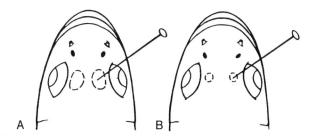

Figure 38. Dorsal view of heads of fishes. A. Supraorbital canals wider than bony space between them. B. Supraorbital canals narrower than bony space between them. Drawings by Anne Musser and Linda Greatorex.

10. Gill rakers short and knoblike (Fig. 37A); pectoral fins short and rounded, less than four times length of pectoral fin base, and less than twice least depth of caudal peduncle; reddish streak on midline of back, before dorsal fin, in life (pallid in preserved specimens) .... Longear Sunfish, *Lepomis megalotis*
Gill rakers long and slender (Fig. 37B), longest when depressed extending to base of second raker below; pectoral fins pointed, their length at least four times length of pectoral base, and at least twice depth of caudal peduncle; no reddish predorsal stripe 11

11. Supraorbital canals (two pitlike depressions atop head between eyes) wider than bony space between them (Fig. 38A); anal soft rays usually nine; length of upper jaw much more than ⅓ length of pectoral fin; opercular projection large in adults and brilliantly white-edged .... Orangespotted Sunfish, *Lepomis humilis*
Supraorbital canals narrower than bony space between them (Fig. 38B); anal soft rays usually 10–12, rarely nine; length of upper jaw less than ⅓ length of pectoral fin; opercular projection short, dusky to its margin .... Bluegill, *Lepomis macrochirus*

KEY TO THE PERCHES (FAMILY PERCIDAE)

1. Preopercle saw-edged; 7–8 branchiostegal rays (Fig. 39A, C)................. 2
Preopercle smooth-edged; 5–6 branchiostegal rays (Fig. 39B, C) 4
2. Jaws with strong canine teeth (Fig. 39A); anal soft rays 12–13; body lacking distinct vertical bars of color in adults 3
Jaws without canine teeth; anal soft rays 6–8; body with series of vertical bars over yellow ground-color .... Yellow Perch, *Perca flavescens*
3. Cheeks well-scaled; dorsal soft rays 17–19; spinous dorsal fin spattered with distinct black spots, without large dark blotch at posterior base of fin; lower lobe of caudal fin not white-tipped .... Sauger, *Stizostedion canadense*

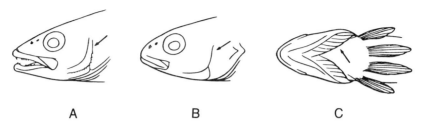

Figure 39. Views of heads of fishes. A. Lateral view showing saw-edged preopercle. B. Lateral view showing smooth-edged preopercle. C. Ventral view showing branchiostegal rays. Drawings by Anne Musser and Linda Greatorex.

Cheeks sparsely scaled; dorsal soft rays 19–22; spinous dorsal fin without distinct dark spots, but with large dark blotch at posterior base; lower lobe of caudal fin white-tipped....................... Walleye, *Stizostedion vitreum*

4. Belly naked or with median row of enlarged spiny scales (one such scale usually present between pelvic fins); pelvic fins separated by space about as wide as base of each pelvic fin (Fig. 40A); anal fin about as large as soft dorsal fin; lateral line complete 5

   Belly usually covered with ordinary scales (sometimes partly naked, but never with enlarged spiny scales on midline or between pelvic fins); space between pelvic fins less than length of fin base (Fig. 40B); anal fin usually smaller than soft dorsal fin; lateral line complete or incomplete 9

5. Snout with conical protuberance projecting forward beyond mouth; lateral-line scales usually more than eighty; sides with alternately long and short vertical bars, interrupted ventrally; large dark spot at base of caudal fin.. Logperch, *Percina caprodes*

   Snout not protruding, jaws terminal or nearly so; lateral-line scales fewer than eighty; color not as above 6

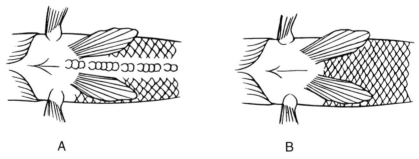

Figure 40. Differences in scales on the belly and in bases of the pelvic fins in darters. A. Belly with a median row of modified scales that are sometimes lost, leaving a naked strip; pelvic fins separated by a space about as wide as the basal length of each pelvic fin (genus *Percina*). B. Belly with scales like those on sides (sometimes partly naked anteriorly, but never with a median scaleless strip); pelvic fins separated by a space less than the basal length of each fin (genus *Etheostoma*). Drawings by Anne Musser.

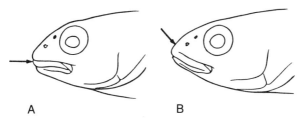

Figure 41. Lateral view of heads of fishes. A. Groove separating upper jaw from front of head continuous. B. Groove separating upper jaw from front of head interrupted. Drawings by Anne Musser and Linda Greatorex.

6. Groove separating upper jaw from front of head continuous across tip of snout (Fig. 41A) (premaxillaries protractile), sometimes finely bridged to snout in *Percina shumardi;* lateral-line scales fewer than 65... 7

   Groove separating upper jaw from front of head interrupted at tip of snout (Fig. 41B), bridged by narrow band of tissue (premaxillaries non-protractile); lateral-line scales more than 65 8

7. Gill membranes connected, their juncture nearer base of pelvic fins than tip of snout (Fig. 42A); cheeks scaly; prominent dark bar below eye; sides with diffuse, vertically elongate blotches
   .... River Darter, *Percina shumardi*

   Gill membranes separate, their juncture nearer tip of snout than base of pelvic fins (Fig. 42B); cheeks usually naked or with embedded scales (sometimes scaly); midsides with line of narrowly connected small dark spots, upper sides with irregular pattern of dark checks
   .... Channel Darter, *Percina copelandi*

8. Gill membranes broadly connected at midventral line, their juncture nearer base of pelvic fins than tip of lower jaw (Fig. 42A); spinous dorsal fin with orange submarginal bar; sides plain dark-colored or blotched (blotches, if present, more than eight and vertically elongate)
   .... Slenderhead Darter, *Percina phoxocephala*

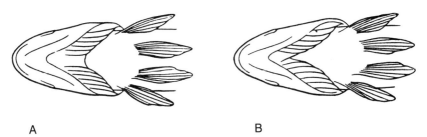

A   B

Figure 42. Ventral view of heads of fishes. A. Gill membranes broadly connected, with juncture nearer to base of pelvic fins than to tip of snout. B. Gill membranes separate, with juncture nearer to tip of snout than to pelvic fins. Drawings by Anne Musser.

A   **B**

Figure 43. Lateral view of anterior portion of anal fins. A. Two anal spines present. B. One anal spine present. Drawings by Anne Musser.

Gill membranes separate, their juncture nearer tip of lower jaw than base of pelvic fins (Fig. 42B); spinous dorsal fin without orange bar; 7–8 horizontally elongate dark blotches on midsides
.... Blackside Darter, *Percina maculata*

9. Premaxillaries protractile (groove, separating upper jaw from front of head, continuous across snout; Fig. 41A)... 10

Premaxillaries nonprotractile (groove along margin of upper jaw interrupted medially; Fig. 41B) 13

10. Anal spines two (Fig. 43A); dorsal spines 11–14 11

Anal spine usually one (Fig. 43B); dorsal spines usually nine 12

11. Mouth ventral, snout rounded; maxillary adnate to preorbital (Fig. 44); lateral line complete; sides with prominent W-markings, breeding males green with scattered red dots
.... Greenside Darter, *Etheostoma blennioides*

Mouth terminal, snout acute; maxillary free from preorbital (Fig. 41); lateral line incomplete; sides without W-markings, breeding males with blue lateral spots and brassy sheen
.... Speckled Darter, *Etheostoma stigmaeum*

12. Lateral line complete; dark bridle on snout interrupted at midline
.... Johnny Darter, *Etheostoma nigrum*

Lateral line incomplete, terminating near middle of body; dark bridle continuous from eye to eye across front of snout above upper lip
.... Bluntnose Darter, *Etheostoma chlorosomum*

Figure 44. Head of Greenside Darter showing ventral mouth and rounded snout. Maxillary not evident. Drawing by Anne Musser and Linda Greatorex.

13. Lateral line absent or nearly so; fewer than 38 scales in lengthwise series; total spines and soft rays in dorsal fins seventeen or fewer
.... Least Darter, *Etheostoma microperca*

Lateral line present, with more than seven pored scales; more than 38
scales in lengthwise (lateral-line) series; total spines and soft rays in dorsal fins usually more than seventeen 14

14. Gill membranes broadly connected at midventral line (Fig. 42A) 15

Gill membranes separate (or only narrowly joined; Fig. 42B) 17

15. Cheeks and opercles fully scaled; snout bluntly decurved, mouth horizontal, lateral line complete; breeding males with bright green vertical
bars .... Banded Darter, *Etheostoma zonale*

Cheeks and opercles mostly naked; snout pointed, mouth oblique; lateral line incomplete; never with bright green pigment 16

16. Dorsal spines usually 10–11; breeding males with red and blue pigment
on fins, scattered red dots on sides ..... Redfin Darter, *Etheostoma whipplii*

Dorsal spines usually 7–8; breeding males lacking red and blue pigment
(fins barred and sides lined by brownish black pigment)
.... Fantail Darter, *Etheostoma flabellare*

17. Lateral line arched anteriorly, parallel with dorsal body contour; cheeks
scaly; caudal peduncle slender, its least depth much less than half its
length .... Slough Darter, *Etheostoma gracile*

Lateral line nearly straight; cheeks usually naked; least depth of caudal
peduncle not less than half its length 18

18. Infraorbital canal incomplete (interrupted below eye; Fig. 45A); upper
jaw terminating below anterior margin of orbit (length of upper
jaw, when projected into snout length, not intersecting pupil); sides
horizontally lined or with dark vertical bars on caudal peduncle; breeding males with much blue pigment
.... Orangethroat Darter, *Etheostoma spectabile*

Infraorbital canal complete (Fig. 45B); upper jaw extending posteriorly
beyond vertical line from anterior rim of orbit (length of upper jaw,
when projected into snout length, intersecting pupil); sides mottled

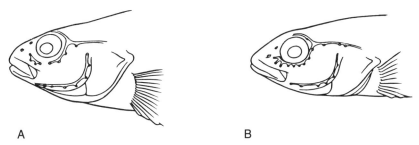

A   B

Figure 45. Lateral view of heads of fishes. A. Infraorbital canal incomplete below
eye. B. Infraorbital canal complete below eye. Drawings by Anne Musser.

brown, never lined or barred on caudal peduncle; breeding males lacking blue pigment 19

19. Lateral line with more than 25 pored scales; total spines and soft rays in dorsal fins 23 or more; snout acute, usually longer than eye
.... Stippled Darter, *Etheostoma punctulatum*

Lateral line with fewer than 25 pored scales; total spines and soft rays in dorsal fins 22 or fewer; snout rounded, usually shorter than eye
.... Arkansas Darter, *Etheostoma cragini*

GLOSSARY

Abdominal: pertaining to the belly; pelvic fins abdominal when inserted far behind the bases of pectoral fins (Fig. 3A).

Acute: sharply pointed.

Adipose fin: fleshy, rayless fin on the midline of the back between the dorsal and caudal fins (Fig. 3A).

Adnate: grown together or joined (Fig. 35B).

Air bladder: membranous, gas-filled sac in the upper part of the body cavity.

Anal fin: ventral unpaired fin (Fig. 3).

Axillary process: A thin free flap of a membrane at the inner base of the pectoral or pelvic fin.

Barbel: slender, flexible process located near the mouth; tactile and gustatory in function (Figs. 3A, 17D, 18A).

Basioccipital: hindmost bone on the underside of the skull. In the minnow genus *Hybognathus*, the basioccipital bone can be exposed by cutting across the isthmus (throat) and bending the head upward. The posterior process of the basioccipital bone is then seen as a posterior projection into the anterior part of the body cavity; the bone and its attached muscles pivot downward as the head is bent back (Fig. 30).

Belly: ventral surface posterior to the base of the pelvic fins, anterior to the anal fin (Fig. 3).

Branchiostegal: one of the bones supporting the gill membranes, ventral to the operculum (Figs. 3C, 39C).

Breast: ventral surface anterior to the insertion of the pelvic fins (Fig. 3).

Canine teeth: in fishes, conical teeth, in the front part of the jaws, that project beyond the others.

Caudal fin: tail fin (Fig. 3).

Caudal peduncle: narrow region of the body in front of the caudal fin (from the posterior end of the base of the anal fin to the base of the caudal fin; Fig. 3).

Cheek: area between the eye and the preopercle bone (Fig. 3C).

Compressed: narrow from side to side (flattened laterally).

Concave: curved inward (hollowed).

Convex: curved outward (arched).

Depressed: flattened from top to bottom; wider than deep.

Distal: remote from point of attachment (free edge of fins, farthest from their bases).

Dorsal: pertaining to the back; often used as an abbreviation for the dorsal fin.

Dorsal fin: median unpaired fin (or fins, but excluding the adipose fin) atop the back (Figs. 3, 22).

Entire: in fishes, having an edge (as of a spine or bone) that is smooth rather than notched or toothed (like a saw).

Falcate: sickle-shaped (with a concave margin).

Fin ray: a bony or cartilaginous rod supporting the fin membrane. *Soft rays* usually are segmented (cross-striated), often branched, and flexible near their tips (Figs. 2, 3, 8), whereas *spines* are not segmented, are never branched, and usually are stiff to their sharp distal tips (Fig. 3B).

Fontanelle: aperture or opening in a bony surface.

Gape: refers to the mouth. In fishes, width of gape is the transverse distance between the two ends of the mouth cleft, when the mouth is closed; length of gape is the diagonal distance from the anterior (median) end of the lower lip to one end of the mouth cleft.

Gill membranes: membranes that close the gill cavity ventrolaterally, supported by the branchiostegals (Fig. 6).

Gill rakers: projections (knobby or comblike) from the concave anterior surface of the gill arches (Fig. 5).

Gonopodium: modified anal fin of the fish genus *Gambusia* and its relatives, used in the transfer of sperm to the genital pore of the female.

Gular plate: large, median, dermal bone on the throat (as in the Bowfin).

Heterocercal: the caudal fin is heterocercal if the vertebral column turns upward into the dorsal lobe (Fig. 2).

Homocercal: the caudal fin is homocercal if the posterior vertebra is modified to support the entire fin; neither lobe is invaded by the vertebral column (Fig. 2).

Infraorbital canal: segment of the lateral-line canal that curves beneath the eye and extends forward onto the snout (Fig. 3C).

Insertion (of fins): anterior end of the bases of paired fins (Figs. 3, 22).

Interopercle: small bone of the gill cover situated between the preopercle and the subopercle (Fig. 3C).

Isthmus: contracted part of the breast that projects forward between (and separates) the gill chambers (Figs. 3, 6).

Lateral line: system of sensory tubules communicating to the body surface by pores; refers most often to a longitudinal row of scales that bear tubules and pores. *Incomplete* if only the anterior scales in the row have pores; *complete* if all scales in that row (to base of caudal fin) have pores (Fig. 3).

Mandible: principal bone of the lower jaw (Fig. 3C).

Mandibular pores: pores along a tubule that traverses the underside of each lower jaw (part of the lateral-line system; Fig. 3C).

Maxilla (maxillary): bone of each upper jaw that lies immediately above (or behind) and parallel to the premaxilla (Fig. 3C).

Melanophore: black pigment-cell.

Nape: dorsal part of the body from the occiput to the origin of the dorsal fin (Fig. 3).

Nares: nostrils; in fishes, each nostril usually has an anterior and a posterior narial opening, located above and in front of the eyes (Fig. 3).

Nonprotractile: not protrusible; premaxillaries are nonprotractile if they are not fully separated from the snout by a continuous groove (Figs. 3C, 16A).

Nuptial tubercles: hardened, often thornlike projections from the skin, seen in adult males of many fishes during their breeding season; also called pearl organs.

Occiput: in fishes, the posterior dorsal end of the head, often marked by the line separating scaly and scaleless portions of the skin.

Opercle: large posterior bone of the gill cover (Fig. 3).

Orbit: eye socket; orbital diameter is measured from the anterior to the posterior bony rim of the eye socket, whereas eye diameter is measured across the cornea only (and is slightly less than orbital diameter).

Origin (of fins): anterior end of the base of a dorsal fin or anal fin (Figs. 3, 22).

Papillose: covered with papillae (as contrasted with *plicate* when applied to lips of suckers; Fig. 31C).

Pectoral fin: paired fin on the side or on the breast, behind the head (Fig. 3); corresponding to forelimb of a mammal.

Pelvic fin: ventral paired fin, lying below the pectoral fin or between it and the anal fin (Fig. 3).

Peritoneum: membranous lining of the body cavity (Fig. 26).

Pharyngeal teeth: bony projections from the fifth gill arch, which is nonrespiratory and is embedded in tissues behind the gill-bearing arches (Fig. 7).

Plicate: having parallel folds or soft ridges; grooved lips (Fig. 33).

Premaxilla (premaxillary): paired bone at the front of the upper jaw. The right and left premaxillae join anteriorly and form all or part of the border of the jaw (Figs. 3, 35).

Preopercle: sickle-shaped bone that lies behind and below the eye (Fig. 3).

Preoperculomandibular canal: branch of the lateral-line system that extends along the preopercle and mandible (Fig. 3C).

Preorbital: bone forming the anterior rim of the eye socket and extending forward on side of snout.

Principal rays: fin rays that extend to the distal margin of median fins, especially if those fins have a straight leading edge; enumerated by counting only one unbranched ray anteriorly, plus subsequent branched rays (Fig. 8).

Procurrent ("rudimentary") rays: small, contiguous rays at the anterior bases of the dorsal, caudal, and anal fins of many fishes; excluded from the count of *principal* fin rays.

Protractile: capable of being thrust out; in fishes, descriptive of the upper jaw if it is completely separated from the face by a continuous groove (Figs. 3C, 16).

Snout: part of the head anterior to the eye, but not including the lower jaw (Fig. 3).

Soft-ray: see fin ray.

Spine: see fin ray.

Spiracle: orifice on the back part of the head (above and behind the eye) in some fishes (Paddlefish and some sturgeons).

Standard length: distance from the tip of the snout to the structural base of the caudal fin (point at which central caudal rays originate; Fig. 3B).

Subopercle: bony plate immediately below the opercle in the gill cover (Figs. 3C, 32).

Subterminal mouth: mouth that opens slightly ventrally, rather than straight forward from the front of the head; lower jaw closes within the upper jaw rather than being equal to it in its anterior extent.

Supramaxilla: small, movable bone adherent to the upper edge of the maxilla near its posterior tip.

Supraorbital canal: paired branch of the lateral-line system that extends along the top of the head between the eyes and forward onto the snout (Figs. 3C, 38).

Supratemporal canal: branch of the lateral-line system that crosses the top of the head at the occiput, connecting the lateral canals (Fig. 3C).

Terete: cylindrical and tapering with circular cross-section; having a rounded body form, the width and depth about equal.

Thoracic: pertaining to the thorax, including especially the chest in fishes; pelvic fins are thoracic when inserted below pectoral fins (Fig. 3B).

BIBLIOGRAPHY

The following list of books and papers is divided into two sections. The first part is General Works, which are not directly concerned with Kansas fishes. Readers may use these 31 publications to further their knowledge of other aspects of fish biology not covered in this book. In addition, some of these references can help familiarize the reader with fishes in nearby states. The second part is a selected Bibliography for Kansas Fishes, an extensive list of 276 books and papers that in some way deal with or mention fishes in Kansas. This compilation is reasonably comprehensive from 1850 to date with the exception of articles on angling and commercial fish-raising techniques; no attempt has been made to include a complete listing of these, but some appear in our list. With few exceptions, both sections of this bibliography include books and papers in press or appearing in print prior to September 1994.

GENERAL WORKS

Amlacher, E.
    1970.   Textbook of fish diseases. T. F. H. Publ., Jersey City, New Jersey. 302 pp.
Bailey, R. M.
    1956.   A revised list of the fishes of Iowa, with keys for identification. *In* Iowa fish and fishing. J. R. Harlan and E. B. Speaker (eds.). Publ. Iowa Conserv. Comm., Des Moines, pp. 326–377.
Blair, W. F., A. P. Blair, P. Brodkorb, F. R. Cagle, and G. A. Moore
    1968.   Fishes. *In* Vertebrates of the United States. Second ed. McGraw-Hill, New York, pp. 31–210.
Bond, C. E.
    1979.   Biology of fishes. W. B. Saunders, Philadelphia. vii + 514 pp.
Bouc, K.
    1987.   The fish book from Nebraskaland Magazine. Publ. Nebraska Game and Parks Comm. 130 pp.
Breder, C. M., Jr., and D. E. Rosen
    1966.   Modes of reproduction in fishes. Publ. American Mus. Nat. Hist., New York. xv + 941 pp.
Carlander, K. D.
    1969.   Handbook of freshwater fishery biology. Two volumes. Iowa State Univ. Press, Ames.
Collins, J. T. (editor)
    1985.   Natural Kansas. Univ. Press Kansas, Lawrence. xii + 226 pp.
Collins, J. T., S. L. Collins, and B. Gress
    1994.   Kansas wetlands: A wildlife treasury. Univ. Press Kansas, Lawrence. 128 pp.
Curtis, B.
    1949.   The life story of the fish, his morals and manners. Harcourt, Brace, New York. xii + 284 pp.
Eddy, S., and J. C. Underhill
    1978.   How to know the freshwater fishes. Third ed. Wm. C. Brown, Dubuque, Iowa. viii + 215 pp.
Everhart, W. H., and W. R. Seaman
    1971.   Fishes of Colorado. Publ. Colorado Game, Fish and Parks Div., Denver. 77 pp.
Harlan, J. R., E. B. Speaker, and J. Mayhew
    1987.   Iowa fish and fishing. Iowa Dept. Nat. Res., Des Moines. 323 pp.

Herald, E. S.
    1961.   Living fishes of the world. Doubleday, New York. 304 pp.
    1972.   Fishes of North America. Doubleday, New York. 255 pp.
Hocutt, C. H., and E. O. Wiley (editors)
    1986.   The zoogeography of North American freshwater fishes. John Wiley & Sons, New York. xiii + 866 pp.
Johnson, J. E.
    1987.   Protected fishes of the United States and Canada. Publ. American Fisheries Soc., Bethesda, Maryland. 42 pp.
Lee, D. S., C. Gilbert, C. Hocutt, R. Jenkins, D. McAllister, and J. Stauffer, Jr.
    1980.   et seq.
            Atlas of North American freshwater fishes. Publ. North Carolina Biol. Surv., Raleigh. x + 854 pp.
Marshall, N. B.
    1966.   The life of fishes. World Publ., Cleveland and New York. 402 pp.
Matthews, W. J., and D. C. Heins (editors)
    1987.   Community and evolutionary ecology of North American stream fishes. Univ. Oklahoma Press, Norman. viii + 310 pp.
Mayden, R. L. (editor)
    1992.   Systematics, historical ecology, and North American freshwater fishes. Stanford Univ. Press. xxvi + 969 pp.
Miller, R. J., and H. W. Robison
    1973.   The fishes of Oklahoma. Oklahoma State Univ. Press, Stillwater. xii + 246 pp.
Moore, G. A.
    1968.   Fishes. In Blair, W. F., A. P. Blair, P. Brodkorb, F. R. Cagle, and G. A. Moore. Vertebrates of the United States. Second ed. McGraw-Hill, New York, pp. 31–210.
Morris, J., L. Morris, and L. Witt
    1972.   The fishes of Nebraska. Nebraska Game and Parks Comm., Lincoln. 98 pp.
Moyle, P. B., and J. J. Cech, Jr.
    1988.   Fishes: An introduction to ichthyology. Second ed. Prentice-Hall. xii + 559 pp.
Nelson, J. S.
    1994.   Fishes of the world. Third ed. John Wiley & Sons, New York. xvii + 600 pp.
Page, L. M., and B. M. Burr
    1991.   A field guide to freshwater fishes of North America, north of Mexico. Peterson Field Guide 42. Houghton Mifflin, Boston. xii + 432 pp.
Pflieger, W. L.
    1971.   A distributional study of Missouri fishes. Univ. Kansas Publ. Mus. Nat. Hist. 20(3): 225–570.
    1975.   The fishes of Missouri. Publ. Missouri Dept. Conserv., Jefferson City. viii + 343 pp.
Robins, C. R., R. Bailey, C. Bond, J. Brooker, E. Lachner, R. Lea, and W. Scott
    1991.   Common and scientific names of fishes from the United States and Canada. Fifth ed. American Fish. Soc. Spec. Publ. 20: 1–183.
Robison, H. W., and T. M. Buchanan
    1984.   Fishes of Arkansas. Univ. Arkansas Press, Fayetteville. xviii + 536 pp.
Sublette, J. E., M. D. Hatch, and M. Sublette
    1990.   The fishes of New Mexico. Univ. New Mexico Press, Albuquerque. xiii + 393 pp.

Tomelleri, J. R., and M. E. Eberle
  1990.   Fishes of the central United States. Univ. Press Kansas, Lawrence. xv + 226 pp.

SPECIFIC BIBLIOGRAPHY FOR KANSAS FISHES

Abbott, C. C.
  1860a.   Descriptions of four new species of North American Cyprinidae. Proc. Acad. Nat. Sci. Philadelphia 12: 473–474.
  1860b.   Descriptions of two new species of *Pimelodus* from Kansas. Proc. Acad. Nat. Sci. Philadelphia 12: 568–569.
Albaugh, D. W.
  1969.   Sources of growth variation among individual black bullheads, *Ictalurus melas,* and channel catfish, *Ictalurus punctatus.* Trans. American Fisheries Soc. 98(1): 35–44.
Al-Rawi, A. H., and F. B. Cross
  1964.   Variation in the plains minnow, *Hybognathus placitus* Girard. Trans. Kansas Acad. Sci. 67: 154–168.
Anonymous
  1987.   Cheyenne Bottoms: An environmental assessment. Executive summary. Publ. Kansas Biol. Surv. and Kansas Geol. Survey 29 pp.
  1994.   1994 Kansas reservoir and lake fishing forecast. Kansas Wildlife and Parks 51(4): 18–22.
Bailey, R. M.
  1954.   Distribution of the American cyprinid fish, *Hybognathus hankinsoni* with comments on its original distribution. Copeia 1954(4): 289–291.
Bailey, R. M., and F. B. Cross
  1954.   River sturgeons of the American genus *Scaphirhynchus:* Characters, distribution, and synonymy. Papers Michigan Acad. Sci. Arts Letters 39: 169–208.
Bailey, R. M., and W. A. Gosline
  1955.   Variation and systematic significance of vertebral counts in the American fishes of the family Percidae. Misc. Publ. Univ. Michigan Mus. Zool. 93: 1–44.
Bandel, E.
  1932.   Frontier life in the army, 1854–1861 (Ed. by R. P. Bieber.) Southwest Historical Series, 2. Arthur H. Clark, Glendale, California. 330 pp.
Bass, J. C., and J. R. Triplett
  1968.   An addition to the known Kansas fish fauna. Trans. Kansas Acad. Sci. 70(3): 411.
Bass, J. C., J. R. Triplett, and W. T. Walker
  1970.   Fishes in the Kansas segment of the West Fork of Drywood Creek. Southwest. Nat. 15(1): 138–141.
Bonneau, D. L., J. W. McGuire, O. W. Tiemeier, and C. W. Deyoe
  1972.   Food habits and growth of channel catfish fry, *Ictalurus punctatus.* Trans. American Fish. Soc. 101(4): 613–619.
Braasch, M. E., and P. W. Smith
  1967.   The life history of the slough darter, *Etheostoma gracile* (Pisces: Percidae). Illinois Nat. Hist. Surv. Biol. Notes 58: 1–2.

Branson, B. A.
  1962.   Observations on the distribution of nuptial tubercles in some catosto-
           mid fishes. Trans. Kansas Acad. Sci. 64(4): 360–372.
  1963.   The olfactory apparatus of *Hybopsis gelida* (Girard) and *Hybopsis aesti-
           valis* (Girard) (Pisces: Cyprinidae). J. Morphology 113: 215–229.
  1964.   Additions to the known Kansas fish fauna. Trans. Kansas Acad. Sci.
           66(4): 745–746.
  1967.   Fishes of the Neosho River system in Oklahoma. American Midland
           Nat. 78(1): 126–154.
Branson, B. A., and R. Hartmann
  1963.   *Lepisosteus oculatus* (Rafinesque) in Kansas. Copeia 1963(3): 591.
Branson, B. A., J. R. Triplett, and R. Hartmann
  1970.   A partial biological survey of the Spring River drainage in Kansas, Okla-
           homa and Missouri. Part II: The fishes. Trans. Kansas Acad. Sci. 72(4):
           429–472.
Brenner, S. R., and O. W. Tiemeier
  1971.   Lipofuscin accumulation in the channel catfish, *Ictalurus punctatus*.
           Trans. Kansas Acad. Sci. 73(3): 390–393.
Breukelman, J.
  1940a.   The fishes of northwestern Kansas. Trans. Kansas Acad. Sci. 43:
           367–375.
  1940b.   A collection of Kansas fishes in the State University Museum. Trans.
           Kansas Acad. Sci. 43: 377–384.
  1946.   A review of Kansas ichthyology. Trans. Kansas Acad. Sci. 49: 51–
           70.
  1960.   What have I caught? Kansas Forestry, Fish and Game Comm. Bull. 7:
           1–36.
Brown, K. L.
  1987.   Colonization by mosquitofish *(Gambusia affinis)* of a Great Plains river
           basin. Copeia 1987: 336–351.
Brown, L.
  1942.   Propagation of the spotted channel catfish *(Ictalurus lacustrus punc-
           tatus)*. Trans. Kansas Acad. Sci. 45: 311–314.
Burrage, B. R.
  1962.   Notes on some captive minnows, *Pimephales promelas* Rafinesque. Trans.
           Kansas Acad. Sci. 64: 357–359.
Cairns, J., Jr.
  1969.   The need for regional water resource management. Trans. Kansas
           Acad. Sci. 71(4): 480–490.
Caldwell, J., and J. T. Collins
  1977.   New records of fishes, amphibians and reptiles in Kansas. *In* New
           records of the fauna and flora of Kansas for 1976. State Biol. Surv.
           Kansas Tech. Publ. 4: 63–78.
Call, L. E.
  1961.   Agricultural research at Kansas State Agricultural College (KSU) be-
           fore enactment of the Hatch Act (1887). Agric. Exp. Sta. Kansas State
           Univ. Bull. 411: 1–43.
Calovich, F. E., and B. A. Branson
  1964.   The supraethmoid-ethmoid complex in the American catfishes, *Ictalu-
           rus* and *Pylodictis*. American Midland Nat. 71(2): 335–343.

Chanay, M. D., and O. E. Maughan
  1972.   A recent record of the blue sucker *Cycleptus elongatus* in the Kansas River. Trans. Kansas Acad. Sci. 74(1): 112–113.
Clarke, R. F.
  1986.   The invaders. Kansas School Nat. 33(2): 1–16.
Clarke, R. F., J. Breukelman, and T. F. Andrews
  1958.   An annotated list of the vertebrates of Lyon County, Kansas. Trans. Kansas Acad. Sci. 61(2): 165–194.
Clarke, R. F., and J. W. Clarke
  1984.   New county records for Kansas fishes and amphibians. Trans. Kansas Acad. Sci. 87(1–2): 71–72.
Cloutman, D. G.
  1971.   Notes on the distribution of the Arkansas darter, *Etheostoma cragini* Gilbert, with a new record from Bluff Creek, Clark County, Kansas. Trans. Kansas Acad. Sci. 73(4): 431–433.
Collette, B. B.
  1962.   The swamp darters of the subgenus *Hololepis* (Pisces: Percidae). Tulane Studies Zool. 9(4): 115–211.
Collins, J. T.
  1977.   Rediscovery of the shovelnose sturgeon in the Arkansas River of Kansas. Trans. Kansas Acad. Sci. 79(3–4): 159.
  1979.   New records of fishes, amphibians and reptiles in Kansas for 1978. *In* New records of the fauna and flora of Kansas for 1978. State Biol. Surv. Kansas Tech. Publ. 8: 56–66.
  1980.   New records of fishes, amphibians and reptiles in Kansas for 1979. *In* New records of the fauna and flora of Kansas for 1979. State Biol. Surv. Kansas Tech. Publ. 9: 1–11.
  1981.   New records of fishes, amphibians and reptiles in Kansas for 1980. Tech. Publ. State Biol. Surv. Kansas 10: 7–19.
  1982.   New records of fishes in Kansas for 1981. Tech. Publ. State Biol. Surv. Kansas 12: 17–20.
  1983.   New records of fishes, amphibians, and reptiles in Kansas for 1982. Tech. Publ. State Biol. Surv. Kansas 13: 9–21.
  1984a. New records of fishes, amphibians, and reptiles in Kansas for 1983. Kansas Herp. Soc. Newsl. 56: 15–26.
  1984b. New records of fishes, amphibians and reptiles in Kansas for 1984. Kansas Herp. Soc. Newsl. 58: 14–20.
Collins, J. T., and J. Caldwell
  1976.   New records of fishes, amphibians and reptiles. *In* New records of the fauna and flora of Kansas for 1975. State Biol. Surv. Kansas Tech. Publ. 1: 78–97.
  1978.   New records of fishes, amphibians and reptiles in Kansas for 1977. *In* New records of the fauna and flora of Kansas for 1977. State Biol. Surv. Kansas Tech. Publ. 6: 70–88.
Collins, J. T., S. G. Haslouer, C. H. Fromm, and K. L. Brunson
  1987.   New records of fishes in Kansas for 1984 and 1985 including some earlier records previously unreported. Kansas Chapt. American Fisheries Soc. Newsl. 1987(3): 5–9.
  1988.   New records for fishes in Kansas for 1985 to 1987. Kansas Chapt. American Fisheries Soc. Newsl. 1988(3): 4–6.

1991. New records for fishes in Kansas for 1988 and 1989. Kansas Chapt. American Fisheries Soc. Newsl. 1991(1): 4–7.

Cope, E. D.
1864. Partial catalogue of the cold-blooded vertebrata of Michigan (Part 1). Proc. Acad. Nat. Sci. Philadelphia 16: 276–285.
1865a. Partial catalogue of the cold-blooded vertebrata of Michigan (Part 2). Proc. Acad. Nat. Sci. Philadelphia 17: 78–85.
1865b. Note on the fishes brought from the Platte River, near Fort Riley, by Dr. Wm. A. Hammond. Proc. Acad. Nat. Sci. Philadelphia 17: 85–87.
1871. Recent reptiles and fishes. Report on the reptiles and fishes obtained by the naturalists of the expedition. *In* Preliminary report, U.S. Geol. Survey Wyoming 8: 432–442.

Cragin, F. W.
1885a. Note on the chestnut lamprey. Bull. Washburn Lab. Nat. Hist. 1: 99–100.
1885b. Preliminary list of Kansas fishes. Bull. Washburn Lab. Nat. Hist. 1: 105–111.

Cramer, J. D., and G. R. Marzolf
1970. Selective predation on zooplankton by gizzard shad. Trans. American Fisheries Soc. 99(2): 320–332.

Crevecoeur, F. F.
1903. A new species of fish. Trans. Kansas Acad. Sci. 18:177–178.
1908. A new species of *Campostoma?* Trans. Kansas Acad. Sci. 21(1): 155–157.

Cross, F. B.
1953a. Occurrence of the sturgeon chub, *Hybopsis gelida* (Girard) in Kansas. Trans. Kansas Acad. Sci. 56: 90–91.
1953b. Nomenclature in the Pimephalinae, with special reference to the bullhead minnow, *Pimephales vigilax perspicuus* (Girard). Trans. Kansas Acad. Sci. 56: 92–96.
1953c. A new minnow, *Notropis bairdi buccula,* from the Brazos River, Texas. Texas J. Sci. 5(2): 252–259.
1954. Fishes of Cedar Creek and the South Fork of the Cottonwood River, Chase County, Kansas. Trans. Kansas Acad. Sci. 57: 303–314.
1955. Records of fishes little-known from Kansas. Trans. Kansas Acad. Sci. 57: 473–479.
1967. Handbook of fishes of Kansas. Univ. Kansas Mus. Nat. Hist. Misc. Publ. 45: 1–357.

Cross, F. B., and M. Braasch
1969. Qualitative changes in the fish-fauna of the Upper Neosho River system, 1952–1967. Trans. Kansas Acad. Sci. 71(3): 350–360.

Cross, F. B., and J. T. Collins
1975. Fishes in Kansas. Univ. Kansas Mus. Nat. Hist. Pub. Ed. Ser. 3: 1–189.
1992. *Cliola (Hybopsis) topeka* Gilbert, 1884 (currently *Notropis topeka;* Osteichthyes, Cypriniformes): proposed conservation of the specific name. Bull. Zool. Nomen. 49(4): 268–270.

Cross, F. B., J. T. Collins, and J. L. Robertson
1976. Illustrated guide to fishes in Kansas. An identification manual. Univ. Kansas Mus. Nat. Hist. Pub. Ed. Ser. 4: 1–24.

Cross, F. B., W. W. Dalquest, and L. Lewis
1955. First records from Texas of *Hybopsis gracilis* and *Notropis girardi,* with comments on geographic variation of the latter. Texas J. Sci. 7(2): 222–226.

Cross, F. B., J. E. Deacon, and C. M. Ward
   1959.   Growth data on sport fishes in twelve lakes in Kansas. Trans. Kansas
           Acad. Sci. 62: 162–164.
Cross, F. B., F. J. DeNoyelles, and S. C. Leon
   1982.   Impacts of commercial dredging on the fishery of the lower Kansas
           River. Report DACW 41-79-C-0075, U.S. Army Corps of Engineers,
           Kansas City Dist.
Cross, F. B., and O. T. Gorman
   1983.   The Red River shiner, *Notropis bairdi*, in Kansas with notes on depletion
           of its Arkansas River cognate, *Notropis girardi*. Trans. Kansas Acad. Sci.
           86(2–3): 93–98.
Cross, F. B., and S. Haslouer
   1984.   *Pimephales vigilax* (Pisces, Cyprinidae) established in the Missouri River
           basin. Trans. Kansas Acad. Sci. 87: 105–107.
Cross, F. B., and C. E. Hastings
   1956.   Ages and sizes of 29 flathead catfish from the Kansas River, Douglas
           County, Kansas. Trans. Kansas Acad. Sci. 59: 85–86.
Cross, F. B., and A. L. Metcalf
   1963.   Records of three lampreys *(Ichthyomyzon)* from the Missouri River sys-
           tem. Copeia 1963(1): 187.
Cross, F. B., and W. L. Minckley
   1958.   New records of four fishes from Kansas. Trans. Kansas Acad. Sci. 61(1):
           104–108.
   1960.   Five natural hybrid combinations in minnows (Cyprinidae). Univ.
           Kansas Publ. Mus. Nat. Hist. 13: 1–18.
Cross, F. B., and R. E. Moss
   1987.   Historic changes in fish communities and aquatic habitats in plains
           streams of Kansas. *In* Community and evolutionary ecology of North
           American stream fishes. W. J. Matthews and D. C. Heins (eds.). Univ.
           Oklahoma Press, Norman, pp. 155–165.
Cross, F. B., R. E. Moss, and J. T. Collins
   1985.   Assessment of dewatering impacts on stream fisheries in the Arkansas
           and Cimarron rivers (Kansas). Final Report to Kansas Fish and Game
           Comm. 161 pp.
Davis, B. J., and R. J. Miller
   1967.   Brain patterns in minnows of the genus *Hybopsis* in relation to feeding
           habits and habitat. Copeia 1967(1): 1–39.
Davis, W. J.
   1959.   Management of channel catfish in Kansas. Univ. Kansas Mus. Nat. Hist.
           Misc. Publ. 21: 1–56.
Deacon, J. E.
   1961.   Fish populations, following a drought, in the Neosho and Marais des
           Cygnes rivers of Kansas. Univ. Kansas Publ. Mus. Nat. Hist. 12(9):
           259–427.
Deacon, J. E., and A. L. Metcalf
   1961.   Fishes of the Wakarusa River in Kansas. Univ. Kansas Publ. Mus. Nat.
           Hist. 13(6): 309–322.
Distler, D. A.
   1968.   Distribution and variation of *Etheostoma spectabile* (Agassiz) (Percidae,
           Teleostei). Univ. Kansas Sci. Bull. 48(5): 143–208.
   1972.   Observations on the reproductive habits of captive *Etheostoma cragini*
           Gilbert. Southwest. Nat. 16(3–4): 439–441.

Distler, D. A., and A. L. Metcalf
    1962.   *Etheostoma pallididorsum,* a new percid fish from the Caddo River System
             of Arkansas. Copeia 1962(3): 556–561.
Doze, J. B.
    1925.   The barbed trout of Kansas. Trans. American Fisheries Soc. 55: 167–183.
Dyche, L. L.
    1914.   Ponds, pond fish, and pond fish culture. Kansas Dept. Fish and Game
             Bull. 1–208.
Eberle, M. E., G. W. Ernsting, W. J. Stark, J. R. Tomelleri, and T. L. Wenke
    1989.   Recent surveys of fishes from western Kansas. Trans. Kansas Acad. Sci.
             92(1–2): 24–32.
Eberle, M. E., G. W. Ernsting, and J. R. Tomelleri
    1986.   Aquatic macroinvertebrates and fishes of Big Creek in Trego, Ellis, and
             Russell counties, Kansas. Trans. Kansas Acad. Sci. 89(3–4): 146–151.
Eberle, M. E., G. W. Ernsting, J. R. Tomelleri, and S. L. Wells
    1993.   Assessment of restored streamflow on fish communities in the Arkansas
             River of southwestern Kansas. Trans. Kansas Acad. Sci. 96(1–2):
             114–130, with corrections in Trans. Kansas Acad. Sci. 97(1–2): 68.
Ellis, M. M., and B. B. Jaffa
    1918.   Notes on Cragin's darter, *Catonotus cragini* (Gilbert). Copeia 59:
             73–75.
Ernsting, G. W., and M. E. Eberle
    1989.   Distributional records of the Arkansas darter in the Arkansas River of
             central Kansas. Prairie Nat. 21(2): 111–112.
Ernsting, G. W., M. E. Eberle, and T. L. Wenke
    1989.   Range extensions for three species of madtoms (*Noturus:* Ictaluridae)
             in Kansas. Trans. Kansas Acad. Sci. 92(3–4): 206–207.
Evermann, B. W., and U. O. Cox
    1896.   Report upon the fishes of the Missouri River Basin. Dept. U.S. Fish
             Comm. (1894): 325–429.
Evermann, B. W., and M. W. Fordice
    1886.   List of fishes collected in Harvey and Cowley counties, Kansas. Bull.
             Washburn Lab. Nat. Hist. 1: 184–186.
Fisher, H. J.
    1962.   Some fishes of the lower Missouri River. American Midland Nat. 68(2):
             424–429.
Fitch, H. S.
    1958.   Home ranges, territories, and seasonal movements of vertebrates of the
             Natural History Reservation. Univ. Kansas Publ. Mus. Nat. Hist. 11(3):
             63–326.
Fowler, H. W.
    1910.   Notes on the variation of some species of the genus *Notropis.* Proc.
             Acad. Nat. Sci. Philadelphia 62: 273–293.
    1925.   Notes on North American cyprinoid fishes. Proc. Acad. Nat. Sci.
             Philadelphia 76: 389–416.
    1945.   A study of the fishes of the southern Piedmont and Coastal Plain.
             Monogr. Acad. Nat. Sci. Philadelphia 7: 1–408.
Fuselier, L.
    1993.   Habitat restoration and seasonal habitat use by Neosho madtoms (*Noturus placidus*), and spatio-temporal variation of fish assemblages in the
             Cottonwood River, Kansas. Masters thesis, Emporia St. Univ. Emporia,
             Kansas. 113 pp.

Fuselier, L., and D. R. Edds

1993.   *Phoxinus erythrogaster* (Cypriniformes: Cyprinidae) range extension in Kansas. Trans. Kansas Acad. Sci. 96(3–4): 227–228.

1994.   Seasonal variation in habitat use by the Neosho madtom (Teleostei: Ictaluridae: *Noturus placidus*). Southwest. Nat. 39(3): 217–223.

Gabelhouse, D. W., Jr., R. L. Hager, and H. E. Klaassen

1987.   Producing fish and wildlife from Kansas ponds. Publ. Kansas Dept. Wildlife and Parks, Pratt. 57 pp.

Gash, R., and S. Gash

1973.   Helminth fauna of Centrarchidae from two stripmine lakes and a stream in Crawford County, Kansas. Trans. Kansas Acad. Sci. 75(3): 236–244.

Gash, S. L., and J. C. Bass

1974.   Age, growth and population structures of fishes from acid and alkaline strip-mine lakes in southeast Kansas. Trans. Kansas Acad. Sci. 76(1): 39–50.

Gash, S. L., R. Gash, J. R. Triplett, R. Tafanelli, and J. C. Bass

1973.   Helminth parasites of Drywood Creek fishes in Bourbon and Crawford Counties, Kansas. Trans. Kansas Acad. Sci. 75(3): 245–250.

Gibbs, R. H., Jr.

1957.   Cyprinid fishes of the subgenus Cyprinella of *Notropis*. II. Distribution and variation of *Notropis spilopterus,* with the description of a new subspecies. Lloydia 20(3): 186–211.

1961.   Cyprinid fishes of the subgenus Cyprinella of *Notropis*. IV. The *Notropis galacturus-camurus* complex. American Midland Nat. 66(2): 337–354.

Gier, H. T.

1967.   Vertebrates of the Flint Hills. Trans. Kansas Acad. Sci. 70(1): 51–59.

Gilbert, C. H.

1884.   Notes on the fishes of Kansas. Bull. Washburn Lab. Nat. Hist. 1: 10–16.

1885a.   Description of three new fishes from Kansas. Proc. U.S. Natl. Mus. 7(32): 512–514.

1885b.   Second series of notes on the fishes of Kansas. Bull. Washburn Lab. Nat. Hist. 1: 97–99.

1886.   Third series of notes on Kansas fishes. Bull. Washburn Lab. Nat. Hist. 1: 207–211.

1887.   Descriptions of new and little known etheostomids. Proc. U.S. Natl. Mus. 10: 47–64.

1889.   Fourth series of notes on the fishes of Kansas. Bull. Washburn Lab. Nat. Hist. 2: 38–43.

Gilbert, C. R.

1964.   The American cyprinid fishes of the subgenus Luxilus (genus *Notropis*). Bull. Florida State Mus. 8(2): 95–194.

Gilbert, C. R., and R. M. Bailey

1962.   Synonymy, characters, and distribution of the American cyprinid fish *Notropis shumardi.* Copeia 1962(4): 807–819.

Gill, T.

1862.   Descriptions of new species of Pimelodinae. Proc. Boston Soc. Nat. Hist. 8: 42–46.

1864.   [Untitled description of *Percopsis hammondii*]. Proc. Acad. Nat. Sci. Philadelphia 16: 151.

Girard, C.

1856.   Researches upon the cyprinoid fishes inhabiting the fresh waters of the United States, west of the Mississippi Valley, from specimens in the museum of the Smithsonian Institution. Proc. Acad. Nat. Sci. Philadelphia 8:165–213.

1858. Fishes [in general report on zoology]. U.S. Pacific Railroad Surveys 10(4): 1–400.

Graham, I. D.
1885a. Some Kansas fishes now in the college museum. Industrialist 10(30): 4.
1885b. Preliminary list of Kansas fishes. Trans. Kansas Acad. Sci. 9: 69–78.

Gray, M. W.
1968. Water pollution and agriculture. Suppl. Trans. Kansas Acad. Sci. 70(3): 30–38.

Greer, J. K., and F. B. Cross
1956. Fishes of El Dorado City Lake, Butler County, Kansas. Trans. Kansas Acad. Sci. 59: 358–363.

Hall, H. H.
1934. An ecological study of the fishes of Mineral Lake, Kansas. Trans. Kansas Acad. Sci. 37: 225–233.

Harms, C. E.
1960a. Checklist of parasites from catfishes of northeastern Kansas. Trans. Kansas Acad. Sci. 62: 262.
1960b. Some parasites of catfishes from Kansas. J. Parasit. 46(6): 695–701.

Haslouer, S. G., M. S. Cringan, and J. E. Fry
1987. New county records for fishes in Kansas. Trans. Kans. Acad. Sci. 90: 85–86.

Hastings, C. E., and F. B. Cross
1962. Farm ponds in Douglas County, Kansas. Univ. Kansas Mus. Nat. Hist. Misc. Publ. 29: 1–21.

Hay, O. P.
1887. A contribution to the knowledge of the fishes of Kansas. Proc. U.S. Natl. Mus. 10: 242–253.

Herin, K. C.
1987. South Lawrence Trafficway wetlands functional assessment. Publ. Kansas Dept. Transportation. ii + 13 pp.

Hesse, L. W., G. E. Mestl, and J. W. Robinson
1993. Status of selected fishes in the Missouri River in Nebraska with recommendations for their recovery. In Proceedings of the symposium on restoration planning for the rivers of the Mississippi River ecosystem. L. W. Hesse, C. B. Stalnaker, N. G. Benson, and J. R. Zuboy (eds.). U.S. Dept. Interior, Natl. Biol. Surv., Biol. Report 19, Washington, D.C. [vii + 502 pp], pp. 327–340.

Hoy, P. R.
1872. Journal of an exploration of western Missouri in 1854, under the auspices of the Smithsonian Institution. Smithsonian Inst. Ann. Rept. for 1864: 431–438.

Hoyle, W. L.
1937. Notes on faunal collecting in Kansas. Trans. Kansas Acad. Sci. 39: 283–293.

Hubbs, C. L.
1930. Materials for a revision of the catostomid fishes of eastern North America. Misc. Publ. Univ. Michigan Mus. Zool. 20: 1–47.
1945. Corrected distributional records for Minnesota fishes. Copeia 1945(1): 13–22.
1951a. The American cyprinid fish Notropis germanus Hay interpreted as an intergeneric hybrid. American Midland Nat. 45(2): 446–454.

1951b. Identification of cyprinid fish reported from Kansas as *Squalius elonga-tus.* Trans. Kansas Acad. Sci. 54(2): 190–192.

Hubbs, C. L., and J. D. Black
1941. The subspecies of the American percid fish, *Poecilichthys whipplii.* Occ. Papers Univ. Michigan Mus. Zool. 429: 1–27.
1947. Revision of *Ceratichthys,* a genus of American cyprinid fishes. Misc. Publ. Univ. Michigan Mus. Zool. 66: 1–56.

Hubbs. C. L., and K. Bonhan
1951. New cyprinid fishes of the genus *Notropis* from Texas. Texas J. Sci. 3(1): 91–110.

Hubbs, C., and M. D. Cannon
1935. The darters of the genera *Hololepis* and *Villora.* Misc. Publ. Univ. Michigan Mus Zool. 30: 1–93.

Hubbs, C. L., and W. R. Crowe
1956. Preliminary analysis of the American cyprinid fishes, seven new, referred to the genus *Hybopsis,* subgenus Erimystax. Occ. Papers Univ. Michigan Mus. Zool. 578: 1–8.

Hubbs, C. L., and C. W. Greene
1928. Further notes on the fishes of the Great Lakes and tributary waters. Papers Mich. Acad. Sci. Arts Letters 8: 371–392.
1935. Two new subspecies of fishes from Wisconsin. Trans. Wisconsin Acad. Sci. Arts Letters 29: 89–101.

Hubbs, C. L., and G. A. Moore
1940. The subspecies of *Notropis zonatus,* and cyprinid fish of the Ozark Upland. Copeia 1940(2): 91–99.

Hubbs, C. L., and A. I. Ortenburger
1929a. Further notes on the fishes of Oklahoma with descriptions of new species of Cyprinidae. Publ. Univ. Oklahoma Biol. Surv., 1(2): 15–43.
1929b. Fishes collected in Oklahoma and Arkansas in 1927. Publ. Univ. Oklahoma Biol. Surv., 1(3): 45–112.

Hubbs, C. L., and E. C. Raney
1944. Systematic notes on North American siluroid fishes of the genus *Schilbeodes.* Occ. Papers Univ. Michigan Mus. Zool. 487: 1–41.

Hubbs. C. L., and M. B. Trautman
1937. A revision of the lamprey genus *Ichthyomyzon.* Misc. Publ. Univ. Michigan Mus. Zool. 35: 1–113.

Jennings, D.
1942. Kansas fish in the Kansas State College Museum at Manhattan. Trans. Kansas Acad. Sci. 45: 363–366.

Johnson, D. W., and W. L. Minckley
1969. Natural hybridization in buffalofishes, genus *Ictiobus.* Copeia 1969(1): 198–200.

Jordan, D. S.
1877a. Contributions to North American ichthyology: Notes on Cottidae, Etheostomatidae, Percidae, Centrarchidae, Aphododeridae, Umbridae, Esocidae, Corysomatidae, Cyprinidae, Catostomidae, and Hyodontidae, with revisions of the genera and descriptions of new or little known species. Bull. U.S. Natl. Mus. 10: 5–68.
1877b. Contributions to North American ichthyology: Synopsis of the freshwater Siluridae of the United States. Bull. U.S. Natl. Mus. 10: 69–120.
1878. A synopsis of the family Catostomidae. Bull. U.S. Natl. Mus. 12: 97–230.

1891.   Report of explorations in Colorado and Utah during the summer of 1889, with an account of the fishes found in each of the river basins examined. Bull. U.S. Fish Comm. 9: 1–40.

Jordan, D. S., and A. W. Brayton
1878.   Contributions to North American ichthyology: On the distribution of the fishes of the Allegheny Region of South Carolina, Georgia, and Tennessee, with descriptions of new or little known species. Bull. U.S. Natl. Mus. 12: 7–95.

Jordan, D. S., and B. W. Evermann
1896.   The fishes of North and Middle America. Bull. U.S. Natl. Mus. 47(1): 1–1240.

1900.   The fishes of North and Middle America. Bull. U.S. Natl. Mus. 47(4): 3137–3313.

Jordan, D. S., and C. H. Gilbert
1882.   Synopsis of the fishes of North America. Bull. U.S. Natl. Mus. 16: 1–1018.

1886.   List of fishes collected in Arkansas, Indian Territory, and Texas, in September, 1884, with notes and descriptions. Proc. U.S. Natl. Mus. 9: 1–25.

Jordan, D. S., and S. E. Meek
1884.   Description of four new species of Cyprinidae in the United States National Museum. Proc. U.S. Natl. Mus. 7(30): 474–477.

1885.   List of fishes collected in Iowa and Missouri in August, 1884, with descriptions of three new species. Proc. U.S. Natl. Mus. 8(1): 1–17.

Judd, C. E., and F. B. Cross
1966.   Tissue-damages in livers of channel catfish, *Ictalurus punctatus,* raised on artificial diets in ponds. Trans. Kansas Acad. Sci. 69(1): 48–57.

Kerns, H. A., and S. C. Leon
1982.   The occurrence of the Topeka Shiner *Notropis topeka* (Gilbert) in Buck Creek, Jefferson County, Kansas. Trans. Kansas Acad. Sci. 85(1): 57–58.

Kilgore, D. L., and J. D. Rising
1965.   Fishes from southwestern Kansas. Trans. Kansas Acad. Sci. 68(1): 137–144.

Klaassen, H. E., and F. W. Cook, Jr.
1974.   Age and growth of the freshwater drum in Tuttle Creek Reservoir, Kansas. Trans. Kansas Acad. Sci. 76(3): 244–247.

Klaassen, H. E., and M. K. Eisler
1971.   Age and growth of the channel catfish in the Smoky Hill River of western Kansas. Trans. Kansas Acad. Sci. 73(4): 439–445.

Klaassen, H. E., and G. R. Marzolf
1971.   Relationships between distributions of benthic insects and bottom feeding fishes in Tuttle Creek Reservoir. *In* Reservoir fisheries and limnology. G. E. Hall (ed.). American Fisheries Soc. Spec. Pub. 8, Washington, D.C., pp. 385–395.

Klaassen, H. E., and K. L. Morgan
1974.   Age and growth of longnose gar in Tuttle Creek Reservoir, Kansas. Trans. American Fisheries Soc. 103(2): 402–405.

Klaassen, H. E., and A. H. Townsend
1974.   Age and growth of the channel catfish in Tuttle Creek Reservoir, Kansas. Trans. Kansas Acad. Sci. 76(3): 248–253.

Layher, W. G.
1988.   Taking care of our own. Kansas Wildlife Magazine 45(1): 7–14.

1993. Changes in fish community structure resulting from a flood control dam in a Flint Hills stream, Kansas, with emphasis on the Topeka shiner. Univ. Ark. Aquacult. Fish. Center Res. Pap. Ser. AFC-93-1: 1–20.

Layher, W. G., and K. L. Brunson
1986. New distributional records for some Kansas fishes. Trans. Kansas Acad. Sci. 89(3–4): 124–133.

Layher, W. G., and F. B. Cross
1987. New distributional records of the rosyface shiner and slender madtom in Kansas. Trans. Kansas Acad. Sci. 90(3–4): 150–152.

Layher, W. G., and O. E. Maughan
1987. Spotted bass habitat suitability related to fish occurrence and biomass and measurements of physicochemical variables. North American J. Fish. Mgmt. 7: 238–251.

Layher, W. G., J. Terrell, and L. D. Zuckerman
1991. Designing statewide stream surveys for multiple benefits. In The warmwater fisheries symposium I, Phoenix, Arizona. U.S. Forest Serv. Gen. Tech. Report RM-207 [407 pp.], pp. 183–188.

Layher, W. G., and R. D. Wood
1986. Collections of threatened, endangered, and unique fish species in Kansas streams. Trans. Kansas Acad. Sci. 89(1–2): 1–8.

Limbird, R. L.
1993. The Arkansas River—A changing river. In Proceedings of the symposium on restoration planning for the rivers of the Mississippi River ecosystem. L. W. Hesse, C. B. Stalnaker, N. G. Benson, and J. R. Zuboy (eds.). U.S. Dept. Interior, Natl. Biol. Surv., Biol. Report 19, Washington, D.C. [vii + 502 pp], pp. 282–294.

Lynch, J. D.
1988. Introduction, establishment, and dispersal of western mosquitofish in Nebraska (Actinopterygii: Poeciliidae). Prairie Nat. 20(4): 203–216.

Martin, R.
1983. Absent king of the Ark. Explore (Fall issue): 16.

Matthews, W. J., and R. McDaniel
1981. New locality records for some Kansas fishes, with notes on the habitat of the Arkansas Darter (Etheostoma cragini). Trans. Kansas Acad. Sci. 84(4): 219–222.

Maupin, J. K., J. R. Wells, and C. Leist
1954. A preliminary survey of food habits of the fish and physico-chemical conditions of the water of three strip-mine lakes. Trans. Kansas Acad. Sci. 57: 164–171.

Mayden, R. L.
1988. Systematics of the Notropis zonatus species group, with description of a new species from the Interior Highlands of North America. Copeia 1988(1): 153–173.

Metcalf, A. L.
1959. Fishes of Chautauqua, Cowley and Elk counties, Kansas. Univ. Kansas Publ. Mus. Nat. Hist. 11(6): 345–400.
1966. Fishes of the Kansas River system in relation to zoogeography of the Great Plains. Univ. Kansas Publ. Mus. Nat. Hist. 17: 23–189.

Michl, G. T., and E. J. Peters
1993. New distributional record of the Topeka shiner in the Loup drainage basin in Nebraska. Prairie Nat. 25(1): 51–54.

Miller, R. R.
    1955.   An annotated list of the American cyprinodontid fishes of the genus *Fundulus,* with the description of *Fundulus persimilis* from Yucatan. Occ. Papers Univ. Michigan Mus. Zool. 568: 1–27.
    1960.   Systematics and biology of the gizzard shad *(Dorosoma cepedianum)* and related fishes. U.S. Fish and Wildlife Serv., Fishery Bull. 173: 371–392.
    1972.   Threatened freshwater fishes of the United States. Trans. American Fisheries Soc. 101(2): 239–252.

Miller, R. V.
    1968.   A systematic study of the greenside darter, *Etheostoma blennioides* Rafinesque (Pisces: Percidae). Copeia 1968(1): 1–40.

Minckley, C. O.
    1969.   A new record of the quillback carpsucker *Carpiodes cyprinus* (Le Sueur) from the Kansas River basin. Trans. Kansas Acad. Sci. 72(1): 108.

Minckley, C. O., and H. E. Klaassen
    1969a.   Burying behavior of the plains killifish, *Fundulus kansae.* Copeia 1969(1): 200–201.
    1969b.   Life history of the Plains killifish, *Fundulus kansae* (Garman), in the Smoky Hill River, Kansas. Trans. American Fisheries Soc. 98(3): 460–465.

Minckley, C. O., and W. L. Minckley
    1968.   Fishes of Deep Creek, Riley County, Kansas recording establishment of spotted bass *(Micropterus punctulatus).* Trans. Kansas Acad. Sci. 71(1): 87–89.

Minckley, W. L.
    1956.   A fish survey of the Pillsbury Crossing area, Deep Creek, Riley County, Kansas. Trans. Kansas Acad. Sci. 59: 351–357.
    1959.   Fishes of the Big Blue River Basin, Kansas. Univ. Kansas Publ. Mus. Nat. Hist. 11(7): 401–442.

Minckley. W. L., and F. B. Cross
    1959.   Distribution, habitat and abundance of the Topeka shiner, *Notropis topeka* (Gilbert) in Kansas. American Midland Nat. 6(1): 210–217.
    1960.   Taxonomic status of the shorthead redhorse, *Moxostoma aureolum* (Le Sueur) from the Kansas River Basin, Kansas. Trans. Kansas Acad. Sci. 63: 35–39.

Minckley, W. L., and J. E. Deacon
    1959.   Biology of the flathead catfish in Kansas. Trans. American Fisheries Soc. 88: 344–355.

Moore, G. A., and D. H. Buck
    1955.   The fishes of the Chikaskia River in Oklahoma and Kansas. Proc. Oklahoma Acad. Sci. 34: 19–27.

Moore, G. A., and F. B. Cross
    1950.   Additional Oklahoma fishes with validation of *Poecilichthys parvipinnis* (Gilbert and Swain). Copeia 1950(2): 139–148.

Morris, M. A., and L. M. Page
    1981.   Variation in western logperches (Pisces: Percidae), with a description of a new subspecies from the Ozarks. Copeia 1981(1): 95–108.

Morrissey, J. R., and D. R. Edds
    1994.   Metal pollution associated with a landfill: Concentrations in water, sediment, crayfish, and fish. Trans. Kansas Acad. Sci. 97(1–2): 18–25.

Mosher, T. D.
    1984.   An evaluation of threadfin shad *(Dorosoma petenense)* introduction in Kansas. Publ. Kansas Fish and Game Comm., Pratt. 54 pp.

Moss, R. E.
    1981a.   Life history information for the Arkansas darter *(Etheostoma cragini)*. Contract No. 38 Final Report, Kansas Fish and Game Comm., Pratt. 15 pp.
    1981b.   Life history information for the Neosho madtom *(Noturus placidus)*. Contract No. 38 Final Report, Kansas Fish and Game Comm., Pratt. 33 pp.
    1983.   Microhabitat selection in Neosho River riffles. Doctoral thesis, Univ. Kansas, Lawrence. 294 pp.

Moss, R. E., and K. Brunson
    1981.   Kansas stream and river fishery resource evaluation. Publ. Kansas Fish and Game Comm. 71 pp. + detached map.

Moss, R. E., J. W. Scanlan, and C. A. Anderson
    1983.   Observations on the natural history of the blue sucker *(Cycleptus elongatus Le Sueur)* in the Neosho River. American Midland Nat. 109(1): 15–22.

Mulhern, D. W.
    1989.   Status report on Arkansas darter *(Etheostoma cragini)*. Publ. U.S. Fish and Wildlife Serv. Manhattan, Kansas. 75 pp.

Nicholson, H. P.
    1968.   Pesticides: A current water quality problem. Suppl. Trans. Kansas Acad. Sci. 70(3): 39–44.

Olund, L. J., and F. B. Cross
    1961.   Geographic variation in the North American cyprinid fish, *Hybopsis gracilis*. Univ. Kansas Publ. Mus. Nat. Hist. 13(7): 323–348.

Osbaldiston, G. W., A. L. Kelly, E. C. Stone, and H. E. Klaassen
    1971.   Bacterial flora of the intestines of fishes taken from an unpolluted freshwater reservoir. Trans. Kansas Acad. Sci. 73(2): 257–266.

Pfingsten, D. G., and D. R. Edds
    1994.   Reproductive traits of the Neosho madtom, *Noturus placidus* (Pisces: Ictaluridae). Trans. Kansas Acad. Sci. 97(3–4): 82–87.

Platt, D. R., F. B. Cross, H. Klaassen, T. Wenke, J. C. Bass, D. Distler, and R. Boles
    1974.   Rare, endangered and extirpated species in Kansas. I. Fishes. Trans. Kansas Acad. Sci. 76(2): 97–106.

Polson, J.
    1964.   New reservoirs—new fish species. Kansas Fish and Game, 21(3): 3–6.

Potts, G. D., and J. T. Collins
    1991.   A checklist of the vertebrate animals of Kansas. Univ. Kansas Mus. Nat. Hist. Spec. Pub. 18: 1–42.

Prophet, C. W.
    1970.   Limnological features of Lyon County Lake after drainage and reflooding. Southwest. Nat. 14(3): 317–325.

Reno, H. W.
    1969.   Cephalic lateral-line systems of the cyprinid genus *Hybopsis*. Copeia 1969(4): 736–773.

Rostlund, E.
    1952.   Freshwater fish and fishing in native North America. Univ. California Publ. Geog. 9: 1–314.

Rues, T.
    1986.   The Kaw River nature and history guide. Publ. Kansas State Hist. Soc. 28 pp.

Sanders, R. M., Jr., D. G. Huggins, and F. B. Cross
    1993.   The Kansas River system and its biota. *In* Proceedings of the symposium on restoration planning for the rivers of the Mississippi River ecosystem. L. W. Hesse, C. B. Stalnaker, N. G. Benson and J. R. Zuboy

(eds.). U.S. Dept. Interior, Natl. Biol. Surv., Biol. Report 19, Washington, D.C. [vii + 502 pp], pp. 295–326.

Schaefer, J.
1984.   New life for nongame. Kansas Wildlife 41(2): 26–30.

Schelske, C. L.
1957.   An ecological study of the fishes of the Fall and Verdigris rivers in Wilson and Montgomery counties, Kansas, March 1954 to February 1955. Emporia State Research Studies 5(3): 31–56.

Schoonover, R., and W. H. Thompson
1954.   A post-impoundment study of the fisheries resources of Fall River Reservoir, Kansas. Trans. Kansas Acad. Sci. 57: 172–179.

Schwilling, M.
1985.   Cheyenne Bottoms. Kansas School Nat. 32(3): 1–15.

Setzer, P. Y.
1970.   An analysis of a natural hybrid swarm by means of chromosome morphology. Trans. American Fisheries Soc. 99(1): 139–146.

Shipley, F. S., and R. E. Moss
1982.   First record of the tadpole madtom, *Noturus gyrinus* (Mitchill) from the Kansas River basin. Trans. Kansas Acad. Sci. 85(1): 59–60.

Simco, B. A., and F. B. Cross
1966.   Factors affecting growth and production of channel catfish, *Ictalurus punctatus*. Univ. Kansas Publ. Mus. Nat. Hist. 17(4): 191–256.

Snow, F. H.
1875.   The fishes of the Kansas River, as observed at Lawrence. State Board of Agric. Annual Rept. 4: 139–141.

Sparks, R. E., J. Cairns, Jr., and F. B. Cross
1969.   Some effects of a neutral mixture of calcium oxide and sulfuric acid on channel catfish *Ictalurus punctatus* (Rafinesque). Trans. Kansas Acad. Sci. 72(1): 1–15.

Stark, B. J., M. E. Eberle, G. W. Ernsting, and T. L. Wenke
1987.   Distributional records of some Kansas fishes. Trans. Kansas Acad. Sci. 90(3–4): 153–156.

Stark, W. L.
1990.   A survey of the ichthyofauna in the tributaries of the Missouri River in northeastern Kansas. Masters thesis, Fort Hays St. Univ., Hays, Kansas. 29 pp. + 43 maps.

Stucky, N. P., and H. E. Klaassen
1971.   Growth and condition of the carp and the river carpsucker in an altered environment in western Kansas. Trans. American Fisheries Soc. 100(2): 276–282.

Summerfelt, R. C.
1967.   Fishes of the Smoky Hill River, Kansas. Trans. Kansas Acad. Sci. 70(1): 102–139.

Summerfelt, R. C., and C. O. Minckley
1969.   Aspects of the life history of the sand shiner, *Notropis stramineus* (Cope), in the Smoky Hill River, Kansas. Trans. American Fisheries Soc. 98(3): 444–453.

Suppes, C., O. W. Tiemeier, and C. W. Deyoe
1968.   Seasonal variations of fat, protein, and moisture in channel catfish. Trans. Kansas Acad. Sci. 70(3): 349–358.

Tabor, V. M.
1992a.   Status report on Topeka Shiner *(Notropis topeka)*. Report U.S. Fish and Wildlife Serv., Manhattan, Kansas. 22 pp.

1992b. Temporal changes in the ichthyofauna of the South Fork of the Cottonwood River and Cedar Creek, Chase County, Kansas. Master's thesis, Univ. Kansas, Lawrence. 43 pp.

Tafanelli, R. J., and J. C. Bass
1968. Feeding response of *Lepomis cyanellus* to blister beetles (Meloidae). Southwest. Nat. 13(1): 51–54.

Tanyolac, J.
1973. Morphometric variation and life history of the cyprinid fish *Notropis stramineus* (Cope). Occas. Pap. Mus. Nat. Hist. Univ. Kansas 12: 1–28.

Taylor, W. R.
1969. A revision of the catfish genus *Noturus* Rafinesque with an analysis of higher groups in the Ictaluridae. Bull. U.S. Natl. Mus. 282: 1–315.

Tiemeier, O. W.
1962. Increasing size of fingerling channel catfish by supplemental feeding. Trans. Kansas Acad. Sci. 65: 144–153.

Tiemeier, O. W., and C. W. Deyoe
1968. Growth obtained by stocking various size combinations of channel catfish *(Ictalurus punctatus),* and efficiencies of utilizing pelleted feed. Southwest. Nat. 13(2): 167–174.

1969. A review of techniques used to hatch and rear channel catfish in Kansas and proposed restrictions on nutritional requirements of fingerlings. Trans. Kansas Acad. Sci. 71(4): 491–503.

1973. Producing channel catfish. Kansas State Univ. Agric. Exper. Sta. Bull. 576: 1–24.

Tiemeier, O. W., C. W. Deyoe, and R. Lipper
1970. Influence of photoperiod on growth of fed channel catfish *(Ictalurus punctatus)* in early spring and late fall. Trans. Kansas Acad. Sci. 72(4): 519–522.

Tiemeier, O. W., C. W. Deyoe, and C. Suppes
1967. Production and growth of channel catfish fry *(Ictalurus punctatus).* Trans. Kansas Acad. Sci. 70(2): 164–170.

Tiemeier, O. W., C. W. Deyoe, and S. Weardon
1965. Effects on growth of fingerling channel catfish of diets containing two energy and two protein levels. Trans. Kansas Acad. Sci. 68: 180–186.

Tiemeier, O. W., and J. B. Elder
1960. Growth of stunted channel catfish. Prog. Fish-Cult. 22(4): 172–176.

Tiemeier, O. W., M. A. Lambert, and C. W. Deyoe
1971. Length–weight relationship of supplementary fed and non-fed channel catfish. Trans. Kansas Acad. Sci. 73(2): 252–256.

Todd, B.
1962. Explosive new fish in Kansas. Kansas Fish and Game, 20(1): 3–5.

Trautman, M. B., and R. G. Martin
1951. *Moxostoma aureolum pisolabrum,* a new subspecies of sucker from the Ozarkian streams of the Mississippi River System. Occ. Papers Univ. Michigan Mus. Zool. 534: 1–10.

Tsai, C., and E. C. Raney
1974. Systematics of the banded darter, *Etheostoma zonale* (Pisces: Percidae). Copeia 1974(1): 1–24.

Uhler, F. M., and F. A. Warren
1929. [Survey of] Cheyenne Bottoms, Barton County, Kansas. Unpubl. report. 9 pp.

Wagner, B.
    1984.   Information for Exhibit E. Environmental report. Bowersock Dam. Lawrence, Kansas. 15 pp.
Wedd, G. R.
    1985.   Observations on Neosho River larval fish in Coffey County, Kansas. Emporia St. Res. Stud. 34(1): 1–56.
Wenke, T. L., Eberle, M. E., G. W. Ernsting, and W. J. Stark
    1992.   Winter collections of the Neosho madtom *(Noturus placidus)*. Southwest. Nat. 37(3): 330–333.
Wenke, T. L., G. W. Ernsting, and M. E. Eberle
    1993.   Survey of river fishes at Fort Riley Military Reservation in Kansas. Prairie Nat. 25(4): 317–323.
Werden, S. J.
    1993a.   Status report on sturgeon chub *(Macrhybopsis gelida)*, a candidate endangered species. Publ. U.S. Fish and Wildlife Serv., Bismarck, North Dakota. 58 pp.
    1993b.   Status report on sicklefin chub *(Macrhybopsis meeki)*, a candidate endangered species. Publ. U.S. Fish and Wildlife Serv., Bismarck, North Dakota. 41 pp.
Wheeler, W.
    1879.   A partial list of the fishes of the Marais des Cygnes, at Ottawa. Trans. Kansas Acad. Sci. 6 (for 1877): 33–34.
Wilson, W. D.
    1957.   Notes on cestodes in paddlefish, *Polyodon spathula* (Walbaum), from the Missouri River. Trans. Kansas Acad. Sci. 59(4): 459–460.
Witt, L. A.
    1970.   The fishes of the Nemaha Basin, Nebraska. Trans. Kansas Acad. Sci. 73(1): 70–88.
Zuckerman, L. D.
    1988a.   Fishing. Clown prince of the Arkansas basin. Kansas Wildlife and Parks 45(5): 40.
    1988b.   Fishing. Lake Sturgeon. Kansas Wildlife and Parks 45(6): 22.
    1989.   Rainbow trout in the South Fork Ninnescah River. Part I. Modified habitat evaluation procedures analysis. Abstract. Ann. Meet. Kansas Chapt. American Fisheries Soc.
    1991.   Fishing. Kansas' newest cardinal. Kansas Wildlife and Parks 48(2): 45.
    1992.   Rudd: A new fish species in Kansas. Abstract. Ann. Meet. Kansas Acad. Sci.
    1993.   Conservation reserve program impacts on fish communities of Delaware River basin, Kansas. Abstract. Ann. Meet. Kansas Chapt. American Fisheries Soc.

INDEX TO COMMON AND SCIENTIFIC NAMES

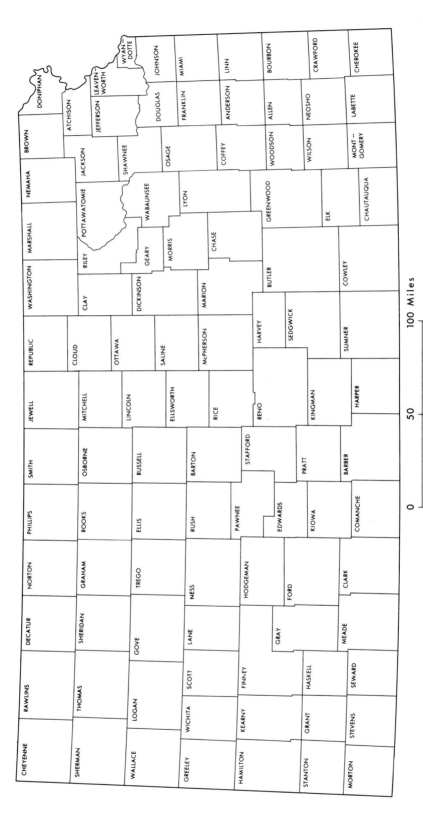

Scale

0   50   100 Miles